# YARNS

## STORIES FROM THE
## WAY WE WERE

# *YARNS*

## STORIES FROM THE
## WAY WE WERE

### BASED ON A FEW ACTUAL FACTS

*Frank Loudin*

# FRANK LOUDIN

I'll Be Frank

FIRST EDITION
EASTSOUND, WA

*YARNS: Stories from the Way We Were,*
*Based on a Few Actual Facts*

Cover and Book Designer: Jonathan Sainsbury
Editor: Donna Lane
Production Manager and Assistant Editor: Edee Kulper

Some of the places and some of the characters in these stories are real. Real names were used fondly and respectfully by the author to enhance the memories of those times and acquaintances in order to add a necessary reality.

Front cover: *The Way We Were* painting by Frank Loudin
Back cover: Frank Loudin on Orcas Island

*YARNS* was typeset in Sabon Next™, which was designed by Jan Tschichold in 1967 and revived by Jean François Porchez in 2002.

Library of Congress Control Number: 2023908114
ISBN: 979-8-35091-115-2 (print)

Printed in the United States of America

Published by I'll Be Frank
First Edition, Eastsound, Washington

Other Books by Frank Loudin

*Capture the Charm of Your Hometown in Watercolor*

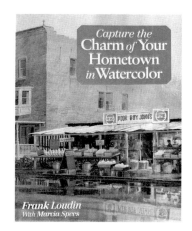

*T*his book and these stories are dedicated to my heritage as a son of a son of the hills of West Virginia, and to my dear wife who has allowed me the freedom to do what I love to do, that being a storyteller. Spinning yarns so to speak. For sixty-eight years I told stories in paint, dabbing colors here and there to represent a country back porch or a small berg, a grocery, a service station, a deserted gold mine's monumental headframe, or a gaggle of geese in a shady lane, all close to the heart of Americana.

I've retired my paints and brushes in exchange for a laptop computer and colorful verbiage. The purpose is the same.

I dedicate this book to my dear Jannie who is gone now but I still feel her support in all my endeavors and her gentle enjoyment of my corny metaphors. I write these in sheer pleasure and I hope you will appreciate them in that spirit.

Frank Loudin
Orcas Island, Washington
2023

# ACKNOWLEDGMENTS

First of all, if it weren't for my friend Edee Kulper, there wouldn't be any reason for me to be writing this. I have been writing these short stories for at least fifteen years and waiting for someone to come along who would help; no, who would do it for me—organize a manuscript for a book. Through a mutual friend, there she was. I thank her more than words can express.

Though at the time I didn't know it, my father was imbuing in me the enjoyment of a good story, not to mention the value of the same to the world in general.

I spent more time than I care to remember in classes of various subjects learning the how-tos of being a creative artist. Good and sincere teachers, yes, but the subject is vague. The great examples are at The University of Colorado, Pasadena's ArtCenter College of Design, and Qvale and Associates (which is no longer in operation).

I feel indebted to the many artists I have admired from a distance and who have influenced my career—too many to name—as well as an art show entrepreneur, Irma Eubanks, for showing me what selling art is all about.

Today, I thank my good friend Dane Steck for his friendship. JoEllen Moldoff for our weekly conversations. Chama Anderson for her care. My niece Leslie and her husband, Rich. John Steach, B. J., Patsy and Stu, Marti, Jim S. and Ken, Jim C., Wilma, Marsha, Heidi—all of them my good friends. I also wholeheartedly thank Mark and Carolyn Bledsoe of the original Teezer's, where so many of these stories happened.

And of course, my dearest Jannie, who loved me even when I wasn't that good.

# CONTENTS

---

# *PREFACE*

---

## YARNS MY FATHER TOLD ME

*I*'m not sure just what a PREFACE might be, but I think it is an explanation or maybe an excuse for the following malarkey.

My father was a country boy from the hills of West Virginia, and I mean THE HILLS. He was the oldest son in a family of nine saplings from parents of simple and pious stock, around the turn of the twentieth century. Their country was rutty and rocky with little land even close to being flat enough to plant anything. Their corn fields were so tilted that a determined farmer could stand downhill from his rows of corn and chop weeds uphill without having to bend over. Their hogs were just turned loose in the woods to be rounded up after the first frost to take part in the annual porker round-up. But I digress, which is so like a true spinner of yarns.

These folks would gather at the drop of a litter of coon hounds to potluck at Pine Grove Church or Blue Rock School in celebration, eating, singing and storytelling into a weathering night. Yarns were spun by the oldsters to be absorbed with wonder by the big-eyed younger generations. Traditional stories yes, but told with a somewhat new twist every time. These folks were creative.

My father took it one step further. With a bit of higher education, he became a professional minister of the gospel. Not your fire and brimstone revivalist but a quiet gentle man with a fine sense of humor. Every night at bedtime, my stories were Peter Rabbit, but with a different line every time. Peter was joined on these lyrical journeys by Old Bounce the coon dog, Uncle Zed Cutright, Grandma Saucy, Lovey Loudin (distant relation), Gideon Turkey-Trot, etc. No two stories were alike! I learned that the best stories can be stretched and molded just a bit with the innocent intent of story improvement. My family have all passed on now, so there is nobody who can deny any of this. That's one of the benefits of being an old guy. I can tell it any way I want to without fear of contradiction.

After years as a creator of watercolor paintings which leaned to the story illustration gender, wherein I could make up anything I thought appropriate, it was an easy jump from painting dabs of color to typing words of color. These yarns are meant to entertain and are roughly based on my experiences from young whippersnapper to dotage.

# MORNING GLORY CAFE

US 101 goes right by the Morning Glory Café. I mean, right by. The spray and dirt clods fly from the rumbling eighteen wheels of the continuous parade of loggers and chip trucks to splatter across the narrow sidewalk, settling on the front porch and the two tiny patio tables in a coat of fine umber-colored film.

Inside the atmosphere is warm, almost humid, from the rain-pelted jackets and overalls mixed with the heady aroma of buttermilk pancakes and Starbucks premium. A full order of biscuits and sausage gravy is more than a mere mortal can manage. It's a large platter of quantum-size drop biscuits, peppery and salty as the wind-blown mist off the surf line across the highway.

This stretch of the Oregon coast mixes timber and tourism like an oil and vinegar dressing that never quite reaches a comfortable blend.

"Coffee or breakfast?" Crystal, the youngish waitress chirps as a skinny fellow in a lumberjack shirt and wide red suspenders clomps through the door in jeans that have either been worn off or torn off at the top of his muddy, lace-up safety boots.

Four dressy folks from Urbana look up from their lattes but try not to meet the tired, hard eyes of the trucker who has already completed two round trips in a Kenworth rig that would fill the entire footprint of the Morning Glory Café. These rogues of the highway wrestle lumbering eighteen-wheelers up the mountainside on makeshift temporary trails in all kinds of foul weather, from before dawn to after dusk. Then it's back to civilization on US 101 to do battle with summer tourists in rented RVs who are usually lost or slowly approaching every view spot for a Kodak moment. No love lost there.

Bettina is bundled up like she is facing a nor'wester, old blue wool jacket with turned up collar, a pink knit scarf that goes around her neck and over her head in a tumble of faded colors. Her straight gray bangs hang down over her forehead to very large, guy-style sunglasses that she never takes off, at least not in the café. She walks carefully in white nurse's shoes with white calf-length athletic socks. Because of the dark glasses it's as if she is blind.

"Did you hear the thunder last night?"

Karen's voice comes from the pass-through to the kitchen as she gives the order-up bell a good whack.

This opens up a general conversation among the cluster of locals who perch in the corner booth every morning and stirs up the tourists who just want to be friendly. The thunder topic morphs into weather in general, weather history, storms, tides, tsunamis, fishing, bait, road closures, highway departments, local representation, a guy named Monk, slow pitch softball, the price of a cord of wood, taxes, and back to the clap of thunder that occurred at 4:17 a.m., as per general consensus.

There comes a period of quiet when everybody stares into their respective morning brew while contemplating their individual choice of the above-mentioned subjects.

Casey, a mostly sheep dog, sits on a bench on the front porch and looks in the window at Dave, who sits in the only corner booth in the place.

"No. That ain't my dog. Belongs to my wife. She goes to work and Casey comes down here with me. I guess he don't like to sell real estate much." A general round of grunts and snorts accompany a raspy scratch of laughter from the tiny kitchen.

Dave has already pulled his few crab pots for today. Actually he's retired but can't stop.

Karen comes out with a plate of crumbled sausage bits and

gives them to Casey, who twirls around her ankles in a flurry of tongue and tail.

"Don't you ever feed that dog? Ha ha haaaaaaaaaaaaaaaa."

"Don't have to. Gets all he wants down here," Dave replies. His three companions appreciate his humor with snorts and sips of Starbucks.

Crystal brings out a hammer, turns one of the tables upside down, and gives the base a good healthy pop.

"You could get a job over at the construction site. You look better than any of those whoppers from Portland," George, the retired railroad man, suggests.

"Yeah, but they don't have fresh cookies nor the intelligent spectators that come in here."

"She could open a hardware store with all the tools she keeps down under the counter. I bet she has a 24-inch Stihl saw down there and maybe a jackhammer, huh?"

"Well, somebody fer sure should open a hardware store, since Harold gave it up to go off to wherever he went off to."

"He never knew nothing about hardware anyhow."

"T'wasn't him at all wanted no store. Was her, Emma. She wanted one of them boutiques and such."

The conversation went around the little gathering like a case of the winter colds.

"God knows, we got enough of those, and junk shops, huh?"

Bettina sings a few words out loud but nobody pays her any mind. She sits there at a table by the door talking to an empty chair. Sometimes she speaks out loud and sometimes she sings a few words. Bettina looks like a fashion statement for a Goodwill store.

"More coffee, Bettina?" Crystal comes by with two pots of coffee.

Bettina just shoves her mug over to the edge of the table wordlessly, then sings out a few husky notes as Crystal goes around the room with the pots.

She suddenly puts down her jelly bear claw, gets into her yellow slicker over her red polar-fleece vest over her green Rockaway sweatshirt over her whatever else and is gone. The four tourists utter some niceties to Crystal and leave. Dave and his buddies get up and gather around the cash register.

"Well, I reckon we better get on with it, whatever it is," George drawls.

A very young couple comes in with a tiny new baby in a huge carrier thing that looks like a space-age ejection capsule. A crowd gathers about cooing and gurgling the traditional sounds. It turns out the new baby is the great granddaughter of Gloria the owner. I would guess that Gloria herself was in her forties. They make three quick phone calls on the house phone and leave.

Crystal fills the coffee maker, Karen goes out back for a cigarette, and another logger drives south on 101 leaving another coat of dingy spray on the Morning Glory sign.

# *TEEZER'S TWISTS 1*

---

*T*here are great seats of higher learning around this old world. You are perhaps thinking The American University in Cairo, or maybe the University of Saint Andrews in Edinburgh, or perhaps just Pacific Lutheran University. One of the great seats of learning that I know of is right here in my hometown. That great seat is Teezer's.

Of course, if you wish to confer with brainy old guys who can expound on the mating habits of the Arctic muckhog, then you should go to Krakow A&M, or if your interests are in the origin of the square hole in some ancient Chinese coins, then you should take the slow boat to Shanghai Polytech.

But if it's just everyday stuff you're curious about, then Teezer's is your spot. On any given day there will be, in residence, experts on a constellation of matters from Alpha to Omega from the most common to the obscure. If a question remains, then someone will fabricate a perfectly logical solution unsubstantiated by facts.

It is just a small place in a really small town that doesn't even have a parking meter, a town marshal, or a street sweeper. Well, it does have a street sweeper, but it belongs to the county, as do all the streets, so we get street services through the capricious whims of some folks in an office over at the county seat on another island.

Originated by four sisters with the name Ortiz, armed with their mother's cookie recipes, they adopted their nickname for their shop, and Ortiz became Teezer's.

Teezer's sits on a busy corner that everyone passes on their way to the post office. There is one handsome shade maple and a garden-like patio out in front with four tile tables where there is usually at least one tethered dog—usually a black Lab—and maybe an untethered companion, plus some small kids playing chase.

The patio is decorated in accordance with the season, with pumpkins in the fallen maple leaves for Halloween and Thanksgiving, colored lights and snowflakes—real or plastic— for Christmas, etc. On a nice day, there might be a silver-haired woman reading a poetry book and taking notes. Or a young man, too well dressed for our town, filling out a business order on his laptop. Sometimes, there will be a family with backpacks and a border collie. Maybe a cluster of bikers clomping around in their tight little outfits of matching colors.

Inside, there are seven tables with seating for maybe twenty-four close friends or eighteen perfect strangers. The only time there are that many strangers in Teezer's would be on a rainy Fourth of July, when all of the regulars are out on the street watching our famous parade while the tourists gather inside, out of the wet.

You can always tell the locals from the tourists. We have all been trained to bus our own tables. In fact, if a stranger leaves his cup on a table, one of the regulars will usually pick it up and take it to the dirty dish trash.

Mark, the co-owner/baker, starts his day at 1:30 a.m. By 7, when he allows the first customer in, he has the display case filled with seven flavors of scones: cinnamon, pecan, blueberry, raspberry, raisin, pumpkin and chocolate chip, plus breakfast egg sandwiches, pumpkin bread, brownies, cinnamon rolls, bran muffins, various chip cookies, and quiche. He also has several gallons of coffee (regular and decaf Starbucks), a big crock of cold water, and an espresso/latte machine that's warmed up and ready to go.

By the time the early crowd gathers, Carolyn, Mark's wife and co-owner, will be there presiding over the roaring espresso machine, turning out everyone's special desire as Mark hands her pink Post-it Notes at machine-gun speed, with orders such as venti nonfat, quad shot, caramel mocha with whipped cream, and one percent foam on top.

While Carolyn talks to a friend, she doesn't even look up but operates the machine like a mad chemical engineer.

Tony grabs a coffee to go. "I gotta catch a ferry," he says over his shoulder to a gathering of regulars at the three favorite tables in the corner. Favorite because from there you can see everything that goes up and down the street as well as everyone that might come through the Dutch door.

"Catch a ferry? What are you using for bait?"

"Yeah, I hope you are using a mighty big net."

"He thinks he'll get the first spot on the ferry."

"I have never gotten the number one spot on the ferry."

"How do they load the ferries anyhow?"

The comments run around the group like a game of Button, Button, Who's Got the Button.

"Well, it's my theory that vehicle color is the primary guide," Frank poorly imitates the raspy voice of an old man. "One loading master, or mistress in this case, was overheard asking for two more reds, a silver, and a green to complete her ensemble on the port mezzanine."

Bob interjects, "That one loading master, that really tall blond guy with the bad posture, doesn't seem to really care. With a lackadaisical flick of his bony wrist, he guides innocent islanders to indiscriminate spots on his precious Elwha which, in the big picture, could seal their fate to some gruesome catastrophe which might occur on the high seas between Shaw and Lopez."

"Well, if you just hang back a little when you get to the ramp, they don't seem to know what to do with you, so they just put you down the middle," George informs the crowd in a low voice, like he is sharing a state secret.

"Do they really call them 'loading masters?'" Jannie asks.

"I've heard them called other things," Frank replies.

"In Anacortes, how come they let the latecomers for Shaw

and Lopez just drive right in and get onboard?"

"How come they let the Island Hardware Truck drive on anytime he shows up, while the rest of us have been sitting there for hours?"

"Why don't they open more ticket booths on Fridays?"

"Why do they have the air conditioning on in the winter and the heat on in summer?"

Why, oh why? Since all—rich or poor, young or old, islander or tourist, Republican or Democrat—have to use the ferries, they all have their horror stories and theories.

"Just wait 'til they build the bridge. You'll all have to go live in Ballard," Steve, the perpetual skeptic, growls.

There is a pause. Some folks have to go to a board meeting, or up the street for teeth cleaning while others get refills.

They all sip and look out the window as our town's own demented street character hustles across the street to stop and stare at some distant figment that only he can see.

"I wonder where he sleeps at night?" Jannie asks.

"Maybe in someone's garage or crawl space in one of those summer homes on the mountain."

"I sometimes think we should try to help him, but he seems to get along okay. Don't you wonder what is going through his mind?"

"Nothing. He went to WSU and is on the board of directors that set up the loading system for the ferries."

Everyone snorts and sips.

Both Bobs get up to leave. Two telephone guys come in and take the one remaining table in the corner.

"Do you guys have cell phones so that headquarters can get in touch in case there is a communication emergency?" Frank asks.

"What'd you mean? We are headquarters!" Rob answers.

There is general laughter until two well-dressed strangers come in, look around, and check their oversized wristwatches and leave.

"Boy, do those guys have government written all over them," Jannie observes.

"Yeah, who else wears gray slacks, blue button-down shirts, and blue blazers with red ties?"

"Yeah, and where do you get a haircut like that?" Al rubs his hand over his bald head.

"Maybe at the police academy."

"Maybe at Les Schwab."

"They could be Republican congressmen or FBI, or maybe even the CIA."

"Or maybe even military intelligence."

"Naw, they don't have that anymore. If they ever did."

"The big one had a Marine Corps pin in his lapel button-hole."

"Hey Frank, they want that landing barge back."

"Yeah, you were supposed to turn that thing in when you came home. And what about all of your green skivvies?"

They all sip on their coffees and watch a young mother give a huge blackberry scone to a toddler, who immediately drops it on the floor.

"Quick! Three second rule!" four people shout.

The little girl looks around with saucer eyes, takes two steps backwards, and sits down on the scone.

Mom picks her up, with not too much damage done—except for the scone. Mark whips over in his usual efficient manner and cleans up the floor. One of the tables takes up a collection to replace the terminal scone. The little girl hiccups a couple of times and takes a big bite out of the berry side of the new pastry.

There is always a sampling of tiny tots around because Teezer's is a family-run place. Mark and Carolyn are the owners/managers with lots of help from two of Carolyn's sisters and one daughter. A few years ago, during the summer, three daughters and an assortment of nephews were behind the counter most of the time, while Mark continued to do the baking, banking, and carrying out the trash.

There is a gallery of black and white photos on the walls that covers a slew of grandchildren who show up from time to time. Carolyn, a great hand with her new digital camera, provides a continuous sampling of her family on the walls. They all have wonderful dark eyes, so the walls seem to be watching all the goings on.

By eleven o'clock, the crowd thins and a quiet settles over the place. The espresso machine is down to a timid gurgle, Mark has wiped off all the tables, taken out the trash, washed most of the dishes, and gone to the bank.

Anyone who shows up now is of another vintage. Not so prone to conversation or lingering discussions. Tomorrow, there will be the same faces ... with some new twists.

# FERVOR ON BACA MESA

---

*I*t was now lunchtime and they were all sitting under the double green fly of the dining tent pretending that nothing had happened. Maybe nothing had happened, but they had seen what they had seen.

Several women were clustered around Mrs. Londa Tallow there in the dining tent. Their conversation was muted and intermittent, punctuated with exclamations like, "rascal," "scoundrel," "scalawag," and "well I never." They were hunched around a picnic table like setting hens, shifting now and then to better arrange themselves.

The men had gone out to a grove of piñon trees. Some worried the ground with the pointed toes of their underslung western boots while others hunkered down in cowboy fashion, picking out choice bits of grass to fondle between their suncracked lips.

The rumble of Claude "Crump" Tallow's deep voice rose occasionally, drifting down over the rim of the mesa to be purified by the high desert morning.

Cowboy Camp Meeting was the annual summer week that found these good folks camping on the rim of Baca Mesa, suffering the yellow jackets in order to find some sort of Christian experience.

Early this day the camp had been shocked completely out of its schedule by an event that just might dismiss the whole meeting.

---

Normally, there would be the daily Sunrise Service where the women would stand in a circle, hold hands, and sing. The men would hike over to Pulpit Rock and gaze out across the valley, pondering beef prices and too long of a dry spell. They would congregate for a breakfast of overdone, lumpy gravy, scrambled eggs, and pancakes. Gallons of boiled coffee with crumpled eggshells were consumed, including some of the eggshells that gathered in the bottom of each cup.

Every meal came with gravy of some description: white to gray, always too salty, and sometimes laced with yesterday's chili leftovers or lumps of mysterious origin.

The camp cook, Cotton Dubbs, a cowboy himself, was perfectly comfortable including gravel in his pinto beans and little green inch worms in his iceberg lettuce "salad."

Cotton had been a rodeo clown until he was crippled in a pile-up in a chuck-wagon race and sent home to stay with his wife, Myrna, who supported them from her teller's cage at the Bank of Lincoln County.

With the questionable assistance of a few hard-bitten old hands and his daughter, Ruth June, Cotton could indeed turn out a classic Southwestern feed for lunch. The same every day for the whole stay, would be tri-tip, mesquite-roasted beef that was black on the outside and raw on the inside, but tasty. Always the biscuits, always the pinto beans, in a sauce right out of The Jornada del Muerto, ending with rice pudding and raisins covered with yellow jackets. Red or green Kool-Aid or lemonade out of a five-gallon barrel with a chunk of ice that showed Ice Age crustaceans was consumed by the gallon. Daily volunteers would do the serving and clean up.

Their only child, Ruth June, was an adult with the IQ of a recalcitrant seven-year-old and the personality of a roll of barbed wire. She was built like one of those balloons in the Macy's Thanksgiving Day Parade. She always wore a blue denim tent-like dress that came just below her knees, so that her pink, trunk-like legs showing traces of black hair over comparatively tiny feet in white tennis shoes gave her the appearance of floating.

Her face was fixed into a permanent scowl with her lower lip protruding under a fat nose and squinty eyes that watered a lot, showing stains down those chubby cheeks. Her mop of black hair had been cut short, like a boy's, to keep her from chewing on it.

Services of some sort continued throughout the day except for the traditional softball and horseshoe competitions.

Preachers of various faiths guested voluntarily on a daily basis, but the main attraction this year was a traveling evangelist named Wesley L. Wesley. The Reverend Wesley was a little man with a short neck and round head crested by a smooth pommel of black hair that didn't quite match his bushy sideburns. Narrow black eyes and eyebrows that met in the middle over a beak of a nose made him look like some sort of shore bird photographed in stark black and white.

Wesley performed in a white, western, double-breasted suit with plenty of black piping and padded shoulders. He wore studded white boots that were built up about as far as possible that made him look like he was prancing about on the stage on his tiptoes. His habit was to intimidate the congregation by waving a large white bible, also with black piping, shouting, "Evil doers perish at the rebuke of the divine countenance!" All in all, he looked like a black and white ink cartoon.

The Reverend was accompanied by Magdalena, one name only, a young woman with physical attributes that made cowboys gawk and pious ladies blanch. Magdalena played the accordion and led the singing with more than necessary fervor.

Her rendition of "In the Highways, In the Hedges" or "Snow White Wings" was enough to get the most reluctant old cowhand to repent and spit out his cud of Red Dog at least for the duration of the revival.

Ruth June would set quietly on the front row nearest Magdalena, rocking back and forth, chewing on a stick, mouthing words from some obscure source.

Last night the Reverend Wesley had told a few inspirational tales of his own epiphany then brought out Magdalena, who performed a solo rendition of "I'm In Heaven When I'm in My

Mother's Arms" that had the tender-hearted dabbing at their eyes and the cowboys looking out across the mesa with thousand-yard stares.

By the time Wesley L. Wesley launched into his main topic of temptation and redemption, with a fervor that only one of like experiences could possibly address, the crowd was in a revival mood.

There were nods of agreements and extemporaneous "amens" throughout, so that when the Rev asked those sinners to come forward and witness for the Lord, a small flood of pilgrims confessed to sins they never knew they had committed.

After the last amen, when folks trailed off to their family tents and Reverend Wesley snuck out behind the cook tent for a Lucky Strike and a nip out of a paper sack, the Big Dipper turned up and the desert horned owls were whooing in their soft-throated way.

The Rev retired to his bunk in the bachelor's tent while Magdalena bedded down on an air mattress in the supply tent where Ruth June had her steel army cot. Magdalena let Ruth June hold the accordion and finger the white ivory keys with her stubby fingers. The big face almost broke into a smile at the thrill.

The camp was silent except for a variety of snores, wheezes, and occasional feet padding to the outhouse.

Then just before dawn, the Reverend Wesley tiptoed out of the bachelor's tent in his stocking feet and slipped into the supply tent with lust in his heart. Being an early riser, it was his habit to mingle with Magdalena after a good night's sleep and recovery from his performance the night before.

He found the object of his desire on a grounded air mattress in supine attitude. Beneath a heap of thin blankets in the back of the supply tent, he proceeded into those soft white arms with fervor, being oblivious to the proximity of another sleeper. Magdalena was either too tired or too arduous to remember that just over there was that dark cloud of pent-up violence, Ruth June.

The large one awakened to see a dark figure assaulting Magdalena in a vigorous manner, and sprang to the rescue. She got Wesley's throat in a hammerlock that would have been the envy of any grizzly, and with a mighty heave, hurled him across the tent into an array of empty milk cans.

The clamorous clanging rang through the camp then out over the mesa, arousing all and any that might have been asleep.

Wesley scrambled up with his trousers and skivvies down around his ankles and tried to make his escape. Ruth June, in a move so quick for someone so large, got a handful of Wesley's oily hair in one big fist and twisted him around in preparation for another toss when the Rev pulled loose and scampered out of the tent, leaving Ruth June with his expensive hair piece in hand.

With one hand holding up his pants, Wesley tried to make some space between himself and his assailant, whom he assumed to be some formidable force of vengeance. Which she was.

He stumbled around the corner of the cook tent and fell flat on his front, right in the middle of the Ladies Sunrise Sisters who were just gathering for their morning devotional walk to the rim of the mesa to watch the sun rise.

Screams mingled with the still-tumbling milk cans and Ruth June's bellowing brought forth a crowd in time to witness Wesley's bare buns skittering into the bachelor's tent on his all fours.

They all turned to see Ruth June standing in the door of the supply tent in just a pair of baggy bloomers and they naturally assumed the most unholy.

Now, Ruth June was indeed a difficult situation, but they all felt some degree of responsibility for her welfare, and this was unacceptable.

In less than fifteen minutes, Crump Tallow had Wesley L. Wesley, Magdalena, and her accordion in his GMC pickup winding down the dirt road off Baca Mesa.

The sunrise sisterhood didn't meet that morning, but instead sat there under the green fly of the dining tent pretending nothing had happened.

# THE CUSTODIAN KID

---

**"D**on't pull too hard on the rope," Dad said, as he gripped the bell rope just above my hands. "If you don't watch out, the bell will turn over and come tumbling down on all of us."

My sister, Mary, and I were allowed, for the first time, to stay up late enough to usher in the new year, which in this case was 1942.

We were huddled in the vestibule of the First Methodist Church in Ripley, West Virginia, a small farm town suffering proudly through the war effort like the rest of America—rationing, deprivation of nice things and many necessities, and the like. Folks were plagued with worry, fear, sadness, pride, and sacrifices of untold variety.

And, there was no bubble gum! There were no hot patches for innertubes that were wearing thin. Retreads were a joke and V-mail was a poor substitute for an actual letter. And SUGAR!

More and more blue stars appeared on the windows along Church Street, plus the trauma that affected the whole town when a gold star appeared in a neighbor's window.

My dad was the Reverend John J. Loudin, a fully ordained Methodist minister. My mom did everything for the church except preach and pray.

There was an official custodian, Aunt Clara Sayer, who had been in service since the church was built back during the Civil War. Last Sunday, she had detected the faint odor of gas in the sanctuary and thrown open all of the windows that weren't stuck. That was probably a good idea, except that at the time the temperature was hovering around twenty degrees with a determined west wind heading a snappy cold front coming up the Ohio Valley into the ridges and hollers of the Mountain State. As a result, the room temperature rested in the low thirties at nine o'clock when she rang the bell calling the faithful to Sunday school. That was the last straw. As a result of all this confusion, Mom and Dad decided to take things into their own hands and quietly released Aunt Clara from her duties, which surprisingly made her happy.

"Anyhow, I'm just tuckered out," she sighed.

After a private conference between Mom and Dad, Mary and I were appointed as joint custodians for which we would receive twenty-five dollars a month, cash.

Custodianship consisted of keeping the dusty old building semi-clean, vacuuming the carpet runners in the aisles, dusting every one of the bleacher-like seats, distributing the hymnals and little paper pledge envelopes, and ... ringing the bell when scheduled. That in itself was worth the price in time spent. Oh yeah! I would get five bucks extra to keep the front steps and walkway clear of inconveniences like lots of huge maple leaves and a goodly amount of snow.

I was the envy of my Sunday school peers with the bell-ringing. I wouldn't let anyone even touch the rope. "No way, kid. You might turn it over and make the bell come crashing down through the steeple and kill us all."

I didn't really understand the scientific theory of all that but my threats were sincere and seemed to work okay.

I was very proud of my exalted position and wouldn't even let Mary touch my precious rope. I felt like Henry Fonda ringing the church bell in *Drums along the Mohawk*. Didn't Paul Revere's cousin ring the bell in the Old North Church the night the redcoats landed in Boston? Charles Laughton's hunchback didn't appreciate his bells in Notre Dame more than I loved that bell rope. And, what about the Liberty Bell? Yes, my little ego ran wild there at the end of that bell rope.

That particular New Year's Eve my little family had supper, did the dishes, listened to the discouraging war news with Lowell Thomas, caught Fibber McGee and Molly, made popcorn over the open fireplace, caught Fred Waring's Pennsylvanians and Kate Smith, listened to H.V. Kaltenborn's late news, and it was still only ten-thirty. I would never make it!

Mary suggested pickup sticks, one of my favorites. I could hardly keep my eyes on the jumble of colored sticks. Then at eleven forty-five, Mom shook me awake from my nap, my head on the dining room table.

"It's time to do the bell, big boy. Up and at 'em."

As we went across the short open space between our house and the church, a blast of frigid air in my face snapped me into a wide-awake state. The dark, empty sanctuary was even colder, and the vestibule was even more so with a large crack under the door that allowed a blast of winter to reach along the wooden floor. A bare bulb in the ancient wall sconce gave us just enough light to see Dad's pocket watch.

"You both get a good grip on the rope, and I'll let you know when to start."

Mary opened the door a crack. "Let's listen to hear when the Baptists start ringing."

"Okay, but we want to be first, don't we?" I suggested.

Just then we heard the distant dong of a bell echoing through the starry night.

"It's the Episcopalians," hissed Mary. "They always think they are better than the rest of us."

"Now, now Mary. It's okay," Dad soothed.

"Yeah, but I just bet'cha ours is louder, huh Dad?"

Mary and I gave a tug on the rope and were rewarded by a wonderful sonorous BONG from above that made the walls tremble.

"Let's open the door so we can hear everybody." Dad opened one side of the big, paneled doorway.

The midnight sky was crowded with stars as if each heavenly body wanted to be included in the festival of the bells there in this dinky village in the hills.

"Wow!" Mary exclaimed, as she leaned through the doorway while still holding onto the rope.

Dad stepped out and leaned over backwards so that his face was lit by stars. The jagged black pattern of bare maple branches framed the crystal sky into artful segments like a stained-glass window.

Now, a caroling of bells echoed through the night.

"I bet every bell in the county is ringing!" Mary shouted in my ear.

"Maybe even the fire bell down the courthouse," I added.

The bell up above seemed to be ringing itself once it got into the rhythm. Mary and I were both leaning out the door just barely touching the rope. Dad's face wore a smile with closed eyes as he took in the midnight melody.

Then, as the different bells dropped into silence, Dad put his hand on the rope.

"That's enough children. At least for this year"

The silence was deafening, broken only by the shifting sounds from the bell above us still creaking back and forth, settling in for the New Year.

By July of that year, our little family had made a dramatic shift in direction. Dad had always suffered from a respiratory disorder picked up during his service in WWI. In 1940, the VA decided he should try the dry desert climate of the Southwest. After a healthier summer in the Tucson, Arizona, VA Hospital, he decided to apply for a church in a dryer climate. This turned out to be Carrizozo, New Mexico, a little cowboy railroad town in the high, dry southern part of the state. Actually, Lincoln County, more famous for a once-upon-a-time delinquent named Billy. Yes, *that* Billy.

Carrizo means desert reeds, which abound in that particular valley. Back in the early 1900s when the railroad founded a watering and fueling stop there, a wise old railhand decided there were so many carrizo clumps around that the town called for an additional syllable. So the extra 'zo' was added to carrizo, which came to indicate plural zos.

The day we got into town, Mary and I were designated custodians of the church. This church was more like a bank, or maybe a Carnegie Public Library. No steeple, no bell, no stained-glass windows, no carpet, a front porch with four plain cement-gray columns in the style of a concrete underpass. There was a yard with things that were impossible to mow or trim. It was a weed patch with more tumbleweeds than actual grass, and a few scrawny elm trees that needed slight attention like water once a month. There were no leaves to rake, and the snow was just a myth.

There was dust—oh yes—there was dust. The wind blew at regular intervals, like every day and some nights. The tumble-weeds changed fences with the winds, north or west.

There was one bit of a plus to the building itself in the form of a small class/cry room in the back of the sanctuary that was blessed with an ancient wind-up Victrola that had been rescued from a house in a mostly abandoned Gold Rush town in the nearby mountains. It actually worked, in a fashion, with a tiny speaker included in the needle arm.

Along with my best buddy, Sonny Smoot, I was really into popular Big Band records, mostly due to the good fortune of Sonny's Aunt Bee owning and servicing all of the jukeboxes in Lincoln County. She stored hundreds of the hottest platters in an old house that included her office, phones, and Regina Apodaca, who took orders, etc.

Sonny and I did odd jobs for Aunt Bee in exchange for a few moments alone in the storehouse with Regina and her golden load. As a result, we amassed a hit parade of top-of-the-chart '78s.

One dull summer day with nothing to do, Sonny's Aunt Bee gave us the task of cleaning out the walk-in freezer of a closed restaurant that she intended to lease out. The job was horrendous to say the least, but Aunt Bee gave us six current hits each. *Wow!*

It's a long story, but at that particular time neither of us had an operating record player. I came up with the idea of using the old Victrola in the church cry room. I had the key, I was the custodian, it was Saturday afternoon, "what could go wrong?"

As we parked our bikes at the back door of the church, Janet May and Betty Jewel pulled up in Janet May's daddy's pick-up, so we invited them to come on in and listen to our brand new records. Artie Shaw, Vaughn Monroe, Peggy Lee, Sinatra, "what could go wrong?"

On the old Victrola with its steel needle, Paula Kelly and the Modernaires sounded like The Chipmunks and Vaughn Monroe sounded like Bugs Bunny.

Janet May and I were sharing the one adult chair, snuggling a bit and laughing heartedly while Sonny and Betty were trying to dance to the squawky tunes, when suddenly the door swung open and there stood Mrs. L. Simon Petty, scion of Methodism in all of Lincoln County.

Mrs. Petty stared at my hand until I realized that it was resting on Janet May's knee. I jerked it up but didn't know what to do with it, so it just hung there in space while I tried to get my breath. After a long and pregnant pause, "I came to put these flowers on the altar for tomorrow's service," Mrs. Petty said icily. "But now I see I should have called ahead, maybe to your father, Frank."

"We were just trying out some new records on this old machine." I was thinking fast with little success.

"Oh, Mrs. Petty, what a beautiful bouquet. Are they from your garden? You do such a great service to the church. We are so lucky to have you with us." Janet May was spreading it on real well.

Betty reached out and gently touched a blossom. "Is this a nasturtium?"

Sonny joined in. "You must have taken some art in college, Mrs. Petty."

I just sat with my mouth open and nothing in my mind as my friends laid it on.

"We-we-we have some great vases behind the piano. I'll just run and get one for your beautiful bouquet."

I jumped up, leaving Janet May to fend for herself.

Vaughn Monroe moaned into his closing, "There I've said it again," leaving the needle to grind into the center groove's endless whumpa-whumpa-whumpa. Mrs. Petty was first to return to action as she moved over to the Victrola and touched its quivering lid tenderly.

"This came down from White Oaks. It was in Hoyle's Castle when I was a girl." She struggled to open the cabinet doors in the lower section of the rather large piece of furniture. Sonny helped swing the stiff doors to a partially open position revealing a row of dusty records and a stack of what looked like sheet music.

Mrs. Petty pulled out one of the old records, one of those double-thick ones. She held it up to her lips and gave it a gentle puff, then squinted at the faded label.

"Animal Crackers in My Soup." Shirley Temple. I used to play this record when I was your age. The Hoyle house was always empty but my father had a key, so my sister and I would go in and pretend we were princesses that lived in the house and played this Victrola, this actual record, Shirley Temple. Every girl had a Shirley Temple doll. We all wanted long curls like Shirley. We all wanted to tap dance like Shirley in *The Littlest Rebel*."

"Let's give it a spin, Mrs. Petty," I suggested, removing Vaughn in favor of little "Curley Locks."

Shirley didn't sound any better than Vaughn on the scratchy old player, but Mrs. Petty got a serene look on her face and almost danced there in the cry room of the Epworth Methodist Church, lost somewhere in the past.

I went to get the vase and by the time I got back, Little Shirley had squeaked to a halt and my friends were looking at Mrs. Petty in wonder.

"Well, I must be on. Things to do you know. Always busy. Go, go, go." She twirled gracefully about and went out the door singing "In every bowl of soup I seeeee."

The four of us stood with open mouths.

"What about that?" Sonny broke the spell.

"Yeah, I thought we were toast."

I turned off the Victrola, placed Shirley back into her crypt, closed the door, and dusted off my hands.

"Let's get out of here. I think I just dodged a bullet."

Mary started college in September, so the custodian job was all mine. It became an act of tedium that I hurried through unsupervised, but still got paid thirty-five dollars a month, which I accepted without too much guilt.

Dusting was easy. Sweeping was easy. We didn't even have a snow shovel. The so-called lawn took watering, and I ran a rusty mower over it on occasion. There were just lumps of grass. But digging out the healthy tumbleweeds was a job.

My only responsibility was lighting the one cranky oil-burning stove early Sunday morning. Actually, that wasn't bad, as I had acquired an early morning paper route, so I was already up and about.

The town marshal, Jim Chisholm, commissioned me to turn off the city street lights every morning. There were fifteen of them located at strategic spots around town. The switches were located on each pole, and I was going that way anyway so it was a snap.

The one big plus I had was the ability to turn off any light I wanted to at any time, like the one at the corner of Court and Sixth, which incidentally lit up the front porch of a certain girl. Whenever I walked her home from the movies, I would just turn off the streetlight in order to enjoy our privacy there on her front steps. I dutifully switched it back on when I had captured my last kiss.

It also came in handy when we had a neighborhood Kick the Can game. I could bring darkness to the whole field of play.

My custodial career was at a low ebb for four years until Dad decided to move again. This time to the northern New Mexico town of Springer. A good promotion for my dad, and a new custodial challenge for me. This was my biggest responsibility.

Now my new charge had a steeple, bell, windows, kitchen, and a large social/class/dining room that demanded almost daily attention. Oh yeah! There was a large, old coal-burning furnace hunkered down in a dark crypt-like basement with a lot of junk and a mountain of dusty coal.

The biggest challenge I faced was Mrs. Porterfield, who

could show up any time to influence my custodial direction. Mrs. P. was a powerful force in town—a member of the Rebekahs, the PTA, the Women's Club, a Colfax County Fair board member-cum-lady, a Daughter of the Rough Riders, etc. I had to be on the lookout constantly, which interfered with my work and a bit of my pleasure.

There was a large classroom off the main sanctuary with folding doors that could be opened for unexpected crowds like Christmas or maybe Easter, or even an important guest minister—some transient revivalist like Sonny Jim with the big voice and ego to match. This room had folding chairs along with a big couch, end table, and small bookshelf that served as a library with mostly children's books and old copies of *The Christian Advocate*, plus a heap of out-of-date church notices and calendars.

This nest became my man cave with a couple of comic books secreted under the couch cushions and two bottles of Dad's Old Fashioned Root Beer in the back of the cluttered refrigerator in the kitchen.

I had been in my new school only two weeks before I attracted the attention of several female classmates. A new preacher in town is highly noticeable and a callow, reddish-haired teen boy who is already varsity basketball material will cause a primal uproar in the nervous system of a bevy of girls.

Judith C. led the pack. Cheerleader, sophomore, tall and slim with dark brown hair, who I soon discovered had several endearing features. A maverick of a sort, she smoked Philip Morris cigarettes occasionally and had the enhanced reputation of lighting them herself with an Ohio Blue Tip struck on her classic Levied posterior.

It wasn't long before we hit it off, so to speak. After school we might join "the gang" down at the Springer Pharmacy for a round or two of lime rickeys. She lived across town but I lived next to the church right on the main route up to the high school on the hill.

One dark and stormy afternoon we were, as usual, walking home past the church, when opportunity struck my fevered mind. Why should we stand in the rain to be together when my man cave sat there beside the way, offering shelter and privacy and maybe a root beer, and maybe ...

We entered the semi-obscure side door and were soon in the library. I helped her out of her cheerleader jacket, enjoying her aroma, slightly imbued with a hint of Philip Morris, but mostly girl.

I sat as close to her as I could, what with the cushion arrangement, as she pulled out a pack of smokes and lit up, waving her hand gracefully about in the manner of Lauren Bacall.

I had just made my first move when I heard the side door open and close. Snatching my trembling hand from her knee, I hissed, "In the closet, quick!"

Judith jumped up but just stood there. I could hear someone moving about in the room next door.

"In here," I muttered, grabbing her arm and shoving her into a nearby closet, pulling out a broom in a countermotion.

Closing the door on a wide-eyed Judith, I began to sweep the floor. Then I noticed a wisp of smoke hovering over the couch. Grabbing a current copy of *The Christian Advocate*, I frantically fanned the surrounding air space.

Mrs. Porterfield caught my last pirouette with the broom in one hand and the Methodist Church newspaper in the other, spinning about in the middle of the room.

"Frank, isn't it?" Mrs. P. gasped.

"Uhhhhh," I muttered, tossing the Christian periodical onto the table, trying to disguise the two root beer bottles. "It's a kinda exercise we do in basketball to improve our foot work. You know, like Meadowlark Lemon takes ballet to learn to make graceful moves on the court."

"Who? What? How? Meadow, huh?" Mrs. P. was speechless, which was just fine with me. "But certainly not in the church, not in this church." She regained her composure, and I went skittering around the room in a mock sweeping motion. She put her hand on the closet door and stopped, as did my heart.

Shaking her head like she had forgotten something, she turned and left without noticing the root beer bottles on the table. Judith was just standing there facing in when I opened the door.

"Who was it?" she snickered.

"Mrs. Porterfield. She left," I sighed.

"What if she had caught us?" Judith squinted at me and grinned.

"We would have been excommunicated forever and doomed to burn in hell."

"Yeah, but wasn't that exciting?" Her eyes were big and sparkling as she came over and kissed me right on the lips. I heard the church bell ringing in my chest!

That hot romance didn't last very long. Judith was a little too much for my timid self, but the custodian part continued. I was even promoted to taking up the collection and assisting Dad with the communion services.

After one winter of struggling with the old coal-burning furnace, we got a new oil burner, which made my early Sunday morning job a lot easier. The negative part of that move was that it became part of my job to shovel the now-unwanted coal up out of the cellar through a small window that was higher than my head and difficult to get to. I did get paid extra for that.

Dad was continually getting me jobs around town that I didn't particularly want. One good one was at the telephone office just across the street. Three mornings a week I would spend about an hour dusting, sweeping, and mopping the office where the switchboard girls did their "number pleases." They liked to flirt with me and vice versa. One in particular caught my imagination even though she was probably ten years older than I. Georgiana was a pert Chicana lady who called me honey and faithfully attended my basketball games to cheer me on, or so I thought.

Then, all too soon, the time came for me to fly the nest. I was off to college, never again to dust church pews or ring the bell, but I still get a tug in my heart on Sunday morning at ten or so when a distant bell echoes across our small town, calling my memories to service yet one more time.

# TEEZER'S TWISTS II

---

## STREET WORK

*T*t's a rainy morning at Teezer's. The rain quietly started sometime in the night. One of those light but persistent rains that locals don't really notice until somebody points it out.

"Looks like rain," some wise guy will say when two meet at the post office door with water dripping from the ends of their noses.

"Uh huh," the other guy will reply. "I heard it's supposed to be this way all week. If you want to believe those hot shots in the office down at KING 5."

Folks are jammed inside Teezer's. The regulars are split up because some high schoolers have the front tables and a perfect stranger is all by himself at the back, hovering over his laptop, sipping from time to time on a tall exotic espresso. He is oblivious of the hard looks he is receiving from the regulars.

"Another day of Orcas sunshine," someone is bound to remark.

You're supposed to give some unique reply, but most of us have run out of clever rejoinders having to do with Northwest rain.

---

Out in the front patio, a couple of umbrellas lie open, like grounded spaceships. Two Labs are circling for an advantage that only dogs understand, and a smattering of the very first red leaves have fallen to decorate everything. It's autumn, and the cool September rain is as welcome as the empty parking spaces down the side streets. This kind of rain doesn't really affect anything. The air is still warm off the Sound and windshield wipers just smear the dead bugs and dust.

Inside though, the lights seem a bit warmer and the hot drinks seem a bit tastier. Everybody knows everybody, even if you don't recall their names just at the moment.

You know where they work and which committee they are on and just who is apt to ask for a donation or a commitment of some kind.

"One mocha grande!" Carolyn shouts.

Three people jump up and go to the counter.

"I forget what I ordered," Terry says.

"You can have this one."

"No, you take it."

"No, you were first."

The two friends try to out-nice each other.

"One mocha grande!" Carolyn calls, putting up another drink without looking up.

The third person takes this one and the two break into snickers.

When Eric comes in and asks, "How's your back?" five people start to answer.

"I'm doing as well as any other terminal case could be expected to do," Bob replies.

"Do you all go to the chiropractor or just tough it out?" Frank asks.

"I go to yoga twice a week and do some at home," Jannie adds.

"I do erotic exercises," one of the women says in a low voice.

"Erotic exercises?" Three of the men gasp, almost in unison.

"Do you have any pictures?" Frank asks.

"Do you do them alone or do you have a bronze Adonis to

give you aid and instruction?"

"She means aquatic exercises. Don't get too excited or you'll have an attack."

"Nuts! I thought we had a good thing going there for a while," scoffs Bill.

"Yeah, I was trying to envision erotic exercises for geriatrics, but I guess that's better left alone."

There is a pause in the conversation as all eyes shift to the corner window. A public works pick-up is sitting in the intersection. Three guys in yellow slickers get out and place three orange cones in the street. One studies a piece of paper and points while the others spray orange paint stripes on the pavement. Then they gather at the back of the truck, light up cigarettes, and watch while traffic works its way around them.

"What are they up to?" someone finally asks.

Here comes the rumor mill.

"Looks like they're going to dig up the street," Jannie submits.

"Maybe they're going to build a traffic diversion wall to keep people from getting into Teezer's," Bill says.

"It's in the shape of a cross. I'll bet the Christian school has something to do with it." Frank's imagination is stretching again.

"No. They're going to put in a pedestrian overcrossing there so you can go direct from here to the post office," someone adds.

"They're going to put in a bike lane for John, so he won't get lost between here and the fitness center," Bob says.

'This building here's been condemned and that out there's where it's going to fall the next time it thunders," Steve says.

"It's a navigational device for flying saucers searching for intellectual life to abduct."

"They're really looking for Hooters."

The three yellow-slickered men finish their cigarettes, then tromp inside and up to the counter for coffee.

"What are you guys getting ready to do out there with all the orange markers?'

"Oh, just patch some cracks, I guess."

"How dull," Pat grunts. "We thought maybe you guys were actually going to do something we could watch, you know?"

Mark steps around the counter with his bar rag in hand.

"Last time they did that, a garbage truck came along and ran over their cones."

"Yeah. And I'll just bet they didn't stop to pick them up either," Eric adds.

The high school girls come in and the conversation pauses as each member of the old guard is reminded of previous conversations on the matter. The women frown and the men pretend to appear uninterested. The girls twitter for a while and leave with their chosen lattes.

"Well, we've got things to see and people to do," Frank grunts.

"You suppose the mail is up yet?" Bob asks.

They all gather up their cups and saucers, crowd over to the bus tray, speak their goodbyes, and tromp out into the rainy day. One of the orange cones is lying on its side and the fresh orange paint is running into the crack that needs to be repaired. The rain is getting a little harder and Turtleback Mountain is fading into the mist, while Mark puts on a new pot of Starbucks and wipes off the tables.

# SALSA VERDE

_____

O n a map of Arizona, about halfway up, a major geographic feature, the Mogollon Rim, baffles the tourists who are already having a time pronouncing Spanish names when ordering breakfast with tortillas and huevos rancheros, along with cerveza or cafe solo. Mogollon is not pronounced any way like it is written. The Mogollon Rim is ballyhooed on every enhanced road map as a must to explore. Its natural grandeur is beyond the imagination, just like its pronunciation. There is a picturesque old ghost town with the same name, a gully, a ridge, a mine, an ancient Indian tribe, a mountain, a bar on highway AZ 277, and probably a laundromat out on the highway east of town.

Somehow the town of that name slipped across the line into New Mexico. It is a very picturesque collection of ghostly architecture scattered along Graveyard Gulch on a dry creek that also serves as a rut called Main (and only) Street.

If you look in the tourist's guide, there is a list of local towns in Arizona that no one really knows how to pronounce. Yavapai, Sonoita, Mazatzal, and of course, Huachuca. Well anyway, Mogollon is "Mug-ee-yun," according to popular practice.

A few Octobers ago, Jan and I, with our poodle Beanie (Sabrina), were motoring across Arizona trying to find a highway that we had never explored, searching for inspiration for my painting career. Searching along the backroads of America for historic barns, bars, backhouses, tractors, trains, and turnstiles. Anything of the rural countryside.

Checking the map after visiting glorious Sedona, we spotted remote AZ 277 that would lead us into New Mexico at a spot that promised ghost towns and desert mountain scenery. I had read about Mogollon and seen photos, but that doesn't do the job like an actual visit.

During the long first day out of California, we had decided to enhance our trip with a purpose. We agreed to research roadside huevos rancheros and/or New Mexico enchiladas along the way at every opportunity.

Snowflake, AZ, became our first experience. I found out later that this minuscule burg was founded by two country entrepreneurs named Flake and Snow. What are the chances? The only eatery in sight was set back from the highway as if it wasn't sure it belonged. The little scabby, sun-faded white stucco and corrugated tin building was designed along the style of a one-time Foster Freeze gone wrong. Swinging awkwardly on loose screws, a well-seasoned Pepsi sign timidly muttered *Food* in a way that should have included a question mark.

"Are we really going into this place?" Jannie muttered as we turned from our car and got a good look at the overall scene.

"This is the last town for a while and it's getting late for breakfast, and I'm really getting hungry. Aren't we looking for authentic Southwestern cuisine like huevos rancheros?"

"Does that include dead flies and cigarette butts?" Jannie stopped and gave the place a good examination.

I held the Wonder Bread screen door for her, trying to ignore the long-ripped spot in the screen patched haphazardly with duct tape.

Inside was sparse to say the least. Two booths under the front windows and four stools along a counter, plus one stand without a seat accounted for the furniture.

Along the back wall was a row of totally empty shelves if you didn't count the trash and spider webs. Oh, there was a pyramidal arrangement of those little Kellogg cereal boxes along the top shelf, some right side up, some not. In the center of the shelf arrangement was a pass-through window into the kitchen, where a wrinkled face flashed back and forth from time to time. A well-fed woman was presiding over the morning cook top with all the confidence of the Cordon Bleu.

"You'all here fer eats?" A raw-bone fellow burst through a swinging door at the center of the back wall and took a stance that was almost a challenge. The cigarette hanging loosely in the very front of his thin lips bobbed up and down as he grunted in his best Rocky Balboa voice. "You'ns can jest sit anywheres." Jan scooted into the first booth and I sat across from her facing the door in the finest tradition of the Old West.

"Coffee, yeah?" He wore a well-seasoned T-shirt with a pack of smokes rolled up in the sleeve showing a badly executed tattoo rendition of an anchor involved in some way with a rattler on a knotty bicep marbled by blue veins. His small head was blockish with a squinty face on the front and a skid mark of thin black hair on the top.

He shuffled across the room and put one foot up on the bench beside Jan, dropped a plastic-covered, typed menu on the table, grunting "Yeah?"

"Two coffees and two of your huevos rancheros with everything," I confidently requested.

"Comes with bacon er chorizo," Rocky informed.

"I'll have mine just plain." Jannie said.

"And mine with chorizo!" I added with enthusiasm.

"Chorizo?" Jannie gave me a look of astonishment. "You're gonna die."

"Don't worry. It will be so hot it will be totally sterile. Did you see who is cooking back there?"

"Yes, and I'll bet she earned her spurs cooking down at the state pen in Yuma."

Rocky came back with our coffee in well-used USN mugs.

"The chorizo is the best. Mama makes it herself. She is from Nogales. Where you'ns from, huh?"

"We're just traveling through from LA."

"LA, huh? I got the caca beat out of me one time in East LA, man. You'ns from around there, huh?"

"No, we live on Catalina Island, just off of California, you know."

"Where you'ns headed, anyhow?"

"We're going over into New Mexico. Around Carrizozo, thereabouts." I took a sip of coffee and shuddered at the strength of it.

"Carrizozo. I got the caca beat out of me one time out there."

Mama slid two steaming plates onto the pass-through and punched a bell somewhere.

Rocky turned and served up our huevos rancheros. They were on huge plates. Cheese, onion, chili, pinto beans, two corn tortillas, covered with salsa verde, topped with two fried eggs and a dollop of sour cream and more salsa verde dripping over the edge of the plate. Oh yes, mine included two chorizo patties.

"You'ns want a Dos Equis to go with that chorizo? I got some real cold."

"No thanks. I gotta drive you know."

He shrugged and disappeared back into the kitchen where a Spanish conversation erupted that we didn't understand, which is probably just as well.

"Thank God. I was worried that we were about to get the caca beat out of us in Snowflake, Arizona." Jannie snickered.

The food was really good if you didn't look around very much.

We both ate pretty fast, casting our fearful looks at the kitchen door frequently, but all was at peace.

Rocky came back with the check. We settled up and departed with a "You'ns be careful there, hear?"

# WHITE SANDS NATIONAL MONUMENT

Two hundred and seventy-five square miles of glistening, 30-foot, white gypsum dunes. Our dog, Beanie went nuts. She skittered up and down those dunes with total enjoyment. It was like a dream, that beautiful, totally black creature skittering over those stark white dunes under a blue, blue desert sky.

On our way, we had passed up several attractive eateries in Alamogordo, but they all seemed too upscale to suit our enchilada purpose, so we motored on north to Tularosa and a highway cafe where a collection of vehicles represented an endorsement from local clientele. Included was a State Highway cruiser, Mountain States Tel. and Tel. repair crew, Tularosa Sewer and Septic, a couple of real cowboys hobnobbing across the flatbed of a vintage international antique, and an assortment of well-traveled sedans.

Blocking the door was a topless Volkswagen convertible with the rear seat removed and replaced by two bales of hay and a dusty old saddle.

## TULAROSA, NEW MEXICO, POPULATION 2,234, ELEVATION 4,511

LIONS INTERNATIONAL Every Tue. 11:45 A.M., the sign proclaimed.

"See there, Jannie. Only the finest choose this spot."

"Does it have a name?" Jannie stood on the step and gave the place a good going over.

"Maybe it's NO SHIRTS NO SHOES NO SERVICE like it says there on the screen door," I snickered.

The heavy glass door gave an irritating rip across the stray gravel strewn across the linoleum floor, getting the attention of everybody inside. They all swiveled around on their stools as if they were expecting something special, like Princess Diana or Geronimo.

The waitress was decked out in a too-short black uniform dress accentuated by a dainty white apron matched by a lacy bow in her severely pulled back salt and pepper hair. Her horn-rimmed glasses sat out on the end of her nose held in place by a glittering string of glass beads. She pointed her pencil in the general direction of the empty booth next to the pinball machine.

We took our assigned seats and reached for the menus that

were in their traditional spot with the napkins and condiment collection.

I looked over the selections listed on the Wurlitzer tabletop coin machine. "We are really out west here. Just look at the musical tastes of the local citizenry. I feel like we just went through a time and location warp." The selections included Willie Nelson, Hank Williams, Patsy Cline, and Loretta Lynn."

"Yeah, and we're Ozzy and Harriet." Jannie added.

"Y'all havin' lunch er jest coffee?" the waitress asked with pencil poised for action.

"It says here that you serve authentic local food. What does that mean, Tina?" I inquired politely.

She peered down at me over her glasses. "In the first place, it means that it's very good and that it is New Mexico style. Especially the enchiladas with stacked tortillas and cheese and real beef and stuff with a fried egg on top with lotsa chile sauce, rojo or verde, you know. Tía Cocinera does it all. Has for as long as we have been here."

"Well Tina, we want two of your local stacked enchiladas with salsa verde." I spoke with authority.

"Did I hear verde?' She raised her perfectly enhanced eyebrows.

"Sí, verde, por favor." I was getting into the moment.

"Okay, verde."

"Verde." She tucked the pencil neatly behind her silver and turquoise ear ornament and whirled into the kitchen.

"How did you know her name is Tina?" Jannie whispered.

"Oh, I can just tell by experience, and it said so on that little thunderbird pin she has on her bosom.

"I might have known you would be looking at that particular spot."

"Just being my usual observant self. I am a professional illustrator, you know. Need to see and reference everything."

Tina came back through the swinging door with authority and placed a large glass pitcher of water and ice cubes on the table in front of me.

"You might need this later on."

"Thanks, Tina. Have you lived in Tularosa long?" I asked.

"All my life. Born in a little adobe out on the west side. Other side of the tracks, so to speak."

"Then you went to school here, like high school, you know."

"Yes. I was a cheerleader senior year. Go Wildcats!" She giggled like a schoolgirl.

"Do you remember a big guy, ball player, named Gallo Bernal? I played for Carrizozo back when, and I remember him well. He was tough."

Her carefully done eyebrows gave a slight wrinkle. "I don't. I'll ask G.W. over there. He played ball before I was in high school, you know."

She went over to a man in khaki work clothes setting at the counter. They both turned and looked at us.

"Gallo was a tough kid I played basketball against. He was Mescalero. Really chunky with huge shoulders and bowlegs. Had a big hawk nose and a crop a black hair that stood up like feathers on top of his head, kinda wild. Gallo means rooster. You can see how he got the nickname." Jannie is used to my farfetched tales.

Tina returned with our enchiladas, which were so big that they spilled out over the rim of the plates.

"G.W. says Gallo is a Ranger with the Forest Service up on the reservation. Fights forest fires and all that. A few years ago, he and another guy picked up the little cub that became Smokey the Bear, you know? Saved it from a forest fire, they say."

"Thanks, Tina. These look really great, and the water."

The plates were stacked at least three inches high, covered with thick salsa verde, a generous dollop of sour cream, and three ripe olives.

Halfway through, our eyes were watering and the pitcher of water was half gone.

"I guess we got our money's worth this time, huh Babe?" I filled both of our glasses again.

Jannie just rolled her eyes and took another sip of water.

The man in khaki got up and sauntered over to us with a big grin.

"You folks handle that green fire pretty well." He had a name patch on his shirt proclaiming G.W. Chapman, Tularosa City.

"This is the best. Hot though!" I proclaimed.

G.W. nodded. "I can only take it once a week," he chuckled. "So you remember Gallo? He is kind of a legend around here. For older folks you know."

"I played for Carrizozo. I don't think we ever beat you guys, though. Actually, we didn't beat much of anybody. But we had fun, I guess."

"I know what you mean. Jest travelin' through, eh?"

"Yep, Zozo for a quick look and then on up to Vaughn for the night."

"Well, make sure you keep gassed up. There are some lonely stretches."

"Yeah, thanks." I stood up to shake his hand.

"Well, you'll take care now."

Tina brought the ticket. I followed her over to the cash register and paid up.

"Great enchiladas, Tina. Give my regards to Tia Cocinera."

"I'll do that," she smiled.

I whispered, "Go Wildcats."

She giggled and gave me a look over her horn-rimmed glasses.

Outside, the hot desert sun was doing its job on the atmosphere as a miniature dust devil went twisting up the highway to the north, the way we were headed.

"Looks like we have an escort. That's only fitting on the way to Carrizozo."

Jannie gave me a look over her sunglasses. "Does that bode evil, ya reckon, buckaroo?"

Five miles out of Tularosa, the highway took a turn for the worse. Gravel! And dusty. It even went down into the arroyos in lieu of bridges. It is real desert with mesquite, yucca, skimpy sage, many thorny things, jack rabbits and some poisonous critters.

There were no fences or electric poles or any other signs of civilization, except for the occasional highway signs decorated with various patterns of bullet holes and rust.

# CARRIZOZO, NEW MEXICO, POPULATION 1,325, ELEVATION 5,425'

I actually lived in Carrizozo from 1943 to 1946, during the height of WWII. At that time, it was a bustling railroad town of probably 5,000 tired railroad workers and attending folks. The three hotels were crowded, as were cafés, boardinghouses, and other supporting businesses.

Every Southern Pacific train, including the special troop trains, east and west, stopped there for water and coal.

Now those big new diesels just go pounding through with maybe a toot or two. The depot foundation is about all that remains of the Southern Pacific complex that once occupied the track side cinders.

Down the main street the only sign of life was a nondescript hound stretched out in a sparse patch of shade by the front door to the Yucca Bar. He reluctantly rolled over and plopped his head back down in the dust.

"That's the town greeter. He fetches the bartender if anybody shows up," Jannie snickered.

"Yeah, he works for tips. Sirloin, that is."

On down the street there were two pick-ups in front of the post office.

"That's a new post office," I said, giving the two cowboys a good look, thinking about some of my old schoolmates.

"I wonder if Billy the Kid picks up his general delivery unemployment checks there." Jannie was getting into the nostalgic spirit of the day.

The two men must have noticed our California license plates because they both turned their backs on us and stared into the tumbleweeds in front of their trucks.

I nodded to their backs and muttered a quiet "Howdy." Jannie snickered. Nothing.

We drove up and down the deserted streets with me pointing out points of memorability with not much interest from Jannie.

Understandable. Like, "On those front steps I kissed my first girl. Her name was Janet, coincidently. That's my dad's church. Methodist if you will. That is where I worked as a grocery boy when I was fifteen. Oh yeah!"

We went by our old house. "Look how the trees have grown!" Right! What happened to our grassy front yard? Years of neglect. "We had a windmill and a big tank, a garage, a small stable with a real corral, and an actual outhouse there in the far back. A real ranchero." There was little sign of life anywhere.

"Let's get out of here," Jannie sighed.

"Okay by me." I performed a wheelie in the middle of my old home street.

Down two blocks and around the corner was Paden's Drug Store in a two-story brick building that showed age with cracked and peeling paint, loose caulking in the brick walls, and sun-faded glass windows. A weathered sign proclaimed Carrizozo's Historic Museum. "Let's go in. Just for a minute. See if they remember me or my dad."

Jannie snorted. "Are you kidding? Do you realize how long it has been since you left here? When was it?"

I thought. "Holy cow, how long ago was that?"

There was a jumble of old stuff in the window that included a copy of *The El Paso Times* featuring a large photo of the first atomic detonation cloud.

"That was 1945. I was here that morning. That thing was only sixty miles west of here. I might have delivered that very newspaper the next day. Wow!"

Jannie opened the front screen door. "Come on, Rip Van Loudin. This is your life," she spoke in a deep voice.

Inside was dark, musty, and kinda eerie. It was actually an old drug store featuring a classic soda fountain with two carbonated water faucets and an impressive row of labeled condiment bins. A marble counter served six authentic 1930s wire stools. The back of the bar was all mirror and stacked soda glasses and Nehi Orange Soda advertisements. A beautifully rendered Chesterfield girl smiled benevolently down at us. "Helloooooo!" came from somewhere behind the clutter.

"Helloooooo yourself," I answered, surprising myself with such bravado.

Jannie took a good hold on my elbow. "It's the spirit of Dr. Paden."

A dumpy little man materialized from among the dim clutter and limped to a station behind the soda fountain, wiping his hands on a once-white apron.

"Howdy. I'm Roy, sole proprietor, soda jerk, janitor, and general all-round stepanfetcher." He did a slight bow and had a big grin.

I scooted up onto a handy wire stool and leaned my elbows onto the dusty marble counter.

"We're Frank and Jan. I used to live here back in the day. Just passing through to give Carrizozo a look. Have you lived here long?"

"Long as I can remember. Mother and Dad too. Four brothers. Most worked for the SP during the war until they modernized and laid off almost everybody."

"My name is Loudin. My father was the preacher at the Methodist church in 1943 to '46. I went to high school here. I—"

He interrupted me. "Oh sure, Loudin. My brother Art went with your sister Mary."

We were getting into it now. "What's your last name?" I saw a big Roy on the wall outside. "Are you Roy?"

"Yeah. I'm Roy Dow. My brother was Arthur Dow, I—"

"Oh yeah! Roy Dow. Arthur Dow. Ran the skating rink one summer. Mary thought he was cute. Mom didn't think so. But there you go, huh?"

"You went with Janet May Shafer, my next-door neighbor. She married a doctor, lives in Denver I think."

"Well, I'll be."

Jannie had found an old magazine in a pile of papers and was trying to ignore all of this good ol' boy stuff.

After the usual spurt of "whatever happened to," we shook hands and parted with, "If you see anybody that might care, please give them my regards."

Back in the car and on the road again, there was a long period of quiet as my memories swirled around and Jannie dozed.

The highway returned to gravel again a mile out of Carrizozo and meandered around desolate desert undulation under a brilliant evening sky through Corona, where I played in my first high school basketball game.

## VAUGHN, NEW MEXICO, POPULATION 737, ELEVATION 5,965

Vaughn was probably founded where two Comanches rested under the only tree in sight for a bit of rattlesnake jerky, then went their separate ways. Subsequently cattle trails, wagon ruts, the first railroads, and highways just happened to repeat the pattern.

Today the Burlington/Santa Fe and Southern Pacific main lines from Chicago to the west coast actually cross there on the way to Albuquerque and El Paso, respectively.

I didn't know this when we innocently selected a motel for the night that was well back from the highway, as claimed on its roadside advertisement. Well back from the highway meant next to the railroads. Not one but two railroads.

As we pulled up to the motel there in what passed for downtown Vaughn, the distant *blaat* of a diesel horn echoed off of the aged Bunk House Inn sign.

"There is something comforting and yet haunting about a distant train horn. Especially at night. When I was a little kid back in West Virginia I could hear the whistles at night and think about those trains full of strangers that came and went to and from distant places like Parkersburg and Grafton. Well, the horizons of little kids are not far from home."

The *BLAAT!* came again. This time much closer.

Jannie elbowed me. "Is that train going to do that all night?"

As we checked in with Rolland the night clerk, there came

a rumble that made the faded drapes tremble, and I noticed a tiny tsunami in the tropical aquarium there at the far end of the counter.

Rolland raised his eyes. "That's an eastbound. They only blow for the crossing downtown."

"And the westbounds?"

Rolland slid the keys to number twenty-six across the counter. "Oh, the westbounds seem to do whatever they want to. Kinda play it by ear, I think."

Jannie nudged me aside. "Do they do it all through the night?"

Rolland slid a collection of travel propaganda at us and turned to answer the persistent phone.

Outside, a giant headlight was pulsating across the fading sunset as another *BLAAT!* came from the east, or was it west?

I could feel Jannie rolling her eyes even though she was facing the other way. Room twenty-six was indeed back from the highway. Way back! All night it felt like we had rented an upper berth in a roundhouse, kept awake for a while discussing which direction the *BLAAT!*s were coming from.

Next morning, we could hardly wait to get out of town and away from the *BLAAT!*s. As a final salute before turning north in the middle of town, the railroad signal was activated, so we sat there for one final toot to AT&SF SP.

## LAS VEGAS, NEW MEXICO, POPULATION 12,483, ELEVATION 6435'

Old Las Vegas, the original Las Vegas, was founded around 1835 as the first town encountered on the west end of the Santa Fe Trail after 700 miles of open prairie. By 1879, when the AT&SF came to town, it was one of the largest "cities" in the Southwest.

There have been economic ups and downs but through them all the town has just mellowed like its classic frontier architecture. La Castañeda is a one-time Harvey House. You know, Judy Garland and all that AT&SF fuss.

I read somewhere that it had been restored into a fine Mexican eatery. So we decided that would highlight our quest for the ultimate salsa verde.

"This place doesn't look very open." Jannie took off her sunglasses for a better look as we pulled into an empty parking lot at La Castañeda.

"Humm." I made a wheelie right there by the impressive front that featured a collection of Mexican icons. "Let me see just what that sign says."

I stepped out of the car and climbed the broad tile entrance pavers to approach a sign on an easel.

"No está aquí, Señora." Looks like they're only open for dinner at 5."

Back into the car Jannie murmured, "Qué malo, Paco." I pulled yet another wheelie back onto the main street.

Directly across from La Castañeda was a once-upon-a-time Phillips 66 station. We could tell because only the very necessary elements had been converted to Bueno's Burritos. Everything facing east or to the highway had been haphazardly painted a garish Tesuque turquoise. The rest still featured a well-weathered Phillips 66 orange. Where these noncompatible hues met along the side of everything, the color clash was to offend even the most insensitive observer. Phillips 66 orange and Bueno's turquoise are not compatible anywhere.

"Well, this will help us forget Snowflake chorizo." I pulled up to the front door to be greeted by a couple of half-empty cans of turquoise just waiting for some artful application. Also, leaning against the can was a crude message. "OPEN SOON—Watch for it."

So we forgot our quest for salsa verde and popped in to an IHOP for Dutch babies with strawberry jam and sour cream.

North on US 85, NM 3 split off and headed into a series of mesas that buttress the foothills of the Sangre de Cristos. The narrow blacktop wanders up and up through Sapello, Buena Vista, La Cueva, and Mora before suddenly making a sharp left turn to climb steeply up Holman Hill into real mountains of Ponderosa forests, alpine meadows, rapid little streams with actual beaver dams, quaking aspen, and three stoic elk lumbering along nonchalantly in the fast lane.

Here was a totally different New Mexico. More like poor man's Switzerland but with no houses. As we descended the western side of the mountains, there appeared more and more little rancheros with adobe houses and log sheep sheds. All with the typical battered red Ford pick-up and cock-eyed TV antennas. Nine miles out of Taos a sign warned, "ROAD WORK AHEAD, WATCH FOR FLAGGER, LOOSE GRAVEL, ABRUPT EDGES, TURNING TRUCKS, FRESH OIL, SLOW FOR WORKERS, LIGHTS ON," and some wise guy added with a spray can, "KILROY WAS HERE IN 1947."

"Somewhere the highway department sign painter is either out of work or out of paint. This is his one-man show," I chuckled, as we slewed around a sharp curve in a mound of loose gravel.

Jannie added, "That sign guy could have used some turquoise just to add some interest."

## TAOS, NEW MEXICO, POPULATION 3,109, ELEVATION 6,965

The Taos city limit sign was a welcome sight as we encountered a larger than usual heap of loose gravel in the middle of the road. As we descended, our car gave a shudder and a bang that rattled our bones and woke up Beanie. She bounced around in the back, barking at her imagination.

Now our vintage Toyota Wagon sounded like a Sherman tank.

The first chance to get off of the highway was by a picturesque sign announcing Los Arboles Cottages. Pulling in under a canopy of ancient cottonwoods, we rested as our Toyota gurgled and hissed and sighed into grateful tranquility.

"I guess we were meant to stop here. Let's just hope they have a spot for us and our faithful companion, Old Beans."

We climbed out of the shuddering old Toyota with relief from too much auto paralysis and went into the office.

We were greeted by a matronly lady who appeared through a macramé doorway. She sported classic Pueblo ornamentation. Squash blossom necklace, a jangling arrangement of delicate silver bracelets, a thunderbird brooch name pin with Martha inscribed in turquoise, salt and pepper hair pulled up into a bun, tiny round glasses on the end of a delicate nose, and a black velvet skirt gathered to a small waist by a concho belt to match her silver necklace.

"Welcome. Looks like you just came down the mountain through our highway improvement project. Probably need a glass of wine." She had a beautiful smile.

I dropped into a wicker rocker. "I'll say. A glass of wine and a good mechanic for Old Paint out there in the corral."

She smiled. "Car trouble?"

"Yes. I think we left some auto parts on a pile of gravel back there."

Jannie joined us. "Our little Toyota sounds like a bulldozer that would be unacceptable in a quiet town like Taos."

Martha placed two small glasses of red wine onto the counter. "Well, there is one cottage left in the back that we call our doghouse, if that's all right with you folks." She slid the registration book over in front of me.

"Sold! Don't know how long we will be here. It depends on what happens with our car." I took a sip of wine. "The way things are right now, it may be for a time."

"I really don't want to get back into that car until my bones stretch out some." Jannie took the other wicker rocker and we settled back.

Martha came over to us. "I'll get Lloyd and we'll work on your car situation."

"Lloyd," she said into the macramé doorway.

"Hello," came from somewhere in the back.

Lloyd came in carrying a small painting. "I just finished this one. Makes twenty-two in all. I never thought there would be so many when I started."

I stood and looked over Lloyd's shoulder at the small watercolor rendering of a patch of healthy chicory.

"It's very well done," I offered with sincerity. I usually don't comment on other people's artworks.

Martha joined us. "He is writing a book on highway horticulture. It's about the so-called weeds that seem to thrive in the gravel and junk that collect on the berms of our roads. You'd be surprised. Some of the names are really delightful. Like this one, it's pussytoes, and this is Angelica, and here is my favorite, everlasting. No, I think this is my favorite, in name anyway, fiddle neck."

"That is really charming. May we see more?" Jannie knows how to treat sensitive artsy types.

Lloyd blushed like a schoolboy. "Really mean it?"

"Sure. I dabble in watercolor myself," I offered humbly.

"We need to work on your car situation, first." Lloyd put down the painting and reached for the phone. "There is a real good young fellow that has a shop just down the alley. His family is one of the old ones from the pueblo. Odegbi, Emerson Odegbi. He keeps our old Buick wagon going."

We all sipped on our wine while he dialed, then spoke quietly. Turning to us, he said, "We're in luck. Emerson was just going to the Napa store and agreed to stop by for a look-see."

"While we wait, let's go get our stuff into the cottage and take care of Beanie."

The cottage, Puesta del Sol, was cheerful and cozy. Beanie attacked her food dish with vigor and made herself at home on the bed.

I went back to the car to find Lloyd talking to a pair of Nikes sticking out from under the rear bumper. Emerson scrambled out and stood up, a well-built fellow with a long black ponytail and a silver earring. He gave my hand a strong grip as I met his green eyes.

"Looks like your tailpipe has come loose from the muffler. Not much wrong, just loose."

"Will you be able to fix it alright?"

"Yep. I'll just drive it down to my shop at the end of the alley to get it up on my rack and weld it back together. No problem"

Lloyd beamed, "Emerson has a master's in engineering and music. Not exactly a wild son of the prairie."

"Lloyd, where would you go to enjoy the most Taos-y of Taos food tonight?"

"Oh, that's an easy one. Kokopelli's. And it is just down the street. Won't need your car to get there. I can call them if you like."

"I hope the salsa verde is not too caliente." Jannie inquired.

"Ask for their elote with cotija cheese and sopa Azteca. They are special and only at Koko's."

We decided to just trust our luck and walk on down to the restaurant for an early dinner. In the middle of the next block—Taos block, which is not necessarily defined by anything in particular—we spotted a very simple hand-carved Kokopelli in an ancient wooden door.

Kokopelli is the coyote clown of native New Mexican folklore represented by a highly costumed dancer who performs comical jigs and gyrations. He can be depicted as a cartoon-like kachina figure, a doll or painting, or just crudely scratched on a rock wall.

Inside was dark after the bright New Mexico afternoon. A young man greeted us with a smile and a gracious half bow. "Buenos días. Are you here for dinner?"

"Buenos días. Lloyd from Los Arboles sent us. We're just two for dinner. He suggested your elote with cotija cheese creme. Martha says they are the best anywhere."

"Oh yes. They come here quite often. I'm Carlos. This is my sister Carlita. She will be your waitress for the evening. This will be your table. That way you can enjoy Abuelo's music and get to meet Kokopelli." Carlita indicated a table in the corner across from a tiny fireplace where a guitar leaned quietly against a carved wooden chair.

By the time we had gotten well into our margaritas a goodly crowd of diners had passed through our room and disappeared down the two steps into somewhere in the back. We could hear muffled kitchen sounds and murmured conversations as our eyes got used to the dim atmosphere. A little boy brought a basket of chips and bowl of salsa verde.

"See, we must be in the right place. Kokopelli knew we are green salsa folks."

Carlita came into the room, gently leading what was obviously a blind man. He had a long silver ponytail, a turquoise shirt, ancient jeans, and huaraches. She guided him to the chair by the fireplace and helped him settle in with the guitar on his lap.

There came a high-pitched "Hola Abuelo."

"Hola Koko" came from the old man that caused a furious fluttering as a large black bird detached from the shadows, then circled the room before settling on the back of his chair.

"Did I just see a crow come in and say 'Hola' to that man?"

Jannie's margarita was poised halfway to her lips. "Yeah, I think so."

After that, there was some tuning and gentle strumming of a few chords that led into "Cielito Lindo," rendered so softly that we weren't sure it was really happening.

Our dinner was served about halfway through the basket of chips and salsa.

"I'm glad that we skipped lunch back there across the mountain." I gazed at the large terracotta taza of corn chowder smothered with Hatch chiles and cotija cheese. Then there was the salsa verde.

"Let's have a cerveza." I was smoldering after my first of taste of the salsa verde.

With our cerveza there was a spirited rendition of "El Rancho Grande."

Jannie sipped lady-like at her cerveza. "This is sure better than Tularosa tacos or Snowflake chorizo, huh Paco?"

Abuelo swung into singing "La Paloma." When he got to the part with the "Coo Coo Roo Coo Coo" there came from the other room a lusty "Coo Coo Roo Coo Coo." Carlos and Carlita answered in kind. The four folks at the large table across the room laughed and joined in.

Then to everyone's surprise, the big black bird fluttered across the room to the fireplace and presented his own version of a loud squawky "COO COO."

Abuelo repeated the musical phrase and Koko continued to flutter excitedly around the room repeating a raspy collection of Coo Coos.

When the performance ended, the house was filled with laughter and happy applause while Koko made the rounds squawking "Buenos Dias, Buenos Dias."

As we meandered back up the street, the sky celebrated the New Mexico setting with a glorious arrangement of more stars than we had ever known to exist.

"There must be a Kokopelli up there someplace along with The Great Bear and Apollo and all of those other Greeks, don't you think?" I put my arm around Jannie's shoulder with a squeeze.

"You may be right there. I think I can just make Lincoln and Washington and maybe Teddy there in the corner."

"Yeah, and not to mention Mickey and Minnie with Pluto, and Kermit the green frog." I stumbled over a lump in the street.

"Be careful what you say. The spirits can be touchy."

Back at Los Arboles we found our car parked in front of the good old doghouse. A note under the wiper from Emerson instructed us to please leave thirty-seven dollars with Lloyd, and adios.

"Boy! That worked out pretty good, didn't it?"

Beanie greeted us at the door like we had been gone for a month.

"I just want to get into bed and rest my eyes and feet." Jannie yawned, tossed her sweater onto a chair, and fell onto the bed.

As we lay there recounting the day, I said "I think I can hear the AT&GN *BLAAT*ing for the town crossing back there in Vaughn."

Jannie giggled and nestled up close to me.

West of Taos, the desert slopes gently down to the Rio Grande Gorge where a spectacular bridge leaps over the river far below, boiling through a volcanic crevice.

We had to get out of our car to listen to the silence that makes one hold their breath in awe. You can feel the sound of the river far below, but you can't really hear it.

West of the river, the land is about as open as it gets. Mostly high desert sage and mesquite, a weathered juniper now and then, and scattered piles of huge boulders that give the appearance of having fallen from the sky eons ago.

The official city signpost was temporarily being used to prop up a dilapidated cattleguard so it was unreadable.

Tres Piedras (three rocks) is aptly named. Don't know how they selected just those three boulders to honor with a title.

"This place should be named Abandonada Comida." Jannie watched as we whizzed past a scattered assortment of empty diners all in a variety of disintegration.

"Looks like a Monopoly game gone sour some time ago. Makes me kinda sad. Somebody's dreams didn't come true."

In contrast, there were isolated homes that showed a decidedly modern flare. The road twisted and turned into high open country with patches of forest and open meadows.

"I think I have been here before with John Wayne and Roy Rogers. They must have shot a bunch of westerns around here."

Jannie rolled down her window. "Just smell that air."

"You know, we haven't seen another car this side of the Rio Grande. It's kinda spooky but in a nice way." I checked the rearview mirror.

Around the next bend we came upon a large herd of cattle and three cowboys. Yes, real cowboys. They were driving those critters right down the highway. Too bad about us.

We stopped and watched as the whole show turned down off of the highway and through a gate toward a very picturesque log barn. By then I was out of the car with my faithful camera.

I felt like John Huston. They were doing everything just right for my viewing pleasure. As the last critter passed safely through the gate, the nearest cowboy doffed his Stetson in true Western style.

"Can you believe that?"

Back in the car, Jannie greeted me with her big smile. "Yeah. That makes the trip worthwhile, doesn't it?

"Not to mention all of the salsa verde."

# TEEZER'S TWISTS III

---

## SHOT FOR SHINGLES

*T*t's just after 10 on a chilly November morning. The pretty leaves in the patio are caught up in a breeze off the Sound, swirling around with a Snickers wrapper and the lid from one of Teezer's coffee cups.

Patsy's yoga class is over. Pam's Power Hour is over. The regulars from the fitness center have dried off and are hungry, and Teezer's Geezers are present in force, gathered at the two back tables and along the wall.

The one common denominator here is silver hair or, in some cases, little or no hair. In fact, that is the subject for discussion.

"Frank! You've lost your ponytail. What happened? Did Jannie cut it off while you were sleeping? Like Samson?"

"No. Suzie the barber did it. I told her I wanted to be the best-looking guy on Orcas, so I needed a new look. You know. Younger, sleeker, faster."

Tony, without even looking up, mutters, "You should get your money back . . . and maybe even bring charges."

"Did you save it?" Dotty asks, running her hand down the back of Frank's head.

---

"Naw, it wasn't long enough for that. I thought maybe the Pentagon would need it to make bomb sights for B-17s, but I guess that time is over. Remember when girls used to do that for the war effort? I bet somewhere there is an old U.S. government warehouse full of ponytails."

Frank stares out the front window at the clouds over Turtleback. "Do you suppose, if I went to that warehouse and rummaged around, I could find Martha Miller's ponytail that I used to lust over when she sat in front of me in study hall?"

Jannie nudges him with her elbow. "If you could find it, it would probably smell like an old groundhog pelt."

"Remember when girls all had ponytails and those long skirts?" Bob asks.

Jannie runs her hand through her short hair. "Yeah. Then we all went to short hair and short skirts."

"I liked that," Frank says, and the other guys nod in agreement. "There was a vice principal in my school, a woman Home Ec teacher named Clarice Phelpery, who would measure the length of the girls' skirts and send a note home to their mothers if they were too short. One mother sent back a needle and a spool of thread and told the teacher to do it herself."

"Yeah! Way to go, Mom!"

"Nowadays we should be satisfied if they have on any clothes at all."

"I think I'll get studded tires this year," Bill announces to the room.

"El Niño or something is supposed to cause a hard winter . . . they say."

"Hmmmm," they all nod and sip.

"I'm gonna get a shot for shingles," Bob announces.

"I knew a guy in the Marine Corps who almost got shot for something like that," Frank says.

"You sure knew a lot of weird guys in the Marine Corps, didn't you?"

"Why do you think they accepted me? They knew I would fit right in."

"We have a friend who had shingles. It is bad stuff, and it

can last a long time," Elsie informs.

Bill butts in, "There was an old woman in my hometown that had shingles so bad she got the shakes."

"Then I suppose she got aluminum siding and a metal roof," Jannie snickers.

"Hmmmm," they all nod and sip.

"The library board is looking for a new member. They need new blood."

"Don't look at me. My blood is old and tired and can't stay awake after dark."

"Every board in town is looking for new blood. You can even be president if you don't watch out. At one meeting I dropped my pencil, reached down to pick it up and when I straightened up I had been volunteered to judge the Fourth of July Parade."

The Geezers have all been on committees and boards and study groups and consulting teams, etc., and are now content to just sit back at Teezer's with a second cup of coffee and watch friends and neighbors come and go. With this group, there is no limit to subjects.

Sometimes the talk can go from the popularity of shark fin soup in Hong Kong, to Sarah Palin, and back again without a hitch.

Rusty comes in, orders "two Debbies and a Rusty" at the counter, then turns to greet the Geezers.

"You have drinks named after you in here?" Frank asks.

"Yeah. Don't you?" Rusty grins.

"Only if I change my name to Venti Nonfat Quadshot," Frank replies. "Actually, that isn't a bad idea. You can call me by my last name, Mr., or maybe Sir Quadshot. What do you think?"

Mike announces, right out of the blue, "You know, the fire chief wants to have a boat for the fire department, in order to take emergency patients to Bellingham when the weather is bad, or at night, or something."

"They gonna dig the ditch right up to the fire station?" Dotty wonders.

"No. They're going to build a giant slide from the station

down the slough to the Sound."

"Yeah, in the summer they can give rides to the tourist kids. It'll be like the Matterhorn at Disneyland," Frank adds.

The crowd breaks up, leaving for the post office, market, Napa Auto Parts, Suzie's Barber Shop, to help at the Food Bank or the Senior Center, heading home to weed bust, stack wood, or any of the myriad chores that seniors have to contend with.

Mark wipes off the tables, picks up a scrap of paper from the floor, carries a tray of dirty dishes into the kitchen, and quiet settles over Teezer's . . . for a moment.

# TILLY McGRAW'S
# GUTTER REGATTA

---

**N**orth Street actually went east and west but it didn't matter because it was only three blocks long anyway and anyone with good sense wasn't about to get lost. The east end of North Street had a nice slope to it. I say nice because that made it perfect for sledding in winter or Indian Ball or roller skating or bike riding stunts the rest of the time.

There were nice houses along the street all the way from Tilly McGraw's at the middle to "Spider" Snider's chicken farm at the lower end.

Oh yes, it was paved but there were no curbs to speak of, but there was a wide strip of grass between the pavement and the sidewalk. This strip of grass served as a sorta gutter for both the street and the sidewalk.

I tell you all of this because to better understand the story you have to know the territory, so to speak.

Anyway, up at the east end of North Street there lived a dear old lady named Tilly McGraw in a modest Victorian house with a tin roof and old leaf-clogged gutters and leaky down spouts.

On a good rainy day, say in April, Tilly's tin roof collected considerable runoff, which drained into a downspout that didn't connect to anything, let alone the cistern at the bottom. It just spewed out into Tilly's treasured grove of hollyhocks, then ran helter-skelter like the North Platte River across the lawn and under the decorative wire fence into the so-called gutter.

This stream attracted the kids like bees to honey. Nothing is more fun for a kid than mucking about in water, a stream, or a puddle after a whole morning of rain-induced confinement.

It all got started one rainy day when Frank and Mary, on the way to the post office, got involved with two leaves racing down the gutter. Being two normal kids, they chose a floating champion to cheer on and a race was initiated.

They began to look for proper streams to race on and started to select odd things to represent racing yachts. Dry leaves soon gave way to candy wrappers, cigarette butts, matchsticks, snail shells, etc.

Other kids began to join in, so the Gutter Regatta was born. Tilly's downspout's output was just right with the perfect amount of water and the dependability of enough flow for their purpose.

Tilly never imagined that she was the origin of a regatta. In fact, she probably wouldn't even know just what a regatta was. Probably not decent or Christian, for that matter. One of them things best not even thought about, she might assume.

In April, the season for great gutter runoff, during a break between showers, Saturday about one thirty, Mary and Frank accidently ran into Little Jimmy Casto and Fuzz Beamer puddling about in the grass gutter.

Great conditions for a race, Mary suggested.

"I double dare you." Little Jimmy took up the challenge.

"I double dog dare you," laughed Mary.

So it began.

Mary came up with an old English walnut half shell. Quite floatable but tipsy, named after the owner, Queen Mary, of course.

Frank sported a folded Fleer's Double Bubble Gum wrapper, artfully folded into a snazzy marine shape, named Bubbles.

"Really dumb," said Mary.

Little Jimmy found a milkweed pod the shape of an Iroquois canoe, named Chief Iroquois.

"Really dumb," said Mary.

And Fuzz Beamer found an unknown celluloid object that floated really well. Being blue it was named Blue Blaze.

"Really dumb." said Mary.

At this point I need to lay out the racecourse. From Tilly's fence, the stream spread out all over the sidewalk but then gathered again into a real stream when it got down in the grassy swale between the sidewalk and the street.

After a straight run past Lester's and Penell's in front of the funeral parlor, it dropped down into a kinda cement basin and swirled around before shooting into a round culvert under the street. When the contents emerged from the culvert, if they did, they dropped into a cement-lined ditch that shot straight past Uncle Charlie's front porch, between his turnip patch and Duncan's barn, onto a dirt alley where the course kinda fooled about in some deep ruts before dropping through a fence down into Bill Shinn's meadow.

In the meadow, the water just spread out all over the place like the Mississippi Delta, heading roughly north through a copse of willows before gathering again into a real stream just as it passed under another fence, under the highway, and into Sycamore Creek. The racecourse ended right as the stream passed under that last fence. Usually, some racers didn't make it all the way. Sometimes none of them made it. Once, all of them were lost in the culvert under the street.

The rules were that you could not touch your ship with your hand but must use a stick to assist any stranded boat.

## THE RACE

A bright ray of sunshine broke through, touching the east end of North Street as the four of them put their boats into the stream just outside of Tilly's front fence.

"Just what are them young'ns up to?" Tilly asked her cat, Fitzbenny, as she peeked out the lace-shrouded front door window.

The overweight tom didn't see anything that might be of interest, so he just jumped up on the dining room table looking for the perfect nesting place for the morning after a hard night on the town. The table was covered with the litter of living alone. Lunch leftovers mixed with bank statements and charity requests surrounded a centerpiece. A white porcelain mug in the shape roughly of John the Baptist or Gary Cooper in his nightshirt. It was a keepsake from the Chicago World's Fair. The cat chose a pile of quilt pieces.

The four kids dropped something onto the sidewalk and went chasing and splashing down the gutter out of sight.

"Well, I never!" mumbled Tilly, testing the knob to make sure the door was locked.

Outside, the Queen Mary went merrily, merrily down the stream, leaving the others behind, confused by clumps of weeds and a discarded garden hose.

The Queen's shell swirled around with indecision on which way to go when a rock plopped down right in front of her. Mary said, "What tha?" Looking up, she saw Ernest "Catfish" Erwin ready to fire again.

"You better not, Fish Face."

He had squinty little eyes and a too-wide mouth. Some said his mother had dropped him on his head as a baby, maybe? He just gave her his fish face grin and tossed another pebble at her ship.

Mary got that look on her face. She walked over to Catfish and, with a lightning-like maneuver, grasped him by the shoulder. With a quick twist, she threw him down, face first in the gutter.

Frank laughed, as he knew his sister's famous twist throwdown well. Mary had practiced it on him many times. The other boys broke into great peals of laughter as Catfish went dripping and whimpering into the back door.

Meanwhile the other contestants had caught up and were forming a cluster. All four entered the black hole of the dreaded culvert test together.

The four of them raced across the street to the other end of the culvert.

Uncle Charlie Kessel observed all of this from his front

porch, tucked into his high-backed wheelchair. He had a special armrest with a cup holder attached for his ever-present amber-colored sipping drink. Some claimed he made it himself in his basement from turnips. TURNIPS? Uncle Charlie loved to watch the kids doing their thing out in the street. Especially Mary.

When she was up to bat, he would pound on the porch rail with his hickory cane and yell, "Go get 'em girlie!"

Mary waved and bowed to Uncle Charlie, which always made him chuckle in delight.

Three of the racers came out of the culvert together. In fact, they were stuck together like one big mess, except there was no Queen Mary. Mary bent over and peered into the black hole, and peered and peered. No luck. No Queen.

Two of the other three went on down the swift-flowing ditch, but Bubbles had come unfolded. Having lost its handsome marine shape, it now was just a soggy scrap of featureless paper lumping along the bottom.

The Blue Blaze and Iroquois were now neck and neck as they entered the maze of mud ruts in the alley. They both meandered in confusion until the town garbage truck came sloshing along and placed one of its huge Uniroyals on The Blue Blaze.

So it was Chief Iroquois that dropped alone into Bill Shinn's meadow. But wait! It was only half there. The faithful milkweed pod had come apart after too long in the water so was no longer a recognizable craft but a collection of scraps drifting along without any direction or purpose.

The rain came first in just a few large but scattered drops, but to the southwest dark clouds and lightning promised something more significant was about to happen.

"Let's get fer home!" shouted Fuzz. But Little Jim had already disappeared.

Back at Uncle Charlie's, Frank had joined Mary on the front porch where Aunt Louisa had brought out a sheet of fresh cinnamon twists and some hot cocoa.

Up at the east end of North Street, Tilly McGraw said to her cat, "Don't you just love to hear the rain on the roof? Sounds like little dancing feet, and the plippity plop of that old broken downspout like toy soldiers at parade." Fitzbenny got up, stretched, tried out his claws on a velvet purse, and curled the opposite way.

# TEEZER'S TWISTS IV

---

## BLUE COLLAR TIME

*A* sliver of a moon plays around a patch of broken fog along the ridge of Turtleback Mountain as a lone '67 Chevy pick-up drifts right through the stop sign in front of Teezer's and pulls into the no parking zone by the side door. A big, scruffy guy slowly gets out the passenger side, takes off his Stihl cap, runs his gnarly hand through a mop of graying hair, reaches into the cluttered truck bed, and pats a big rusty-colored mutt on the nose. The happy dog nuzzles the man's hand, furiously wagging his feathery tail.

The other man, a skinny little fellow with a bent cigarette clinging to his lower lip, slides out of the cab, coughs a deep racking hack, spits into the gutter by the kitchen door, then rubs his face with a sleeve coated with plaster dust.

Inside, warmth and coziness mix with the aroma of fresh baked scones and hot Starbucks. Mark has been there since 1 a.m., working his magic with his own brand of bakery goods. By the 7 a.m. opening time, the glass case is filled with a variety of goodies to suit the tastes of all who might drop in.

The two guys from the pick-up are just the first in a line of early workers that make Teezer's a regular stop. In fact, some of them are already on the clock, meaning that some poor unsuspecting person is paying them hourly wages to do just what they are currently doing.

Every workday, from opening until about 8:30, there is a constant line of workers filling coffee mugs of various descriptions. Most of these mechanical experts seem to have trouble with the lids on the paper cups. They stand there complaining about the job while twisting and crimping those simple plastic lids with their battered and scarred fingers.

The pick-ups in the no parking zone range from huge Dodge crew cabs with GPS, cell phones, and fancy titles emblazoned on the driver's door to a multicolored rust bucket with homemade stake siding that looks like the fence on an Ozark hog farm.

If you have a particular need for concrete pouring, repairing leaded windows, patching a leaking skylight, pumping a septic tank, sitting with some elderly person, or baking pies for the school sailing class, sooner or later someone of that ilk is bound to turn up here.

A couple from a golden state south of here found that if they hung around Teezer's long enough, they could not only find the workers they would need to build their dream house, but could get unsolicited recommendations for same. On the other hand, they would find out just which tile setter would take a job, then go fishing in Alaska—right in the middle of the project—leaving it unfinished until his bait ran out.

Not just the working class gather here. Architects, lawyers, acupuncturists, chiropractors, and retired wealthy professors will show up from time to time. Committees are formed here for the Library Fair, the Fly-In, Christmas Choral Society, kids' soccer, New Year's Polar Bear icy dip in the lake, or just a volunteer work crew for the library park clean-up.

Yes, 7 to 8:30 a.m. is Blue Collar Time at Teezer's. These guys aren't here just for small talk.

Two telephone guys stand at the counter by the coffee urns. "We have to get into her crawl space to get the fax line to the office," Charlie squints over a steaming double latte."

"I bet it's a long time since anybody has gotten into her crawl space," Bud adds with a snicker.

"It's full of cobwebs and rat crap, a lot of old stuff left over from her husband who died fifteen years ago, at least." Charlie is just getting warmed up to the subject.

"Maybe he's in there, too." Bud jams the lid onto his big plastic coffee mug and goes to the door.

Charlie pays Mark, rolls his eyes to the ceiling, and follows Bud, who holds the door open for a big—no, FAT—guy in a set of coveralls that announce "certified some-thing" on a red patch over his left breast. The "something" is a smear of black stuff that disguises just what he is certified for. He has a tail of Teflon tape hanging out of his hip pocket, so that he looks like a big brown Bubba Bear with a skinny white tail.

"Fill 'er up, Marko!" The plumber bellows as he lifts four grande paper cups into one of the gray paper carry-out trays, then proceeds to fill them to the brim, struggling to place lids on top.

The brown Bubba Bear leaves just in time to hold the door for Roy, a good-looking guy with long salt and pepper hair and a well-trimmed beard. He has a fine collection of clip-on pens and pencils in the pocket of his carefully ironed lumber-jack shirt. He has a cell phone as well as a buck knife in a little leather carrier on his belt.

"Has Mr. Summers been in yet this morning?" he asks Mark as he ponders the collection of goods in the glass case.

"Haven't seen him. The usual to go?" Mark asks, while reaching for a pecan and cinnamon scone.

"I'll just sit and wait. He has his wife with him this week, which means a lot of extra stuff for me. She changes her mind every time she comes over and it screws up everything. I've got a whole pile of wasted material stacked around from her changes."

"I hope you included her in your bid," Mark sympathizes.

"Well, I should have paid more attention to what was said by some of the other guys that have worked for them before. She sure is good looking, though. I lose a lot of time from my crew when she's around. One guy tripped over a piece of rebar and fell right into a wet slab when she was walking by. She should be figured into a contractor's job insurance of some kind."

"Yeah," Mark says. "I know."

Uzek, the Orcas Towing guy, comes in to check out the crowd.

"Anybody call for a jumper job?" he asks.

Bob says. "Tony, don't you need a jump start today?"

Tony holds up his latte. "I have mine already."

Uzek meets a stranger as he goes out. They talk a bit and go off together.

Robin, the landscape guy, comes in and five people try to corner him.

"Talk about popularity. This guy is hard to get," Frank says.

"Yeah. And if you do get him, you probably can't afford him."

The electric lights flicker and go out. The three OPALCO linemen, sitting in a corner booth, get up and hurry out.

"What is it this time?" Bob asks.

Mark is already on the phone. The whole place quiets, looking at him.

"It's just a short down the street that only affects this side of town," Mark announces to the room.

"Yeah, I saw that short go by just now. He was about four feet tall, dressed in green spandex, with mud cleats on his slippers and a slick helmet that glowed orange," Frank says, getting up to look down the street.

"What did you say?" Dotty grabs Frank's elbow.

"I said Mark's short just went running up the street."

"I didn't see anyone like that."

"Oh, he was there, all right. You just have to believe."

Dotty punches Frank on the shoulder, announcing, "Come on, Bob, we gotta go."

That's the signal. Everybody gets up, clears their tables, clustering at the front door, patting backs, saying their goodbyes.

Mark and Carolyn are whispering behind the counter as the place clears out.

# *911 (IN CASE OF EMERGENCY)*

*A*ctually, I did call 911 on a wintery evening in 2000 when my chimney was spewing sparks out of the top like a rocket ship bound for Space Station Krypton.

"Just what is the nature of your emergency?"

It actually was a calming voice. I felt better. I was not alone. It was so calming I expected the next question to be "Mother's maiden name?"

"The emergency is my house is ON FIRE."

"Street address?" She was calm and collected. What did she care? It wasn't her house.

"Are all occupants out of the house and safe?"

"No! It's cold and raining outside. Spitting snow. That's why the stove is spewing flames out the pipe. The front door is open. Does that matter?"

"Just what is your complete street address and the nearest cross street."

"No. No. The street is just a country lane. No cross street. Just a dirt road up a hill. A curve, turn left, open gate, watch for Spencer, a big white poodle. He hates trucks. Hurry!"

Silence. More silence.

"Are you still there, 911?"

"Just what is the nature of the emergency?"

"Thank you for your call. Support your local EMTS."

71

Back in yesteryear, before 911, even before "Pennsylvania 6-5000," the alarm was just shouted by a guy running up the street yelling, "FIRE! FIRE!" or down the hall, or from a fourth-floor window. (Never in a crowded theater.)

Once upon a time, when I was around thirteen, I had a real 911 one event. Picture this. Carrizozo, New Mexico, during WWII was a small but busy service stop along the Southern Pacific main line east and west from Chicago to Los Angeles.

From an ugly little cement block and stucco building, my father, a Methodist minister, served his calling faithfully with a gentle hand and open heart.

I was a callow *El Paso Times* delivery boy, timid and shy but punctual.

One blustery Saturday morning as my dad and I drove around my route collecting the weekly fee from my fifty-seven scattered customers, we happened to notice a whiff of dark gray smoke hovering over a licking blaze in a pile of trash beside Omar Spurlock's garage. That in itself was disturbing but then we noticed perched just beyond the flames was a fifty-five-gallon drum, which likely contained something highly combustible.

Dad pulled into the driveway.

"Son, run over to the City Hall and tell them about this." At that he jumped from the car, grabbed a handy garden hose, found the faucet, and bravely advanced on the potential disaster.

Fortunately, City Hall was just around the corner and down half a block, so I was there in a breathless jiffy.

"FIRE! FIRE!" I shouted, bursting through the door upon two stalwarts in faded jeans and well-aged denim shirts with little embroidered FIREs over their left and only pockets.

Vergil Harkey peered over his *El Paso Times*. "Ain't you the preacher's kid?"

"My dad's over at Spurlock's squirting at a fire with a garden hose."

"You ain't Spurlock, are you?" Punk Harkey studied my presence up and down.

"NO. NO. THERE'S A FIRE OVER AT SPURLOCK'S! MY DAD NEEDS HELP! FIRE! I'M TELLIN' YOU!"

"Steady there, son. How come he didn't come his'self?"

"He's squirting it with a garden hose, I'M TELLIN' YOU!"

"Nobody called us." Vergil picked up the phone and held it to his ear, then gave it a good shake. He slid back from the table, slowly got up, carefully folded the newspaper, walked over to a rack of big yellow slickers, chose the third one with a large black V. HARKEY on the back, climbed up into the cab of the homemade 1936 international hose, ladder and tanker, flicked on a battery of emergency lights (red and yellow), ground at the starter until an explosion boomed from somewhere under the rear end, and a cloud of acrid blue smoke filled the room.

Meanwhile, Punk pushed past me and pulled at a tangle of ropes, which somehow connected to the big overhead garage door. He then climbed into the right-hand seat and with a lurch they rumbled out onto the street and disappeared around the corner, leaving me standing there with my mouth open. Alas! I realized that I was not to ride on the fire truck, a lifelong fantasy, so I jogged back to the scene of action.

Dad was holding his own, now supported by the Harkey duo and a tangle of hoses.

Looking about for something to contribute, I spotted Martha Miller across the street, watching with interest. Martha was my dream girl. At least for that week. With a burning desire to impress, I picked up a hose and ran at the fire with as much bravado as possible while dragging such an impediment.

I continued past both Harkeys, then past my dad until I was practically in the fire. It was then I realized that the hose was not only empty but was not connected to anything. Dropping the awkward hose, I side-stepped the fire, stumbling ahead into some assorted trash cans and a stack of empty apple baskets.

By then the Harkeys had control. With their nozzle on super-spray, they were soaking down everything. That included the now-smoldering ashes, the fifty-five-gallon drum, a pile of newspapers, etc., my dad, me, the garage wall, and an open kitchen window. Then in a grand final flourish, the rusty muck from the bottom of the water tank came out in perfect coordination to pass over the fence and decorate the neighbor's fresh laundry with colorful patterns of Navajo terracotta drippings.

Martha, now accompanied by a throng of neighbors, enjoyed the display of first responder coordination that was mindful of Manny, Moe, and what's his name at their hilarious best.

Omar Spurlock never showed up to show his gratification, so as the Harkeys gathered up their hoses, my dad and I quietly got our well-hosed selves into our car and went home.

P.S. Martha Miller never mentioned the event, much to my relief.

About two weeks later, again a Saturday morning as I rode about town on my new red Hawthorne bike collecting twenty-five cents for daily delivery of *The El Paso Times*, I just happened to notice a whiff of smoke coming from under the eaves of the old Thom house which sat alone on the desert about a quarter mile down a narrow dirt trace from the official edge of town. Mr. Tom N. Thom was a general handyman who was familiar with several kitchens in some of the most prominent houses in town. Yes, it was Tom Noble Thom, T.N.T. There was nothing explosive about Mr. Thom, except perhaps his breath.

That day, I was a veteran first responder as I bravely thundered down the short dirt road and into the Thom side yard. Several locals were already there shouting and running back and forth with no apparent purpose. Mr. Thom was nowhere in sight. Smoke was now coming out of the upstairs windows as my buddy G.W. Chapman struggled from the kitchen door with the awkward rocking chair and a pile of quilts. Throwing them down in the weeds, he shouted, "There's more stuff," and ran back inside.

I followed him and two others into the small kitchen where the four of us picked up a wood-burning kitchen stove, including a burning fire within, and proceeded to take it out the door into the backyard. When we returned, we found the stove pipe had come loose and lay on the kitchen floor bellowing smoke and a bit of flame.

Enter the Harkeys, Vergil and Punk, with their rustic fire apparatus and its large spray nozzle. Their truck was now backed up to the back porch allowing the Harkeys easy access to the kitchen where they proceeded to spray liberally the smoky parts of the stove pipe. As this action continued, there was less and less smoke. The stairway cleared. A breeze came through the kitchen.

The Harkeys shut down their spray. We all stopped and looked at each other. There was no more fire. The only smoke was from the scattering of stove pipe parts there on the kitchen floor. Someone started to laugh. Then we all joined in.

As we gathered up our individual belongings and went out the gate, Mr. Tom N. Thom stood with his Mrs. staring at the smoldering kitchen stove setting there in the backyard surrounded by a haphazard collection of household impedimenta.

Oh yeah. The 911 call. Well, they did show up. By the time they got into all their baggy yellow gear and had done all they needed to prepare for, the fire had gone out, but Spencer did enjoy the visit, especially the big red truck in his driveway.

# TEEZER'S TWISTS V

---

## 'TWAS JUST BEFORE CHRISTMAS

*J*an and I go into Teezer's on the Friday morning before Christmas. We go unusually early, at least for us, and it seems kinda empty. Mark is there, but just standing behind the counter full of goodies that he has been working on since really early that morning.

Perry, the Napa guy, is nursing a large paper cup as if he is clinging to his last moment of life. Over in the corner, Valerie the caregiver and a lady we have seen in here many times but, like so many others, we don't really know, are sharing the table in the corner and staring out the window.

Outside is chilly and blustery, dark and gray and kinda ominous. One of those pre-winter days that folks expect only the worst from the weather. We keep looking at Turtleback Mountain for snow, or at least rain, to start blurring the landscape at any moment. A stiff, chilly wind is racing up the Sound to the front door of the post office where it whips the tattered flag around the post and makes the metal clips ring out like "Jingle Bells."

---

Inside, Teezer's is cozy with decorations that accent the dreariness of the empty streets. Across the intersection, the Enzo's sign looks lonely as it stubbornly cries out to the few passing cars: OPEN! WE ARE OPEN!

We get our table of choice where we are able to observe anything that might happen. The coffee is really hot and the pumpkin scone is still warm while background music plays that tune where the dogs bark out "Jingle Bells" over and over, but after all, it's Christmas and you have to put up with stuff like that.

The Napa man tops off his coffee and leaves. Valerie suddenly looks at her watch and goes out without a word, leaving us there with the woman we don't know, but that isn't a problem with Jannie and Teezer's.

"Hi, I'm Jan and this is Frank," Jannie reaches out her hand.

"I'm Carol."

Frank stands up and reaches out his hand.

"I'm Frank."

"Yes, I know, I love your art."

"I get that a lot and it never gets old," Frank smiles.

During the course of conversation about the weather, Carol says that she is from a small town in New Mexico and was, at one time, one of the few female police officers in Albuquerque. The rule was women had to wear skirts and their hair could not touch their collars. Carol describes some of the hairstyles that she came up with to avoid cutting her hair. One came in twin braids down to her ears, then took a hard right angle out over her shoulders. She stiffened it, she said, with some sort of smelly gel that glittered.

"How did that go over?" we inquire.

"Two of the rookie girls copied it the next day, and still, not one of the men noticed. When we wore our regulation uniform hat, you know, those Smokey the Bear things, we looked like space creatures with helmets that were wired to our ears."

"Didn't they ever notice?"

"Yeah. The chief finally issued a memo that all women's hair must be less than three inches long and not attached to the hats in any way. He actually thought that our hair was stuck to the underside of our hats in some way."

She laughs 'til tears come into her eyes, and we can't help but laugh with her. It's one of those infectious times when we're all laughing because somebody else is laughing.

A young man that we all see around town and the market but never speak to, pays Mark for coffee, and then goes over to the pots and spends the next seven minutes concocting his own mix. He pours a half-inch of regular, one spoon of sugar, one squirt of milk, stirs with a white plastic stick, and delicately takes a sip. Then he pours another half-inch of decaf, a spoonful of sugar, a squirt of milk, stirs, and sips. He continues this routine while the line behind him grows and grows. Each time he moves right or left, depending upon the mix, the line shifts in the opposite direction. It looks like a line dance of some sort.

Mark finally asks him to stop. He takes one last sip and walks out without ever acknowledging anyone around him.

Mark just shakes his head as the rest of us poke elbows and snicker.

"Hey, look!" Folks at the counter all turn and rush to the side windows. We hear singing.

Out in the street are about a dozen young people on horseback, all turned toward Teezer's singing "God Rest Ye Merry Gentlemen" while trying to control their nervous mounts. One kid, dressed like an elf, is shoveling up the steaming deposits and dumping them into a wheelbarrow decorated with red ribbon and bells.

"Boy, that is the true spirit of show business."

Mark goes out, passes around some cookies, then they clop on down the street with Santa's little elf chugging along behind with his wheelbarrow full of steaming road apples.

"Wasn't that neat?" Jannie exclaims, and we all nod.

Bob gets his jacket off the hook.

"Well, we have to go to the Holiday Fair at the Legion Hall, the Artisan's Faire at the Odd Fellows, open house at several places, the Library Tea, and then the dump, so we better get going. Merry Christmas, everybody, if we don't see you again before!"

Outside we see that old Turtleback Mountain is fading out at the south end and a couple of wayward white flakes swirl around the Teezer's tree out front. We can still hear those dogs barking "Jingle Bells" as we go to our car there at the corner of A Street and North Beach Road.

# *THE DREADED*
# *GRAPEVINE*

———————

*T*must be the dumbest kid in the whole seventh grade.

I lifted another shovel full of the new fallen snow off the front steps of the old Methodist parsonage that we called home.

*No. Actually the dumbest kid in the seventh grade is definitely Eli Harden. He just sits in the back row and picks his nose and farts. He smells like our dog's old blanket and can't even do the pledge of allegiance.*

That settled, I shoveled off the top step.

"While you are out there you might just as well go over and do the back steps to your dad's office. He has a meeting this morning," my mother's voice came through a crack in the front door.

*Jeez! I'm just getting even dumber.*

Last weekend I had convinced my sister Mary to a deal in which I would have the use of our one bike for all day Saturday in return for the use of our only sled any time she wanted it for the next week.

Then today, Saturday, a bunch of us kids were going to bike up Sycamore Road to explore an old spooky abandoned farmhouse. Flora Jean Powell had asked if I was going. This wasn't a date-like thing, but anything she did, I wanted to be there.

*How was I to know the very first snow of the whole year was just*

———————

*around the corner?*

I shoveled to the end of the paved sidewalk, leaned the shovel on a tree, and tested the snow for snowball quality. It was just a little dry but I still came close to the light pole clear across the street. I carried the shovel back to the garage, put it against the wall behind the now-useless bike, and dug out our ancient homemade wooden sled. This thing went down the hill like a sack of garbage, but it was better than nothing. Barely.

"Did you do the church steps like your dad asked you to? That's part of your job, you know. If you expect to get paid." Mom knew just how to twist the knife.

"I'll do it this afternoon. Maybe it will quit snowing by then." I secretly hoped not.

"See that you do and don't sled in the street. You'll get hit by a car."

Moms always know just how to put the old damper down, don't they? You'll get hit by a car. You'll put out your eye. You'll catch your death. What will they think? Well, *I* care how you look. Would you jump off a cliff if Keith Simmons did?

She said something more as I turned the corner, but I missed it because just then Mr. Beamer came by in his pick-up with snow chains that rattled and banged as he chugged on down the street in second gear. The heavy air was thick with big fluffy flakes that clung to everything. I stuck out my tongue and tilted my face up to the sky. It gave me a chilly tickle.

"Hey Francis. Better get on up there before they wear out all of the snow." Our neighbor, Uncle Charlie Kessel always called me Francis. He liked all of the kids on his street. Watched them play and fight and grow up, even fall in love. He was out with his old-fashioned wooden snow shovel that he probably made himself in his shop off the back porch.

I walked past Flora Jean's big house whistling "I Don't Want to Walk Without You" as loud as I could without spluttering, watching hopefully for any sign. The darkened windows just stared back at me and muttered, *There goes the dumbest kid in the seventh grade.*

As I turned the corner off Maple Street onto Seventh, a heavily clad body on a sled shot under the barbed wire fence and went head first down a steep bank, across the street into a ditch.

As I got closer, the body rolled over and wiped the snow from its face. I could now see it was my buddy, Little Jim Casto. Yes, there was a Big Jim Casto. He was older and bigger.

"Hey Franko. Boy what a ride. I came all the way down from Twin Maples really fast. It's just perfect. Fuzz Beamer already broke his arm, maybe. He crashed into that iron post at the Hey Dad Hole. Anyway, he went home crying."

Fuzz Beamer was always breaking something or other. He liked the attention bandages and slings afforded him. Girls thought he was so brave. Guys thought he was a wimpy hamburger.

Little Jim and I squeezed back through the fence and started the climb to the top of the hill. As we made our way up the steep slope, kids whizzed past us with screams and screeches as some successfully made the run while others spun out into a pile of snow or crashed into a patch of blackberry brambles.

Here and there, kids stood brushing ice and snow from their clothes or wiping their faces and adjusting their assorted outfits.

I recognized my sister, Mary, as her red and white toboggan cap whipped past on our sled.

Flora Jean and Lois Ann Vineyard came by in tandem on Flora Jean's big Snow Queen sled. Flora Jean didn't notice me.

"Get out of the way, kid." Shake Casto—yes, another Casto—a high school kid, yelled at us.

The bigger kids always try to take over.

You could start at "The Hump" like most little kids and girls did, or go on up to the Twin Maples with the big guys. There you could get a quick start at a place where two big maples spread their roots together forming a four-foot drop almost straight down. If you were good or lucky, by the time you got to Death Valley, a straight stretch that was always icy, your speed was hard to manage, so you just hung on.

The really brave would turn off at the Hey Dad Hole, a place where there must have once been a foundation of some sort, because there was a rectangular arrangement of rounded mounds that enclosed a deep hole full of weeds, ice, and gunky black water. An expert sledder could whip off the regular downhill, along the upper shoulder of the hole, make a hard left turn to avoid the iron post, then drop down over the front wall at a speed that turned most sledders into a tumbling ball of snow sled and bodies. Only the best or luckiest could complete that maneuver and get back onto the Dreaded Grapevine.

The Dreaded Grapevine was a twisted series of tracks full of icy lumps and uncontrollable ruts and thrills.

The Hey Dad Hole was so called in honor of Hey Dad Ferguson who, a few years ago, had crashed headlong down into that hoary hollow and broken off the bottom of his two front teeth. From then on, he spoke with a slight lisp, but still was the first kid in our town to get drafted and sent to Fort Dix, New Jersey, where they put him in the Signal Corps as a radio operator and sent him to North Africa.

I stopped at The Hump to watch a couple of girls sitting very close together start   down the hill. The one on back had her arms tightly around the one in front. I thought about Flora Jean. I would never get her on this dumb wooden sled that I was stuck with, but maybe on her Snow Queen. Just maybe.

"You kids get out of the wash," a couple of high school boys yelled at us as they zoomed by in a flurry, their runners making a hissing sound.

"You gonna try from Twin Maples, Frankie Spanky?" Little Jim asked as he wiped his continually dripping nose on his sleeve.

I punched him on the shoulder and turned to start the climb on up to the top. The snow thickened as we got to the top of the hill. We could just barely see the top of the courthouse dome and the clock that had been stuck on 3:47 as long as I could remember.

The Episcopal Church steeple pointed out of the trees, reaching for a higher salvation. Rooftops blended into a delicate pattern of whites. I got a whiff of coal smoke and maybe chicken pot pie. I loved chicken pot pie with biscuits. The atmosphere was more than silent, soft except for snatches of muffled voices from below like KDKA on a windy night.

"You kids, either go or get out of the way," Red Green's voice disappeared down the slope into the building flurries.

"Yeah, pee or get off the pot," John Bob Porter snarled.

"Come on, Frankie Spanky Chicken." Little Jim punched me on the shoulder and dove off the ledge.

I adjusted my cap, pulled up my collar, buckled the straps on my look-alike aviator gloves, and shoved my crummy old wooden sled between the twin maples and dropped down into the challenge of the Dreaded Grapevine.

Wham! I went right on my face. My mom was right. "You'll break your neck." The stubby wooden runners couldn't begin to traverse the steep slope of the jump-off. I rolled over onto my back and tried to wipe the snow from my face but my gloves were as cold as the snow. I sat up and looked around to see if anyone had witnessed my folly. A couple of dim shapes were trudging up the hill but they didn't notice. I quickly shoved the treacherous sled out in front of me and belly flopped on top.

My face was still stinging, and I couldn't really see where I was headed, but it was downhill for sure. By the time I reached The Hump I was up to speed, to the point that I think I left the ground and came down with a whoof, kinda cockeyed, and had to struggle to stay with it. Both feet were dragging to the left, so the sled went to the right up onto the icy slope of Death Valley, which I entered sideways and half off the sled. By the time I had hit the Dreaded Grapevine, all I could do was hang on but that was my problem. On my homemade sled there was nothing to hang on to.

By now I was aware of other kids watching me, so I had no choice but to go on down the hill, which fortunately was just what the sled had in mind. At the bottom, I dug in both toes, determined not to go through the fence and down onto the road like I had seen Little Jim do earlier.

I skidded sideways and rolled over, sat up and wiped my face with the back of my glove like Randolph Scott had done last Saturday afternoon down at The Lyric.

"Hi Frank." Flora Jean was standing right there looking down at me.

"Uh?" I replied cleverly through my frozen face.

"I just saw how you did that. Gee whiz. Will you go down with me?"

She nodded, expecting me to agree, which I did.

I left my old wooden sled leaning on a fence post and took the Snow Queen, rope in hand.

"Here, let me help." Flora Jean reached out and also took the Snow Queen rope. Our hands touched. Well, our *gloves* touched.

"Are you going to the Christmas party at the U.B. Church basement?" Her shoulder brushed mine as we struggled on up the slope.

"Uh. Are you going?" I made sure our gloves touched as much as possible as we pulled on the Snow Queen.

"Oh yes. We're going to dance. I'm taking my new record player and some new Glen Miller. It'll be so much fun." She looked right at me. Her eyes were kinda bluish green and bright. We got up to The Hump with a bunch of other kids, all laughing and yelling as others went whipping past us down the hill.

"Get out of the way, kids." Robert Parsons went by lickety-split.

We put the Snow Queen down in the track. Flora Jean sat in front. I gave it a shove and climbed on behind, putting my feet on the steering handles, which made us into a cozy bundle. She was holding the rope and I put my arms around her tight. My face was right next to hers and it felt hot. She smelled like soap or something nice, and her hair tickled my nose as we went whooshing down The Dreaded Grapevine amid the gently falling flakes.

*I wasn't the dumbest kid in the seventh grade.*

# PAPER BOY

*T*t was one of those early autumn afternoons that inspires poets and balladeers to lazily string together languid words about the hazy golden atmosphere. Kids had settled into their assigned school seats for the year and were shuddering at the unknown information that was hidden there in the back pages of an arithmetic book: long division! And a workbook on diagramming sentences.

Up on the second floor of the aged brick schoolhouse, Frank sat in the second row of Mrs. Kiser's fifth grade between his buddies, Bob King and Jimmy Casto. Most of the gang clung together like overdeveloped puppies, except for Catfish Erwin.

Catfish, because he looked like he had been dropped on his head as a baby. His head was flat on all four sides and top, with squinty eyes and a large wide mouth that kept him in jeopardy most of his waking hours. He always started the school year in the back row, but it wouldn't be long before Mrs. Kiser would move him to the front where she could keep a better eye on the class pest. Catfish wasn't a bully. Anybody could whip him, even Mildred Bailey. He was just a pest.

The top girls, Joyce Simmons and Doris Mills, always liked to sit in the front row where their hands were always waving in answer to any question the teacher would put before the class, but Frank had already learned that it was best to just be somewhere in between, where he would be less noticeable for good or bad.

Also, from this desk he could keep an eye on a certain girl, even though as yet he wasn't sure just why this was important to him.

What *was* important to him was trying to keep up with some of the older boys in school. Sammy McGrew was a boy two years older than Frank, and one of the leaders in everything these kids got involved in. Sammy and his rival, Joe Beamer, were the guys who always chose up sides in any undertaking, be it softball or Kick the Can.

Frank liked the feeling he got when Sammy pointed to him during the early moments of selecting a team. On Sammy's football team, Frank was called "Little Red" because of his dark reddish hair and because he would try to tackle anyone, regardless of size. Sometimes, a high school kid would join in a Saturday morning scrimmage, but Frank would dive at his knees even though he was overmatched. His head usually got a good thumping and his fingers got stepped on. He always had grass stains on his knees and scabs on his nose and elbows.

Frank was a preacher's kid, but seemed to carry that burden pretty well. He didn't want to get into any trouble, but sometimes he did some things with the kids that he knew his dad would be unhappy about, if he found out. During the exciting days working up to one Halloween, when all of the kids were operating at a high degree of energy, he was tested severely when Jerry Conley convinced the gang that it would be fun to remove Judge Lewis T. Sinclair's front gate and run it up the flagpole that he was so proud of. Every day, Judge Sinclair would display a large American flag followed by a Marine Corps regimental flag that he brought back from the First World War. Then, last but not least, there would be a small banner with Latin lettering and a strange symbol that looked like a big eye and an odd-shaped animal in a stone triangle.

What the boys didn't know was that the wily old judge had somehow gotten wind of their plot. He had wired the flagpole lanyard so that when anybody pulled on it, that would trip the switch on two spotlights mounted on the porch roof, flooding the entire front yard with noon-like brilliance. Not only that, a large sprinkler hidden at the base of the flagpole would launch a cold shower on anybody and everybody in the front yard.

The boys fell for it like a herd of goats, and the judge got to enjoy the whole thing from his rocking chair there inside the bay window that hung out into his front yard.

The boys dropped the gate and skittered back to the opening where the gate had been. They jammed into the inadequate opening while being splattered with a considerable shower of cold water. It became a memorable Halloween legend in the town as the story grew into epic proportions.

Frank was a mid-sized boy with freckles on his nose. He mostly went barefoot in summer except on Sundays when his mother made him wear a stupid suit that was too small for him, so that his wrists and ankles stuck out like Pinocchio.

He was the last kid in his class that wore corduroy knickers to school. As soon as he thought his mom couldn't see him, he would loosen the knee buckles and let them hang down loosely on his shins. As he ran along, the corduroy would rub together making a whoomp whoomp sound like the wings of a giant prehistoric flying lizard.

He was relieved one day when he finally wore out the knees in his last pair of knickers and his mom couldn't find anymore in the Sears and Roebuck catalogue. The last of the knickers became lining for his dog's bed in the big old rocker by the fireplace.

Frank lived with his mom and dad and his older sisters Ruth and Mary in the old parsonage next to the Methodist church, just a few blocks from the school. In this town, almost everything was just a few blocks from anywhere else.

The old house leaked and creaked in the winter storms and sweltered under its tin roof that pinged and ponged in the mid-summer heat and made the interior hotter in August than a Biloxi cinder-brick factory. They kept Old Jack Frost at bay with a coal-fired open fireplace that they kept smoldering from November first until sometime around Easter, but there was nothing they could do about the heat except sit on the front porch and try to catch any breeze that might find its way up the valley from the Ohio River that was not far away. The red brick church next door had been built during the Civil War when the Methodists split into North and South like everything else in this part of the country. It was heated by a cantankerous coal furnace that grumbled and belched in the tiny basement under the altar. It was part of Frank's job, as janitor, to start the big awkward thing early, very early, every Sunday morning and keep it chugging along until the final benediction for the day. Mary shared the dusting, sweeping, and general cleaning, as well as placing chairs and tables in accordance with Sunday school scheduling. Frank got extra pay for the outside chores, sweeping, raking leaves, shoveling snow and, best of all, that crowning reward of ringing the large bell that hung high up in the belfry where nobody had ventured since a bell specialist from Cincinnati had checked it out in 1914.

It was 1942 in this small farm town in the low hills of western West Virginia. The war was new with all of the inconveniences just beginning to make their presence known. There was rationing of almost everything except worry, and a busload of young men left every other Tuesday morning to meet their fates somewhere far beyond the Jackson County line. The school band would gather there in front of The Blue Bird Café and bus stop and struggle through "The Star-Spangled Banner" and "God Bless America."

Mayor Bob Goodman would lead them in the pledge of allegiance and say a few cogent words and the bus would growl on down Court Street and out of sight across Mill Creek and around the bend.

Frank's sister, Mary, was fifteen that year, and a sophomore in high school, but she was Frank's best friend. They were about the same size, but Mary was faster and smarter with a bit of a quick temper, so that Frank had to stay on constant alert, lest he be treated to one of her head thumps. Mary, when aggravated to a certain point, would grab the offender around the neck, and with a sudden twist, throw him down so that his head would bounce off the ground.

Two Christmases ago their dad had given them a secondhand bike that had belonged to a neighbor boy who was now flying "The Hump" in Burma. He had fixed it up and painted it red and had it there behind the tree on Christmas morning.

It was an old-fashioned boy's bike that they managed to share with very little disagreement. They named it Francis in honor of the previous owner. They developed several riding stunts that featured both of them on Francis, changing position from handlebars, to seat, to carrier, all without touching the ground. Other kids would marvel at them and occasionally request command performances up on Church Street.

On this particular afternoon, Frank was selling papers on the sidewalk in front of The Candy Corner when a battered, dented Chevy pick-up pulled up across the street.

"Hey kid, g'amme one of those papers."

Frank jumped down off the high curb and ran over to where a grizzled, dirty face leered out from under a John Deere cap that was slightly twisted to the left.

"Ya gotta *Gazette* there, buddy?"

Frank held out one of his newspapers that plainly declared in large black letters, *Parkersburg Sentinel*.

"That's a crappy *Sentinel*. Ain't ya gotta *Gazette*?"

"No. This is what I have. A *Parkersburg Sentinel*."

Frank didn't want to tell the man that Fuzz Beamer was selling the *Gazette* just down the street in front of Tack's Barber Shop.

*The Gazette* was a more popular paper being from Charleston and Democratic in a mostly Democratic state, so it was tough to compete.

"Well, hell. Gimme one anyway. I gotta get goin'." The man held out a dime that was almost lost in his large and battered fingers. "Here, kid. Keep the change. You're gonna need it, trying to sell that crummy rag."

The woman beside him grabbed the paper as the old truck lurched out into the traffic in front of a car driven by Mrs. Maud Nethercutt, with several ladies who had to grab their hats as Maud slammed on the brakes.

With a bang and a cloud of blue exhaust, the truck chugged

on down the street, leaving the ladies sitting in bewilderment after Maud killed the engine in frustration.

Most of the world was in turmoil, so news was mostly bad, but folks had a craving for the latest, so the evening newspapers were popular and easy to sell. The first radio news didn't come on until Lowell Thomas at six o'clock, and people just quitting for the day liked to pick up that day's news on the way home.

Mary and Frank shared the duties of delivering door to door all over town, plus Frank sold extras on a downtown corner while Mary used their only bike to deliver the north end of town. When she finished her part, Frank would take the bike and deliver the south end of town, including across Mill Creek, and all the way out to the old CCC camp.

They had now delivered the *Sentinel* for six weeks and really liked the change that had collected in their pockets and in the little tin box hidden there in the corner closet of the dining room. They were saving to buy a new bike. A girl's bike, by general agreement. It was there in the Montgomery Ward Catalogue. A "Hawthorne!" It cost twenty-five dollars, including shipping. It was green.

One lazy mid-summer afternoon, Frank and Mary were sitting on the front steps hoping that something would happen or someone would come by to entertain them.

What they didn't particularly expect or hope for was Shake Casto. "You kids wanna make some easy money?" Shake was highly excitable and spluttered when he spoke. He was an older kid and usually didn't pay much attention to Frank, but he kinda followed Mary around at school like a slobbering hound dog.

"How and for what?" Mary asked.

"I deliver the *Sentinel* you know. All over town, I make real good money. It only takes an hour or so in the evening. It's easy."

"How easy?" Mary squinted up at Shake as she always did when a bit puzzled.

"Just deliver these papers for next week while I go fishing with my dad down on Tug Fork." Shake got off his bike and sat next to Mary.

He was an awkward kid who always looked like he had just

gotten out of bed. A bed that he had been in for some time. His clothes were rumpled and too small for him, as he sprouted through the teens. His shoelaces were usually untied and the toes were worn out of his high-topped tennis shoes. The chain guard was always broken on his bike so Shake had to keep his right pant leg rolled up to keep from tangling in the sprocket chain. This only contributed to his lop-sided appearance.

Slick black hair draped over his left eye. He thought he looked like Clark Gable but mostly he resembled Frog Mill-house, Gene Autry's awkward sidekick. His large head was always tilted to the left and as a result he usually compensated to the right.

"Come on, you guys. I'll give you ten cents each a day. That's good!" Shake rattled some loose change in his pocket. "You know what you can get for ten cents?"

Yeah, they knew what you could get for ten cents—one Saturday movie double or a model airplane kit of a Piper Cub.

"What do we have to do?" Mary was always suspicious, particularly of Shake. He was constantly working on somebody for something. Shake had convinced the school principal J. J. Harrison that he, Shake, could convince enough kids and their parents to form a school marching band for football games and parades. Even though there was already a music teacher and a band, they didn't march because they didn't have any uniforms or even a drum major, or a football field, for that matter.

Oh, there were football games in Shinn's cow pasture. It was over the hill, clear outside of town and down by Mill Creek that flooded without notice. Shake had convinced Mr. Harrison that a certain group of boys needed Friday mornings off when there was to be a "home" game. This select group of Shake's buddies would troop on down to Shinn's field and clean up all of the cow piles while the school custodian Tom O'Rear lined the field with lime.

Shake was a real politician.

Shake patted Mary on the back and she moved away from him a bit.

"You can ride with me today and I'll show you the customers. They are all in this little receipt book. See? All the names and addresses. They are all in order, so you just follow it around town. I'll show you, come on."

Shake went to his bike and slung a kinda saddle bag thing over his head with newspapers in back as well as in front.

"You can wear this thing or drape it over your carrier in back. I like to wear it so I can get to the papers faster."

He was much bigger than either Mary or Frank so there was no way they could wear that thing.

"Wait a minute. We have to ask our mom." Mary went inside where her mother was again peeling potatoes for supper.

"He said we could make five dollars a week, Mom! Frank and I could share. We could split it up. Huh, Mom?"

Mary came out the screen door. "She said I should go with you today to see what it is like. Okay?"

"When we're half done, we'll come home and Frank will go with you the rest of the way."

By the time they got back, Frank had lost interest and had wandered back into the workshop his dad had in one end of the garage. He was working on a wooden Luger pistol like he had seen last Saturday afternoon in an episode of *Captain Midnight*.

"You have to go with him this time." Mary grabbed him by the arm and shoved him out the door where Shake was rearranging his paper bags.

"Okay, Franko. Let's roll. It's all downhill from now on." Shake was always exuberant.

They went off down the street toward the south end of town that was to be Frank's department, Shake gibbering all of the time.

Frank followed Shake as he crossed the street, jumped the curb, and flung a folded paper at Dr. Rymer's front porch. It ricocheted off a porch post and skittered under a wicker chair into a pile of dead leaves.

"Don't you have to put them behind the screen door?" Frank asked, as they continued down the sidewalk.

"Nah. The dog always chews that one up anyhow. No sweat."

Shake crossed the street and put a rolled-up paper in one of the metal curls in the front gate at Aunt Clara Dodge's ancient overgrown place.

"She can't bend over to get it otherwise. She always gives me a cookie on collection day, too." Shake snickered.

Shake suddenly turned the corner and pulled up in front of "The Central," actually The Central Walgreen Pharmacy. Central, because it was the only one in town or even the county.

"Let's have something to wet our whistles, Franko. I'm buyin."

Shake dropped his bike on the curb, Frank followed suit, and they both went into the drug store. Shake leaned over the white marble soda counter. "Mix up two of your lime rickeys Betty Lou, my darlin."

The girl behind the counter continued drying glasses while giving Shake a squint-eyed look.

"Lemme see your money. The last time you were in here you cheated me out of fifteen cents."

"I did not cheat you. It was a fair and square double or nothin' deal and you lost."

Shake reached over the counter and picked a maraschino cherry out of a stainless steel bin. Betty Lou slapped at his hand.

"She really loves me here, Franko." Shake slobbered around the huge cherry.

"Do you want two lime rickeys or not?"

Shake took a stool, twirled completely around, and placed a dollar bill on the counter, all in one move.

"Money talks, huh B.L.?"

"Shouldn't we do the rest of the papers? I gotta get home for supper."

Frank gulped most of his rickey in one try. "All in good time, my man. We'll get you home before dark if that's what's worrying you."

As the evening progressed, Frank learned that Shake was not too dedicated to the paper route. He thought, "I could do this in about half the time it takes him."

By the time they had gone all the way out to the CCC camp and back, it was truly almost dark.

Mary was not too excited about the paper route but with Frank's enthusiasm and their mother's okay, they decided to do it.

After a week of intermittent introduction from Shake, Mary and Frank took over the paper route for real. As it turned out, they could do the whole town, including the CCC camp, in two hours after school.

Conveniently, the southbound Greyhound called at The Bluebird Café at 4:15 p.m., more or less, notwithstanding high water or drifting snow or cows on the highway. Sometimes the driver would get involved with Elladean, the cashier at The Bluebird, and forget to haul out the bundle of papers from the luggage bin there in the side of the bus.

This snafu would cause the kids to be about an hour late on their route and make their mom a bit testy around suppertime.

One particular evening, Frank was selling papers on the sidewalk in front of The Candy Corner when a battered, once-green Dodge pick-up pulled up across the street.

"Hey kid, you gotta *Gazette*?"

The dusty face with yellow teeth grinned at Frank while the bluetick hound in the back bounded up and down, whimpering and slobbering.

"No," Frank yelled. "I have the *Parkersburg Sentinel*, pointing at the big red and black letters printed on the paper carrier's pouch draped over the basket of his bike.

"Jesus Christ, that piece of crap?"

The big ugly face turned to answer something the woman beside him had said.

"Well, okay kid. Gimme one of those, I guess. How much?"

"A nickel." Frank walked across the street to the pick-up.

"Here's a dime, kid. That's eleven cents more than it's worth."

Frank held out a nickel change.

The guy snorted. "Keep it kid. Give a paper to that lady behind me. Tell her it's from an admirer."

After a couple of months, the kids were so into the job that they could deliver the whole town in two hours, easy. They had always been encouraged to get a job done before taking time to play. They took pride in what Mrs. Nethercutt had told their dad.

"I can set my clock by when that paper hits the screen door. I know it's 4:27 p.m. If the paper isn't here then I know the bus was late," Mrs. Nethercutt pronounced over her expansive bosom.

Frank got so that he could fold a paper while riding the bike without holding onto the handlebars. Then he could float the paper onto the front porch like a Douglas Dauntless dive bomber laying a skip bomb down the funnel of an enemy carrier in the Coral Sea.

One afternoon, when Mary had finished her part of town a little bit late, and Frank knew that a bunch of the guys were into a great football game in Bess Post's huge side yard, he was really whipping around his route. He came down the driveway from Dr. Hileman's office, across Maple Street, and floated a larger than usual *Sentinel* over Mrs. McGraw's hedge in the direction of her large brick and concrete front porch. Just as he was pulling out of his "dive," there came a crash, followed by a series of tinkles sounding like broken glass.

"Jeez," Frank groaned. He parked his bike, then approached the front porch, peering timidly around the thick hedge. Yep. There it was, a smattering of broken glass that once was a pitcher and four fine water glasses. Well, one of the glasses was only slightly wounded and had rolled clear across the porch and wedged itself under the screen door.

Wedged itself so that Mrs. McGraw was struggling to get the door open, but to no avail, no matter how hard she tried. Then came a crack. The screen door opened a little but just at the top. The bottom corner of the old screen door was warped inward and scattered rusty screen bits across the floor, mixing nicely with the broken glass. A complete disaster.

"Land's sakes!" Mrs. McGraw exclaimed as the glass came free, causing the door to swing listlessly on its severely stressed hinges.

Frank was trying to pick up the pieces to put the pitcher

back together.

Pepper, the McGraw sheep dog, came out and tried to mount Frank as he hunkered in the broken glass.

"Pepper!" shouted Mrs. McGraw. "What will people think?" One of the neighborhood's favorite admonishments.

"Well, you should be more careful. One shouldn't be throwing things anyway. Just watch what you're about, I always say. Mr. McGraw will be upset that his mother's pitcher is broken. My oh my," she sighed, shaking her head slowly.

Frank had a big lump in his throat. He knew that Mr. McGraw could be trouble. His mom and dad talked about some of the things he did at the church board of trustees' meetings. He knew that his dad didn't get along with old McGraw, and his dad could get along with anybody.

"I . . . I'll buy you a new one," Frank almost whispered. He wasn't sure what to do.

"We'll see. Let me get a broom and pan to clean up. You wait right here."

Mrs. McGraw gingerly opened the sagging screen door and disappeared down the hall while Pepper tried again to mount Frank from the back.

*I'm doomed*, Frank thought. *That pitcher is gonna cost more than I can make in a month.*

Frank held the dustpan while Mrs. McGraw swept up the remains.

"I'll pay for the damage, Mrs. McGraw, but you'll have to tell me how much." Frank tried not to let the whimper in his voice pass through his lips, but he was scared.

"We'll have to wait to see what the Mr. says. He will want to talk to your father."

Frank was almost crying as he turned to hurry down the sidewalk. He had to finish the daily delivery at any rate, then go home to face his dad.

On the way home, his mind offered a series of possibilities. He could get run over by the train, except the local train didn't go fast enough to do the job. He could take the tin box of money from his hiding place in the loft of the garage and run off to . . . gee, he didn't know. Where could he run off to? Parkersburg? Maybe he would suddenly catch infantile paralysis and die or go blind. Then they would all feel sorry for him.

SPLATT! Something hit him right in the chest. Something hard but gooey at the same time.

"Franko the Cranko!" Catfish Erwin was standing behind a big elm tree with another rotten apple in hand. "Yehaaaaaaa! Franko the Cranko!" He yelled, turned, and ran down the alley to disappear into the old garage that his dad, the undertaker, used to store caskets and other large two-by-eight wooden crates.

Frank couldn't be bothered by Catfish right now. There would be a tomorrow for that. He finished the rest of his paper route in a sort of daze. He knew it so well by now he could do it in his sleep. In fact, there were nights when he did exactly that.

When he got home that evening, everything seemed to be normal.

"Did you remember the new customer out by the county garage?" Mary asked as he put the bike into the garage and hung the canvas bag he carried papers in on the nail behind the door.

"Yeah, but I still have four papers left over. We have to pay for them you know."

Mary sucked on the inside of her cheek. She did that when thinking hard.

Dad was already sitting in his place at the kitchen table. Frank looked at him carefully for any sign of trouble. Nothing.

"Everything go all right, son?" his dad inquired.

Here it comes, Frank thought. He gulped down a half glass of water and felt a hot spot on the back of his neck.

"Yeah, I guess so," Frank mumbled while staring down at a heap of navy beans and onions on his plate.

Mom came to the table with a hot plate of cornbread.

"Oh, yes, Mrs. McGraw phoned just a while ago. Did something happen over there this evening, Frank?"

He put down his fork and looked at his dad.

"Well, I guess I broke a glass pitcher when I threw a paper at her porch."

"Does she know about that?" Dad looked from Mom to Frank and back again.

"You broke a pitcher?" Mary looked at Frank and grew a little frown between her eyes.

"Well, yeah. I threw the paper like I always do, but this time there was a pitcher and some glasses sitting on the rail and the paper knocked them off and broke the pitcher and three glasses. Told her I would pay for them somehow."

The lump in his throat grew into a watermelon and he began to tremble a little.

"Jeez! How you gonna do that?" Mary was leaning on the table, staring at him.

Dad reached over and patted Frank on his shoulder.

"It's okay," Dad said. "I told her that we would give her free papers until it is paid off, and she agreed. She said four weeks would probably do it okay. I think that's very fair, don't you, kids?"

Mary squinted up her brow again. "Gee, Dad. At twenty-five cents a week that's only a dollar. That ain't much."

"Isn't much," Mom corrected.

"Right, it isn't," Mary added.

"Anyway, that's what you can do. Just skip her on collection day for a month, okay?" Dad looked around the table. "Pass the horseradish, please. Let's eat."

Dad liked to spice up the beans and Frank tried to keep up with him, even though the horseradish brought tears to his eyes, but these were good tears.

Usually, Frank went about his deliveries as fast as possible. He and Mary competed in time spent delivering their half of the paper route. Frank's was always a bit longer because he had to go clear out to the old CCC camp where the Coast Guard maintained their vigilance against the Axis Forces in the backroads of the West Virginia hills.

He tended to go a bit slower whenever he approached a certain big white house up on Maple Street. This was where Flora Jean Powell lived with her older sister, Betty Ann, and their parents.

Frank was only twelve, but he felt a tingle in the back of his neck whenever Flora Jean was anywhere near. Even the chance that she might be near made him feel strange. She fascinated him even though he wasn't sure she liked him in the least.

Her daddy owned the town lumber yard and a farm south of town where there were several glass-enclosed greenhouses and a series of carefully tended plots of flowers and vegetables toiled over by members of the Stalnaker clan who were reputed to be the best farmers in Jackson County. They designed and delivered flower arrangements for the various occasions that are typical of most small towns.

The Powells were of "upper class" stock, what with the larger than normal house on Maple Street with a backyard full of more greenhouses and a real potting barn where Bud Wilfreth sold artfully arranged bouquets and professionally potted house plants.

Mr. Marion Powell was always well dressed, usually in a suit coat and a funny kind of tie, like Walter Pidgeon would wear in an English movie. He came to church only on special occasions—Christmas and Easter, or when Flora Jean participated in some special program.

Mrs. Powell seldom appeared anywhere. To Frank, she looked like one of those Hollywood stars like Joan Crawford with a carefully contrived lock of gray hair over her left ear. He had seen her smoking several times, which he knew gave her a questionable moral position, according to his mom.

Flora Jean's older sister, Betty Ann, was away at college, but was still well remembered as Queen of Jackson County Fair two years ago. Betty Ann had deep chestnut hair that accented her green eyes.

Flora Jean was cut from some classy stock, all right. She was a year younger than Frank, so he didn't get to see her much at school. She was slim and tan with short curly brown hair. She could do front and back flips off the diving board and swim the length of the pool underwater. She took tap dancing lessons down in Charleston and played the only flute in the school band. Flora Jean could run like a boy and last winter she and

Frank had spent one whole afternoon sledding together over on Shinn's hill. They took turns sitting behind on her larger-than-most American Flyer so that every other trip he got to hug her and feel the tickle of her hair on his nose.

Is it any wonder that Frank got the willies when he went by her house to toss the evening *Sentinel* onto her front porch? It was like he was sending her a special message. He could only hope that she would be there to perk up a drowsy summer afternoon. The town was totally dull and the swimming pool was closed because of an infantile paralysis scare. Dr. Casto had taken his son, Jimmy, and two of his friends, Frank's best buddies, all the way out to Yellowstone. Frank was not included. His parents wouldn't have let him go anyway.

Old folks were sitting in the shade, swatting flies with fans from Vail's Funeral Home, while several lawn mowers were standing deserted, in mute evidence to the fact that it was just too darn hot, and Frank's dog Chummy was stretched out under the back steps in the cool dirt.

Frank was out on his route, shirtless and shoeless and still sweating from climbing up the Seventh Street hill.

Frank carefully tucked a rolled-up *Sentinel* in Mrs. Wink's front gate and rolled across Maple toward the Powell house.

He felt it first. Then he saw her there on the front porch. She was sitting in a glider with a stack of comic books scattered all over. Flora Jean was sipping on a Coke through two straws while concentrating on *Wonder Woman*. He thought that Flora Jean looked somewhat like a smaller *Wonder Woman*. She could and would do some things that mostly just boys would do.

She was the only girl that would walk across the sagging, wobbly log that served as a bridge across Sycamore Creek to the cow pasture where the guys played softball. Some of the other girls would cross, but they crawled on their hands and knees squealing all the while. Mary would cross, but not with the devil-may-care style that Flora Jean displayed.

Flora Jean started the famous neighborhood crabapple fight one September after school that included half of the kids in town. She started it when Catfish Erwin dared her to throw an apple at him as he taunted her from an upstairs window in the funeral home where he lived. She of course complied, and the thing grew into a neighborhood donnybrook. It went on until it was too dark to distinguish friend from foe, as most of the kids in our section of town joined in. It was Maple Street Methodists against the Court Street Baptists. A glorious event in anyone's boyhood.

"Hi, Frank." Flora Jean didn't even look up as he flicked down the kick-up stand on his bike and walked up the three broad steps to the shady front porch.

"Here is your dad's evening paper," he stammered, standing there like an idiot, holding the *Sentinel* out like a gift offering.

"I know." she replied. "Just toss it inside the screen door." Still, she didn't look up.

"It's hot, huh? Kinda?" Frank studied his bare feet. They were dirty with a scab on the top of one where he had skinned it climbing around in Uncle Charlie Kessel's barn.

Flora Jean tossed a *Wonder Woman* onto the floor and took a long sip from her Coke. "Is that all you do, deliver your papers, play your stupid cowboy and Indian games, and football? Football," she huffed.

"I guess" was all he could think of.

Flora Jean clasped her hands over her head and stretched with her eyes closed.

Frank saw some things about her that he hadn't noticed before.

"Well, I gotta go finish my route."

"Uh huh." She fumbled through her stack of comics and held one up in front of her face, as if reading.

"Well . . . well."

He turned and started down the steps.

"Oh, Frank." She put the comic book down on her lap. "There is a party at Billie Parson's house Saturday night. She has some new Glenn Miller records. "String of Pearls" and "Elmer's Tune." Lois Vineyard is gonna teach us to jitterbug. It'll be so much fun. Will you be there?"

"Uh huh, I'll try."

Flora Jean put *Wonder Woman* up between them again. Frank stood there for a couple of breaths then went back down the big front steps, picked up his bike, and whirled away like William Boyd in *Silver on the Sage*.

There wasn't really any "poorer" section in our town. There were some fairly nice houses but none that were very pretentious. Some were just larger than average.

The large Victorian that Dr. C. Royal Kessel used as a hospital, and Judge J. Lewiston Miller's large brick house at the north end of Court Street were three stories high, with long wraparound porches and "kept" yards. The Powells had a carriage house in back, along with their greenhouses.

The one area that stood out as less average than others was a section squeezed between Mill Creek, the railroad, and the stockyard. On a pot-holed, dusty/muddy, gravel street with no official name that turned off the main street beside Buck Skidmore's garage gathered a haphazard arrangement of small houses that were affectionately known as "Pig Alley." Perhaps intended to capture a bit of the aura of that notorious section of Paris, Pigalle, but falling well short because of the West Virginia understanding of a place named Pig Alley.

In order to get down Pig Alley, one had to negotiate the collection of broken-down vehicles that typically clustered around the back of Skidmore Garage. The street was roughly three blocks long, had there been any real blocks. There were some fences, some grass, a patch of vagrant petunias or two, a scattering of struggling elms, and lots of wooden crates. For some reason crates were popular along Pig Alley. Perhaps collected for future projects, or just firewood. About halfway down, there was a large, rusty hot water tank laying there in a patch of broom sage. Frank always pretended that it was a runaway German torpedo that had somehow found its way up Mill Creek from the Gulf of Mexico.

It added a haphazard effect that made the whole neighborhood look like it had just been spilled off the back of a flatbed harvester.

Down Pig Alley at the very end was the kingdom of Cap

Honeycut and his ever-cantankerous wife, Belle. The Honeycuts kept a scraggly flock of chickens that roamed the neighborhood like a plague of locusts, hunting and pecking anything and everything that might be digestible. There was a huge rooster named Beowolf that dominated not only the herd of free-range hens, but dogs, cats, children, and most adults.

There was one dog that was not to be dominated by anything. "Popeye" had limited eyesight but had a nose that transcended reality. He knew when an outsider turned the corner at Buck Skidmore's and started down the obstacle course of litter called Pig Alley. He would lay in ambush, faking drowsiness, then spring into action when his unsuspecting victim was least expecting.

This atmosphere naturally spawned some independent characters. Ely Short was in the same homeroom as Frank, sat in the back row, and chewed at his yellow fingernails. He couldn't quite fathom long division or fractions. He openly scoffed at the idea of trying to carry a tune. He played the bass drum in the school band but was just barely under control. He loved contact sports, which to him included anything from football to marbles to penny ante poker for matchsticks. Ely once lost his favorite shooter in a fair-and-square marble contest but then became so threatening that Punky Starcher finally just gave it back to him.

Ely was a nice guy compared to Herm Skinner and Dan Hardesty. These two were consistently a threat to every kid in town, and they ruled Pig Alley like the Daltons.

Frank had three regular customers down that street. Buck Skidmore himself, the Honeycuts, and the Rhoads down at the very end, next to the stockyard. In order to deliver to this no-man's land, Frank would move at top speed, keeping to the sides of the street, dodging the crates and clumps of weeds and trying to avoid Popeye on one side and Beowolf on the other.

If this ornery rooster saw anyone on a bike, he would charge out of ambush with his enormous wingspan at full extension, squawking like the avenging angel of death.

Herm and Dan used Beowolf as an alarm system. The

squawking indicated possible entertainment for the two ruffians.

Then one day it happened. Frank got clear down to Honeycut's, tossed his *Sentinel* toward the front porch, and missed. It was one of his rules that if he missed the whole porch, he had to park his bike, open the gate, find the wayward paper, and get it to its proper place.

He parked his bike, went into the yard, tossed the paper against the front screen door, and turned around just in time to see Herm Skinner kick his bike over into the dirt. Then Dan stood on the spilled papers and kinda scuffed them around with his toe.

"Hey paper boy, your stupid bike fell over and spilled your stupid papers into the dirt. Ain't that too bad." Herm looked at him with his squinty eyes and crooked grin that was already stained Lucky Strike yellow.

Dan gave the pile of papers a kick, sending them sprawling.

"Yeah, paper boy. I tried to pick 'em up for you but I guess the wind caught 'em." Dan wiped his big nose on his sleeve.

Frank was scared. He had never had a run-in with these two, but he had witnessed their terrorism before.

He went to his bike and set it back on its stand. Herm and Dan stood back just a bit as Frank gathered up the spilled papers. When he stood up, Herm poked them out of his hands and shoved Frank into the bike, knocking them both over again.

Frank was scared and his face was burning with tears of anger. He was furious as he jumped up and waded into Dan with both fists. He felt contact. It felt good.

"Hey, you stupid little shit. We were just teasing. You don't—" Herm didn't finish as Frank punched him hard in the stomach, bending him over with a hufffff.

Frank felt ashamed for crying now but it was too late. Dan stepped closer and Frank caught him with a flurry of fists. Dan fell backwards over the bike, struggled up, and backed away. Herm was now on his hands and knees crawling away with a trail of snot following in the dust.

Frank got his stuff together and turned back up the street to see Cap Honeycut raise both fists in the air and nod vigorously.

Those two never really bothered Frank again except for occasionally lobbing dirt clods at him from behind a crate.

As evening shadows reached across the now-silent battle-field, old Beowolf herded his harem of Plymouth Rock ladies to their ramshackle boudoir and Popeye rearranged his heap of gunny sacks there under the front steps. Peace settled over Pig Alley but it was never the same.

Frank wheeled around the back corner of the house to the side porch and flicked down the kickstand of his bike.

*Whew. I'm glad that's over,* he thought, as he felt the weight of the money in his pockets. It always made him proud when he had collected for a week's worth of paper delivery and hurried home to count his earnings.

As much as they hated the process, the kids did it faithfully every Saturday morning, rain or shine. The only trouble was, on Saturday mornings most of the other kids were playing football or baseball or something entertaining at least. Certainly more exciting than knocking on a bunch of doors, asking for money.

The *Sentinel* cost twenty-five cents a week for home delivery. At forty-seven customers that amounted to $11.75, but then they had to send three cents a paper to Parkersburg to pay for the papers. What was left satisfied them for spending money for movies, lime rickeys, milkshakes, model planes, comic books, and other necessities of teenage kids of that time.

The trouble was knocking on the doors and having to talk to all of those adults.

The *Sentinel* furnished little pages of dated coupons that served as receipts. Each page had the customer's name and address. The pages were divided into little postage- stamp-like sections by perforations so that they could be torn off and handed to the customer upon payment. The customer would stick it to a calendar as a record of payment. It all worked pretty well.

Some of the places he had to call on were fun. Flora Jean's house was a chance to see her and hopefully not her mother.

It was always a risk to go down Pig Alley and knock on

a door. Herm and Dan could be there, and certainly Beowolf would be on alert as well as Popeye and a couple of mean hounds that roamed the neighborhood looking for any kind of prey for that morning's entertainment.

Perhaps the most exciting place to call was the sheriff's office in the basement of the courthouse.

J.B. "Smokey" Stover, the sheriff, bailiff, jailor, custodian, etc., always had an office full of characters. It was hard to tell the difference between the law enforcement folks and the inmates. The jail was right there through an open door at the back of the office. Half the time, one or more inmates were sitting in the office, sometimes answering the phone and fielding official inquiries.

A crusty fellow called "Turkey-Trot" was there so often some folks wrote in his name in the county elections. Turkey-Trot was our town bum. Folks watched out for him. Gave him rides, let him sleep in the heated chicken house or in the vestibule of the Jackson County Bank on freezing winter nights. Once in a while, he would show up at a church social and the women would fill his plate with all of the good stuff and put aside a paper sack to carry out.

Sheriff Stover would always tell Frank that he didn't really like the *Sentinel* but he paid for it so Turkey could keep up with the world news.

The sheriff was a huge man, always dressed in faded khaki that pretty well matched his complexion. He looked like a live tintype that chewed on a cigar and spit pretty much on the floor because his eyesight was poor and the spittoon was full anyway.

He was called "Smokey" because of an incident that happened some time ago when he was just a deputy.

J.B., as he was called then, thought he would smoke out a hornet's nest that plagued the loft of his shop by setting fire to an old rag soaked in kerosene, tossing it up there, and closing the door.

He did just that, except the loft had about twenty-five years of rats' nests jammed inside, and the loft also had small open windows at either end which made a natural and very effective draft.

The shop soon started smoking like The Capitol Limited charging up the Cheat River grade under a full head of steam. Cool, fresh air was rushing in one end and greenish black smoke was pouring out the other. It truly looked like the old shop was moving uphill.

When J.B. opened the loft door to attempt to put out the fire, he was greeted by an acrid cloud of smoke and debris that cloaked him in a layer of roasted rat guano.

He didn't dare call in a fire alarm. He was a deputy, after all, and had done a stupid thing, but several passersby took note and soon the shed was surrounded by J.B.'s fellows.

The fire as such never caught but it smoldered for several days, and J.B. became "Smokey" Stover.

Saturday, midmorning, Frank leaned his bike on the drinking fountain beside the narrow steps that went down under the large, raised entryway to the Jackson County Courthouse. It had been raining all morning so that the polished granite walls reflected in the wet cement sidewalks like a confused maze of some architectural fantasy. Frank had to pull with all his might to budge the imposing door that announced SHERIFF in large goldleaf civil letters.

Inside had the dank musty air of the Tower of London mixed with decades of tobacco smoke and spit, and unwashed humanity. Male humanity. There was no trace of feminine presence, now or ever. On the rare occasion that there was a woman malefactor, she would be put up across the street at Madge's Curl and Cut Salon, Hair, and Nails, in more civilized surroundings.

Madge and Smokey had an unofficial relationship in civil enforcement, and she was fully capable of carrying out any called-upon force that might become necessary in maintaining judicial security.

"Howdy there, John," Smokey grunted around his well-worn cigar. Lots of folks called Frank "John" because his dad was named John, and folks just supposed.

Turkey-Trot was leaning on a huge dust mop that had more debris collected in its coils than it was intended to carry, so that every time he swirled it around the office, he left a trail of stuff that pretty much defeated the whole operation.

"Ya got today's *Sentinel*, Sammy?" Turkey leaned over Frank as if he was somehow hiding a newspaper behind him.

"No sir. It doesn't come in until the 4:15 Greyhound from Parkersburg."

"Uh, how come they don't send it out earlier?" Turkey looked out the door as if he could see a Greyhound bus coming into town any minute.

"It's an afternoon paper, Turkey. If they sent it any earlier, it would be a morning paper." Sheriff Stover was used to explaining complicated facts to Turkey-Trot.

"How much do I owe you, Francis?" He reached into a vest pocket and pulled out a long change pouch that had a rubber band around the top to secure a long-broken clasp.

"It's twenty-five cents, Sheriff. You are all paid up."

Smokey selected a quarter, flipped it into the air with his thumb, caught it with the same hand and slammed it down on the desk with a bang that rattled the windows.

"Call it, Junior. If you're right, I'll double it up."

"Huh. I don't know, I . . . my dad wouldn't want me to, you know." Frank felt his face getting warm.

"Oh, that's right. Your daddy is the preacher over there at the Methodist. Okay kid, take your quarter, you would probably have won it anyway."

"Turkey, where is yesterday's paper anyhow? He is always hiding it somewhere 'cause it takes him a while to read it. He claims that the governor is his cousin er somepin'. Well, he also claims that Davy Crockett was his great-grandfather and, get this, he says his real name is Cornelius Baltimore an' he can ride on the B&O Pullmans anytime, except they don't go anywhere he wants to go."

Frank picked up the quarter, tore out the little dated stamp, and slid it across the desk toward the sheriff. Smokey opened a drawer and deposited it into a swamp of small notes, rubber bands, and paper clips.

The phone on the desk jingled and before the sheriff could put down his cigar, Turkey-Trot answered.

"Sheriff's office. No, I ain't sheriff. He's busy with a malfeasant. What? No, not Mel Pheasant, we don't know anybody by that name. A malfeasant is like a' outlaw. What?"

"Gimme that thing." Smokey grabbed the phone.

"Sheriff J.B. Stover here." He lowered his voice to a rumbling growl.

Turkey stood there looking at his empty hand.

"I thought it might be Junior Scarborough, you know, the governor, he's my cousin, you know."

Frank tried to picture the governor looking like old Turkey-Trot, shambling down the sidewalk kinda sideways, squinting up and down on his swivel-neck like a searchlight.

"Well, thanks," Frank said to the sheriff's broad back, and pushed open the big door.

Outside, the day had turned into a summer cooker. The sun was beating down through a steamy haze that hovered above the dripping foliage and the simmering pavement. The Jackson County Bank across the street smoldered and pulsated in the vapors like a bad home movie.

Frank turned his bike away from the courthouse, across the sidewalk and, with a good start, tried to jump across the running gutter. He almost made it but had to brake quickly to avoid the Model Grocery delivery truck that was passing by. Over in front of the bank he spotted Punky Starcher and Fuzz Beamer hunkered down on the sidewalk peering into the grate-covered window well in the sidewalk. He pulled up beside them and with one foot on the curb, leaned over his two buddies.

"What are you guys doing? Plotting to rob the bank like Jesse James?"

They ignored him. "Go the other way and up," Fuzz muttered.

"I'm trying, I'm trying. Don't bug me." Punky got his face right down on the grate.

"We gotta get a longer stick and some new gum, I'm tellin'

you." Fuzz straightened up, stretching his back.

Punky carefully pulled a long thin stick up through the heavy grate and inspected the tip. A wad of gum covered with general street debris and some bug bodies was stuck to the tip.

"I told you, we gotta get some new gum and a bigger stick." Fuzz took the stick and snapped it over his thigh, then tossed the two pieces into the narrow passage by the bank.

Frank got off of his bike, stepped closer, and looked down into the window well but saw only the usual trash. "What's the big deal?" he asked.

"I dropped a stupid quarter down there. We can see it, but we can't get the stupid thing out." Punky muttered.

Frank fished around in his pocket. "I got bubble gum. That might do it on a longer stick, but you'll have to give me a nickel out of the quarter if we get it."

"A nickel! Ya crook. Stupid bubble gum ain't worth a nickel." Fuzz snorted.

"It is if you ain't got any and ya need it bad enough." Frank held out a Fleer's Double Bubble in a nice new wrapper. Dangled it in the air, tossed it back and forth from hand to hand, and put it back into his pocket.

"Okay, okay. I'll buy you a lime rickey if we get it out with your gum, okay?"

Punky put his flat hand on Frank's chest and gave him a little shove.

"Deal, but we have to get a better stick. I'll chew up the gum and you guys go find a stick. Frank unwrapped the gum and stuffed the whole thing into his mouth.

"Just where in hell do you expect me to get a stick that long, numb nuts?"

Fuzz looked up and down the street as if he really expected to see a stick leaning on the front wall of Tack's Barber Shop next door.

"Go look at the hardware store. They got sticks," Frank suggested around a mouth full of bubble gum.

Fuzz punched Frank on the shoulder. "I don't have any money to buy a stick."

"Don't buy nothin'. Go round in back and go through their trash. There's gotta be som'pin."

Fuzz and Punky went down the alley behind the hardware store while Frank got down on his hands and knees and peered through the rusty grill into the depths of the musty window well. As his eyes got accustomed to the gloom, he thought he could make out the shape of the lost quarter. As he continued to focus on the collection of debris, he could make out several other small round shapes that suggested other lost coins.

This could turn into a good thing, he thought. He spotted what could be at least five coins down there besides that quarter. If they were just pennies, he probably couldn't see them, so they must all be at least nickels, dimes, or maybe more quarters. Wow!

Fuzz and Punky came out of the alley carrying several yardsticks. They all said Jackson County Hardware in big black letters but looked like they had been dipped in a fresh cow pile.

"It's not what you think, Franko. It's dried axle grease. Well, almost dried," Punky explained, as he gingerly touched one of the soiled sticks and then looked at his fingers.

"That'll do." Frank produced a short string from his pocket and proceeded to tie two of the yardsticks together, making a pretty solid five-foot stick. He then took the wad of bubble gum from his mouth and jammed it onto one end.

"Okay. The partnership owes me five cents for the gum but wait till I show you what else I discovered."

"Never mind nitwit, let's get the quarter!" Fuzz grabbed the stick and worked it down through the grate.

"Wait!" Frank grabbed Fuzz by the shoulder. "There's more than just the quarter down there. I bet there's forty cents or maybe more. We just have to poke around 'til we uncover it and then stab it with the gum stick and bring it up."

"Okay, okay, don't bother me. I gotta concentrate. Like the steady hand of Dr. Frankenstein working tenderly on the monster's balls."

Frank and Punky crowded around watching Fuzz and the end of the yardstick as it carefully touched down on the wayward quarter, then was slowly pulled up through the bars of the grate, just barely clearing the narrow opening.

Fuzz held the quarter up high and then flipped it into the air. "Watch it, stupid. You'll lose it again." Frank yelled.

"What are you geniuses doing now?" It was Lois Ann and Mary Virginia, classmates from the other side of the aisle.

"Nothin' to you guys." Punky stepped in front of Fuzz in order to protect him from those nosy girls.

"We just recovered a lost quarter out of that pit. Cool, huh?" Frank proudly announced. He kinda liked Mary Virginia and wanted to impress her. "It was my idea to use the yardsticks and the gum, see?" He held the messy sticks up for the girls to see.

"Uck. What is that stuff on there, it looks like . . ." Lois Ann covered her mouth and curled up her nose.

"Wouldn't you like to know?" Frank pointed the greasy end toward the two girls and wiggled it around.

"We saved this quarter from the pit." Fuzz rubbed the coin with his thumb and held it up.

"I bet you that money belongs to the bank. You're supposed to give it back to them. You could be arrested for robbery 'er something," Lois Ann said seriously, trying to see into the bank through a window with Venetian blinds pulled down against the bright afternoon.

"I ain't givin' it to them. It's my quarter. I dropped it into their hole and now I got it back and I'm keeping it."

Lois Ann leaned back with her little fists on her hips and took a deep breath preparing for a rebuttal when . . .

"Just what are you kids doing out here?" Mr. Lexton Prattle, assistant manager and head teller, stuck his bald head out of the front door and blinked into the fierce daylight through his steel-framed glasses.

"They just took a quarter out of your pit," Lois Ann quickly replied in her know-it-all voice.

Fuzz held out the quarter. "Just dropped it down in there and then we picked it back out with this stick." He held out the yardstick contrivance for Mr. Prattle to observe.

"Well, that's a pretty clever gadget you have there, boys.

Folks are always complaining about losing some change or other down there. We can't get to it because that window has been bricked up for years."

"Is it okay if we look for some more money down there, Mr. Prattle?" Frank asked in his most polite voice. Mr. Prattle subscribed to the *Sentinel* and always complimented Frank on his dependability and business-like manner whenever he collected his weekly fee.

"Oh, I suppose so, but don't be in the way of our customers, and don't stay very long, and don't make any noise, and be gone before Mr. Parsons gets back from Rotary."

Prattle looked anxiously up and down the street as if Mr. T. Clayton Parsons was already in sight, then slipped into the bank, carefully closing the big door as if it were the entrance to some religious shrine.

"Come on you guys, let's try to get some more of those coins. Let me give it a try." Frank took the yardstick contraption from Fuzz and got down on his knees over the grate.

"I can't really see very good."

"Go in the barber shop and see if you can borrow a flashlight."

"You go, Punky. You get your hair cut there. He knows you." Fuzz shoved Punky toward Tack's Barber Shop next door.

In a couple of minutes he came back with one of those huge flashlights that holds about six batteries and can light up the Carlsbad Caverns from front to back.

Fuzz held the light while Frank stirred the trash on the bottom until he found what looked like a coin.

"I got it. I got one. Hold the light steady."

All three boys held their breath, and the girls leaned over them trying to see, as Frank slowly pulled up the stick with a coin stuck on the end. He took it off and rubbed it between his thumb and finger.

"Crimenently!" Frank snorted. "Look!"

"What is it, a quarter? What is it?" Mary Virginia squealed. "Is it gold? It looks like gold."

"Naw. It ain't gold. It says West Virginia Interurban Transit

Company. It's a streetcar token, for criminy sakes. It says 1928, Good for One Ride."

"Oh, that's hoop-de-doo. If you're ever in 1928, you get a free ride to the dead end of town."

Fuzz looked at the coin. "They don't even have street cars here anymore but maybe someone would want if for a souvenir somewhere."

"Try some more. I bet there's lots more money down there." Fuzz shoved the stick back down through the grate. He stirred around the trash in the bottom of the pit some more.

"Wait a minute. There is something there. Over to the left." Frank tried to guide Fuzz's hand.

"Leave me alone, I'll get it. Don't get your knickers in a twist."

"I got something." Fuzz picked something off of the end of the stick.

"It's just a penny."

"Look over there," Punky whispered. He was shining the light over in a corner piled with debris but something round was plainly visible.

Fuzz moved to the other side of the well and put the bubble gum right down on the round object. "Got it. I'm gettin' good at this. I think I'll become a brain surgeon or a diamond miner."

This time it was a large, dirty-gray coin. Fuzz picked it off of the stick and dipped it into the gutter that was still running water after the recent rain. Then he rubbed it on his shirt tail.

They all crowded around Fuzz. "Let me see it." Mary Virginia reached for the coin. She plucked it out of Fuzz's open hand and began to rub it with her hankie.

All five heads were jammed together when Lois Ann said, "I'll bet you kids are going to get in trouble. Mr. Prattle is going to tell Mr. Parsons and he will tell the sheriff and your dad, Fuzz, and Mr. Davis, and, and—"

"Oh, shut up Lois Ann. You worry too much." Punky elbowed her aside.

Mary Virginia held the coin up to the light. "Oh, look. It says 1890-something. I have never seen any fifty cents like this one."

"Wow! 18-something. That's really old. Is it a real coin? You know, worth money?" Frank, ever the entrepreneur, asked anxiously.

"Yeah, it's worth money. I'll just bet you it's worth more than fifty cents, too."

Mary Virginia squinted closely at the coin. "I think it says 1890. That's really old."

"Yeah. Older than . . . older than . . ." Fuzz frowned at the fifty-cent piece. "That was back during the Civil War," Fuzz proclaimed.

"No. It was more like the First World War," Punky proclaimed.

"No. The Civil War was 1861, you idiots. And World War I was 1917. No wonder you guys don't get good grades in history," Lois Ann spoke in her snooty voice.

"I get good grades. I just can't remember numbers." Punky gave Lois Ann a look.

The bank door opened suddenly and Mr. Prattle stepped out.

"You kids had better leave now. Mr. Parsons is due back any minute and he won't like you cluttering up—what do you have there?" He leaned over Fuzz's hand and looked at the coin.

"It's a half-dollar we got out of the pit," Frank said excitedly.

"Yeah, and it's old. See."

Fuzz held up the coin and Mr. Prattle plucked it out of his palm.

"Oh, good heavens! It's 1890. That's the year the bank opened. See!"

He pointed to a granite plaque over the door. Sure enough. Right there. Established 1890.

"Wow! Do you think that half dollar has been down in there all this time?"

Frank took the coin and squeezed it in his palm.

# TEEZER'S TWISTS VI

---

## EPIPHANY

*T*he day is bright and shiny and, one might add, colder than a polar bear's Jacuzzi. It isn't a day one would expect to witness a real honest to goodness epiphany.

In all of the Bible illustrations, those kinds of things come accompanied by rolling thunder and fierce punctuations of lightning. A guy that looks like Charlton Heston announces epiphanies while reading from tablets of stone. There should be writhing crowds of tormented Philistines, and Roman soldiers wearing those cute bronze briefs and real Italian sandals.

On this unremarkable morning we, the cadre of Teezer's Geezers, are just pondering our second cup of Mark's Starbucks blend. There is a crowd of the usual mix milling around the counter and the front door when a large man, meaning *really* large man, suddenly growls, "THAT'S MY PAPER!"

Conversation stops as all eyes turn to the center of the main dining room to find this man with a face like one of those cloud cartoons the weather people use to indicate a coming storm. He hovers over the room like one of those parade balloon figures. He wears a too-small tweed jacket that struggles to support three tenuous buttons. Real leather elbow patches that don't match and are coming loose anyway indicate some latent academic connection. His baleful eyes peer down at us from a lumpy gray face framed by dishwater colored hair that sticks straight down from his knit watch cap like a spilled pan of yesterday's noodles.

He lumbers over, plops his copy of *The Times* down on the closest table, and turns to the counter to order. An unsuspecting young man pauses and just glances at the paper when the man bellows into his ear.

"THAT'S MY PAPER!" he says, loud enough to startle the two Labs that were dozing in the patio out front. They both jump up and look about for foreign invaders.

"Uh. Oh. I was, I was just looking at the headlines," the poor guy stammers.

"Well, that's my paper. I always have to have my own paper. My father arranged for me to have my very own subscription when I was a child."

He shoulders the poor guy aside, takes possession of the paper and the table, looks around the room like a lion over a fresh kill, and mutters, "I have to have my own paper. That's all."

He settles into his latte and works on the front page of the *Times*, ignoring everybody else.

"Boy, how would you like to be his paper boy?" Frank asks the group in a guarded whisper.

"No thanks. I would rather deal explosives to a band of nervous banditos in a stolen van from Tijuana."

"You wanna bet he reads the obituaries first?" Jan whispers.

"He thinks they are the comics," Bill adds.

"Maybe the news has a reverse effect on him. You know, plague, famine, pestilence, riots, and assassinations probably make his day. Why else would you make such a fuss over the morning news?" Frank surmises.

"He must have loved Katrina and the ongoing fun in Bangladesh." Bob sips on his coffee and hunches down in his chair.

The conversation rambles on over voting yes or no on the recreation bond, local salmon quality, the price of gas at the Indian Casino Chevron station in Anacortes, and personal experience and preference for dermatologists.

A woman comes in, orders a latte, and sits with the "paper man." We hear him say, "I may have hurt some feelings a while ago, but you know how I feel about my paper." The man finishes his latte and paper and stands in the center of the room briefly, as if trying to come to some difficult conclusion. He has a brief conversation with the woman. They both talk with Mark at the counter and calmly walk out.

A few days later, a quiet time at Teezer's brings Mark and Carolyn from behind the counter.

"Remember that big man that made such a racket over his own newspaper the other day?" Mark asks the attending group of Geezers.

"Yeah boy. He reminded me of the wrestling coach at San Quentin." Bill crosses himself and shudders.

"Well, he came in the next day and was meek as a lamb. He apologized to us and has been very friendly ever since."

"Yeah, he is like a different person," Carolyn adds.

"Well, it must have been an epiphany," Bob suggests.

"Yeah, and it happened right here in Teezer's. Hey, Mark, have you ever had an epiphany here at Teezer's before?" Frank asks.

"You remember, he stood right there under those lights and morphed into a human being right before our eyes. It's those lights. Notice how they are placed. How their star-like shapes suggest emitting rays of epiphany, like in Bible stories. That's not by chance." This group can stretch anything to outlandish proportions.

"You know, Oprah has at least three epiphanies on each show, guaranteed. I don't remember ever having one of those unless it was the time in the sixth grade that Joyce Simmons asked me to her birthday party and kissed me on the cheek," Bill laughs.

"Maybe you could feature a Teezer's latte called an Epiphany," Jan suggests.

"Yeah, you could have them stand right here, under these lights, sip a latte, and make an epiphany wish," Dotty laughs.

"I know some people we should drag in here and force them to stand under the epiphany lights. Maybe they would change their evil ways."

"You could put a sign out front like a tanning salon," someone suggested.

"Yeah. Maybe you could get a tan and an epiphany at the same time."

"Yeah. Maybe Oprah would do a show right out there in the patio."

Like a cluster of junior high kids with too much imagination, the conversation reaches a peak and settles back down into important issues like, "Is the theatre closed forever?"

"Did you see what they're doing to the lawn down at the church?"

"Do those kids dress like that at school?" Etc., etc.

"They ARE at school. Going to Teezer's is one of their political science assignments. You know, meeting the public, understanding your peers, dealing with everyday life."

"Yeah, not to mention nutrition. The various ingredients in your favorite latte and how to get the most out of it."

"Well, not like when I was a boy." Frank uses that a lot and everybody pauses to remember.

"They didn't have nutrition when you were a boy. Just look at you!" Jan nudges him and everybody snickers and sips.

Frank gets up, stands in the center of the room, and holds out his arms, looking at the ceiling. "I'm in the epiphany vortex. Give me a sign."

"Your fly is unzipped," Bill whispers loudly and the whole group dissolves into laughter that makes the two Labs in the front patio perk up their ears and look in every direction.

The trash truck comes by and the strange guy that patrols that intersection hurries from southeast to northwest, and things go on.

# RUTS AND ROOTS

---

*T*he midsummer air was so thick and murky, it was hardly noticeable that there was a persistent splattering of raindrops falling through it. The landscape appeared to be an impressionistic painting that was dripping off the canvas.

When the Loudin family turned off the paved highway just east of Valley Bend, the back seat of the '36 Chevy began to tingle with kid enthusiasm.

Maybe, for Mother, who had to drive and shoulder such a burden as three jumping youngsters and one frisky fox terrier, it was more like trepidation, but the kids knew that the more primitive the roads became, the closer to Uncle Jim's farm we were getting.

Mom did most of the family driving because Dad was afflicted by asthmatic respiratory problems that could cause him to break into a fit of coughing at any second. This can be a hazard to the smooth operation of an auto.

As long as they stayed in the rolling valley, the semi-improved road was adequate but as it began to twist and turn into the hills and hollers toward the little hamlet of Adolph, WV, more and more red clay began to show through the gravel.

As they passed the little one-room post office, the gravel petered out completely and Mom's knuckles turned whiter as the front wheels searched the slippery clay ruts for direction while the rear wheels skittered back and forth, digging for any sort of traction. The road got steeper in the soggy afternoon as they ground on up the mountain in second gear and high tension.

The three children and Chummy the dog were all jammed into the back seat, along with jackets and sweaters and Dad's special medicated non-feather pillows. They were tired of playing Highway ABC and were now content to just gaze out the steamy windows.

Dad tried to calm Mom's nerves with, "It's just on up there over the ridge." He was leaning forward, searching through the gloom for any recognizable features.

They passed a farmhouse where a pack of barefooted youngsters, probably cousins of some sort, came from here and there to run alongside the road waving at the Loudins with grimy hands and a dead snake.

"Look," Sister Ruth pointed out. "A couple of them don't have any pants on and that one is buck naked." Well not exactly totally naked. He was partially wearing a battered straw hat that wobbled down over his ears. They stared and giggled.

"That's the Zickafoose place. Now it's just over the next ridge, Mother," Dad said.

Mom stared straight ahead, leaning over the steering wheel. "Why don't these people fix the roads?"

"And why don't they have their pants on?" Mary snickered.

They motored smoothly past a rocky cornfield and a leaning shed of some kind, then made a sharp right turn around a haystack into a wooded ravine where a tall hip-shot man waved a tattered red rag at us. When he was satisfied that the car intended to stop, he tucked the flag into the hip pocket of his bib overalls that were cut off mid-calf to reveal high-top boots laced up with yellow leather thongs.

He leaned over and squinted into the window that Mom had rolled down just enough.

"You'ns holt rat her fer a spell. Them boys yonder bout ta dynermite out a big ol' rocky place outen thu righterway." He let fly with a long brown string of tobacco juice over his left shoulder and wiped his stubbly chin with a well-anointed shirtsleeve.

Mom turned off the engine and leaned back, stiff arms on the top of the steering wheel. "I just don't know," she announced to anyone and everyone.

Dad got out of the car, put on his hat against the drizzle, and leaned over the hood.

"Say, aren't you one of the Van Guilders?" He tilted his chin toward the lanky man who was peering up the road kinda leaning forward-like into the wind.

"Yep, an I'll reckon you'll be Johnny, Amanda's boy, from out." He fired another amber stream into a healthy stand of thistles that held up a failing fence post.

"That's right. Now who's your folks again?" Dad cocked his head, as he was in the habit of doing when particularly interested in a conversation.

"They's Cobber and Monabell from up on South Branch, right on the lick." He hitched up his overalls, took off his hat, slapped it against his leg, and wiped his chin again.

"Oh sure, you must be Elias, then, their youngest boy." Dad took off his hat and slapped it against his leg.

"Reckon." The big fellow seemed embarrassed that anyone would know his name. He hung his head and grinned sheepishly, revealing a mix-matched set of yellow teeth.

"Just what are you fellows doing up there?" Dad tilted his head up the road where the family could just make out some blurry movement in the murk.

"Well, we're a widen' a nary spot yonder." Elias Van Guilder assumed the stance of an informed person of some importance and kinda strutted in place.

"Is it gonna take long?" Mom rolled her window down further, leaned her head partially out, and squinted into the drizzle.

"Any time now, they gonna fire it, ma'am." Elias leaned forward in polite respect to a lady and spit to the side.

The backseat crowd leaned to the left in order to get a better look at Elias Van Guilder. Chummy snarled.

The front of his overalls came to about eye level, revealing the traces of past meals that featured molasses and gravy mixed with tobacco stains. There was the tip of a yellow pencil, a piece of wire, and the drawstring to a pouch of Bull Durham hanging from his breast pocket. Under his overalls, he wore either a collarless flannel shirt or more likely the top of his BVDs. Either way, it was molded to his lanky frame by a history of sweat and dust.

"Looks like he forgot to use his napkin," Mary remarked.

Dad added, "Yeah. And I'll just bet you he uses one end of that pencil to pick his teeth, and the other end to clean out his ears." They all snickered.

"You all better hush. He'll hear you," Mom said out of the corner of her mouth.

Just then a holler came from up the road and Elias straightened up and reached for the red rag in his hip pocket. "They gonna firinthuhole. Ya'all hunker down there." He held up the red rag and waved it back and forth like there was a whole line-up of cars behind them.

"What did he say Mom?" Frank asked.

"Oh, they always have to yell 'fire in the hole' before setting off a blast of dynamite. I think it is a law or something." Dad knew about that kinda stuff.

Elias held up his red rag and waved it over his head.

"Can we get out and watch?" the three children whined together.

"No. You're better off in here. There might be rocks falling all around. One could land on your head and we couldn't go on to Uncle Jim's."

"Yeah. And it would put out our eyes, huh Mom?" the back seat chorused. Mom always had a disaster scenario to any and all kid-inspired activities.

"Fire in the hole!" someone yelled, and Elias repeated it to the empty roadway behind them. There came a lurch and a muffled burp, more than the expected grand explosion.

"Is that it?" Ruth asked.

"I didn't see nothin," Frank added, peering hopefully through the streaked window looking for great boulders falling from the sky.

"Anything. I didn't see anything," Mom instructed. She had been an English teacher at one time and tried to teach her children proper grammar in the midst of their hillbilly influence.

"Me neither," Ruth and Mary murmured together.

"You'all kin get on now. Keep 'er slow and off to thu left. Give yer Maw a howdy fer me, Johnny." Elias waved the car on with his red rag.

As they approached the blast area, several figures in soggy wide-brimmed hats and bib overalls in various stages of wear and fade stopped and leaned on the handles of an assortment of shovels. The road was littered with rocks and roots where a crater had spilled itself out of the hillside. Mom tried to avoid the larger ones with some fine-steering wheel handling, but the old Chevy still hunched and lurched over the helter-skelter of rubble.

The men leaned and gawked as the car bounced by. One removed his hat and slapped it on his leg in respect of the lady driver. In these parts, a woman driver was as unusual as good grammar. Mom kept her eyes on the task ahead, gripping the wheel with both hands.

"That short one there is Rodney Cutright, Emmy's boy. The one with a short leg. He is a first cousin of you children. Emma is my second youngest sister that married Gideon Cutright from over at Camp Six." Dad waved at the lopsided fellow, but he didn't take notice.

"Some people say that everybody up here has one leg shorter than the other because of the steep hills." Ruth was in high school now and was exposed to the prejudices of society.

"That's just a folktale, Ruth. Rodney had scarlet fever when he was a baby and somehow it affected his growth. He couldn't make it in school, but I guess he is able to handle a shovel all right, though somebody had to show him which end to stick in the ground and which end to lean on." Dad was always a good storyteller.

"Wasn't he the one that tried to move the outhouse with a half-stick of dynamite and blew it to smithereens?" Frank always loved it when Dad told that story.

"Yes. Well, the hole got full in the middle of January and he had seen Uncle Gideon use a half-stick of dynamite to blow a new hole for the outhouse because the ground was frozen. Well, Rodney tried to move the outhouse with their old blind mule Hoover, but it was frozen solid. So he got the bright idea of using dynamite to loosen her up."

"Tell us again. What happened?" Mary leaned forward in her seat and put her hand on Dad's shoulder.

"Well, he blasted the outhouse alright, except that he used a whole stick and blew it to smithereens, like you said. The roof went straight up and the heavy hickory two-hole seat became a flying wedge that sailed across the yard and smashed into the side of the house just above the kitchen window.

"Your Aunt Emma was across the room, bending over the flour barrel. She jumped, reared back, and threw a sifter full of buckwheat flour over her head." Dad had to stop here because he always got so tickled that tears came to his eyes.

"And, and, tell us about the ghost," Mary urged.

Dad wiped his eyes with his handkerchief.

"Well, your Aunt Emma had flour in her eyes and went feeling along the wall to get away from whatever had come through the window. So the first thing Uncle Gid knew of the situation was the ghost of your Aunt Emma coming through the dining room door with her hands straight out in front of her, with white powder over her head and moaning, 'Oh Gideon, oh Gideon, a meteor has landed in the back of the house and I've gone blind from the explosion. Oh Gideon. Oh Gideon!'"

Aunt Emma had been expecting the meteorite every day since a fortune teller at the Randolph County Fair had made just such a prediction.

Mom said, "John, you're just filling their heads full of those old tales. None of that ever happened, children."

"Yes, it did Mom. Tell us about Uncle Gid, Dad." Mary patted Dad on the top of his head.

"Well, it went something like this anyway. Uncle Gid was having problems of his own. He was sitting in his rocker with a plug of Bull Durham tucked into his cheek for further enjoyment. He had dozed off with a copy of *The Christian Advocate* in his lap opened to an article about Armageddon and The Holy Ghost and how we should all be getting ready. Whamboozle!! The two-holer hit the side of the house and the kitchen window fell into the sink. Just as he opened his eyes, this powdery figure came lurching through the kitchen door like it was searching for lost souls! Heh, heh, heh." Dad had to stop and dab his eyes with his handkerchief.

"John, you're telling tall stories to the children." Mom took her eyes off the road and gave Dad one of her looks.

That was all it took. The independent front wheels went to the right and the back wheels went to the opposite side of the muddy hump in the road and settled into a ditch full of ooze.

Mom didn't have any habitual words of frustration to cover such a situation, but this was a special event. "Oh Daddy!" she gasped, and leaned back in her seat as if she could will the car to recover or maybe turn back the hands of time just a half-minute or so.

"We're stuck, Mom," Ruth observed.

"We're stuck, Mom," Mary echoed.

"We're stuck, Daddy," Mom admitted.

She put it in reverse and threw mud on the windows on the left side of the car. She tried forward, low gear, and sent a spray of thick brown stuff out the back. Back and forth they lurched, working the rear wheels in deeper and deeper. The motor was beginning to steam, and the smell of burning rubber permeated the blue air. Then the engine quit altogether. They sat there, each with their individual thoughts, listening to the hot parts of the old Chevy relaxing after the strain, and the ever-persistent patter of the rain.

"We're doomed. There is nobody around here. The rain is getting worse, it is getting darker, it'll be night, what about the children?" Mom uttered without taking a breath.

Actually, the children were having the time of their lives. This was all a part of going to Uncle Jim's.

Dad secured his hat onto his head and opened the door.

"What are you going to do, John?" Mom watched him open

the door and start to get out.

"I think maybe if I get out and direct, we can get her out of here." Dad pulled his hat down on his head and turned up his collar.

"We're gonna have to stay here all night," Mary whined.

"Don't be a baby. We'll get out of here when the earth spins closer to the sun and everything dries up." Ruth was more than impatient but relied on sarcasm to release her tensions.

"Git out here and help me son." Dad motioned to Frank, and he climbed out of the back seat along with Chummy the fox terrier.

Together Dad and Frank chucked some rocks and dead branches under the back wheels.

"Okay, Mother, give her a try."

Mom put the old Chevy in low gear and carefully let up on the clutch. The rear tires spun and gave out with a high-pitched whine, threw all of the sticks and rocks out, but didn't make any progress.

"You girls get out too. Maybe less weight will help." Dad leaned over the driver's window.

So Mary and Ruth scrambled around in the back seat getting into their jackets and tying scarves over their heads.

Standing in the weeds by the hole, Dad, Frank, Mary, Ruth, and Chummy all observed and urged as Mom rocked the Chevy to and fro, working feverishly with the gears and clutch.

"Maybe if we all get behind and shove," Ruth suggested.

"Maybe." Dad agreed. "Let's give her a try."

So the four of them worked into position over the rear bumper and Dad yelled, "Okay Mother, give her the gas!"

Mom did and the cranky old car lurched forward and a little bit to the left, slipping sideways into a newer, deeper section of the mudhole where the consistency was more fluid.

As a result, the left rear wheel became the source and dispenser of a goodly amount of deep reddish-brown splatter that affected the lower half of all four of them. Chummy, being by far the most nimble, leapt to the side and escaped the deluge.

"Ooweeee, eeeeeek, spluuuut and Dag-nabit!" The crew

exchanged expletives, looking down at the damage with vary-ing degrees of despair.

Mom leaned out of her window. "Did we do any good?"

"We got rid of some of the mud," Dad replied in his wry tone.

"Look at my shoes."

"Look at my legs."

"Look at my pants."

"Looks like that isn't going to work, huh?" Dad grinned as the girls tried to wipe away the splatter, only to make long smears out of the spots.

"I guess I'll walk back down the road and see if those men will give us a hand." Dad rolled up his pant legs one turn and wiped some thick clay from the soles of his shoes on a clump of broom sage.

"Yeah, maybe old Rodney can blast us outta here with his half-stick of dynamite," Mary offered with a smirk, as she contin-ued to wipe away at the front of her skirt.

"Can I go with you? I want to see the dynamite hole." Frank tugged on Dad's sleeve.

An excited yipping came from somewhere in the nearby field. "Is that Chummy?" Dad asked, staring into the mist.

"Yeah. I think she's after something out there."

"I don't care if she brings back a mastodon. I'm getting back in the car." Ruth took off her gloppy shoes and kinda wadded up her skirt and squeezed into the back seat.

Mary and Frank climbed up onto the rail fence next to their dad.

"What is it, Dad?" The three of them peered into the drizzle as the barking and the clatter got closer.

"What is that noise, Dad?" Frank stood up on the second rail and squinted his eyes.

"I don't know, but I think it's coming this way." Dad took off his glasses and wiped them with his handkerchief.

As they watched, down the inside of the fence came a hulk-ing form that shaped into a huge black mule pulling a clatter-ing mowing machine. The driver was perched on the seat that hung out over the back of the two-wheeled implement, and lurched and swayed like a wild west rodeo bronco. Chummy was circling them, making quick jabs at the mule's huge hoofs from time to time.

As they watched, the big old mule pulled by them and there came a "Woohaaaaa, there, Lightnin'," and the machine came to rest. The driver climbed down using the spokes of the big yellow wheel for a ladder. Chummy sniffed at their high-topped boots.

"Hello there, mister," Dad hollered.

"Hello there yerself, mister. This her' dawg your'n?"

"Frank, get Chummy over here." Dad gave Frank a nudge on the back.

"Come here, Chummy." Frank snapped his fingers and the little dog scrambled through the fence and came to Frank's feet.

"You'ns got yersef into a predicament there aint'cha?" The driver came toward them through the drizzle.

"Yeah. Looks like we slid into a rut. I was about to go back down the way and see if maybe that road crew could give us a pull."

"No need. Ol Lightnin' kin do thu job fer you'ns." The driver came closer and put one foot on the lower rail and spit into the thistles that ran along the fence.

"Well, we'd certainly be obliged." Dad leaned over the fence and held out his right hand. "I'm John Loudin, Jim's brother. I suppose you know of him. He lives on up the mountain at Blue Rock."

"Reckon. I'd be Gingham Mayfield. Folks call me G." G ran her hand around the back of her neck and out fell a long braid of carrot-colored hair. She was wearing overalls that were stuffed into high-top boots. A heavy canvas coat that looked like an old army blanket came down to below her knees, and she wore a black felt hat with a wide brim that drooped to one side where the rain had collected and run off from time to time in a silver string.

"Oh yeah, Mayfields. That would be Scowey and Olive. I knew Scowey's folks from up by Sugar Grove."

"That'ed be right, I reckon. I went to school down at Adolph with some-a Jim's young'ns. I didn't go too long though. Can't jest set long enough to larn good." G took off her hat and wiped her ruddy face with the back of her sleeve. A large purple birthmark spread over the left side of her face and ran down under her turned-up collar. Her china-blue eyes looked straight at them as her cracked lips broke into a buck-toothed grin.

"Let's get at it then. We kin let down the fence right thar 'til I kin get Lightnin' through. You all do that whilst I un-hitch here."

"Sure, we kin—*can* do that, huh Frank?" Dad let the end of the top rail down and, with Frank's help, fashioned a gate.

"What are you doing, John?" Mom called from the car.

"We're gonna tug her out with that old black mule. You just stay there and operate the car and Gingham will do the rest." Dad laid aside the bottom rail, took off his hat, and slapped it on his leg.

Lightnin' came through the opening, dragging his harness, with G coming along behind with the reins, hollering gee and haw and whoa at proper intervals. She maneuvered him into position by thumping him on the chest to make him back in close to the front bumper.

"Here kid. You kin hold him while I hook him up." She handed the dark brown leather reins to Frank. His hands trembled as he stared up at the giant black animal that was steaming and huffing and twitching his hide. Frank got a better grip on the reins and the huge head turned and looked at him with dark eyes that reflected the sky. Lightnin' reached out and put his wet lips on Frank's head and tried to nibble at his hair, then whinnied a chuckle to himself as if he had just pulled off a joke on a city slicker.

"Watch out fer ol Lightnin! He kinna likes ta' take a bite outta whatever's near." G tugged and hauled at the wet harnesses while the big mule flicked at the dripping rain with his tail.

Dad stood with his back to the mule and tried to give some sort of assistance to G. "Can I hold something for you, G?" He put one hand on Lightnin's expansive side to steady himself.

Lightnin' swung his head about, laid back his ears, and snatched Dad's hat right off his head. Dad grabbed at it but Lightnin' tossed his head and took a better grip on the black hat. Dad reached out but Lightnin' was too big and quick, so they played a game of keep away until G saw what was going on.

"Haaaaar, there you gol-danged knob-headed hunk of buzzard bait." She grabbed him by the ear and tugged at the halter, trying at the same time to get the hat. Lightnin' dropped the hat down in the mud and daintily plopped a huge hoof right on top of it.

Naw, you say, a mule doesn't have that kind of intelligence. Lightnin' was well known in these parts because he knew when it was quittin' time, 'cause at the proper time, ol' Lightnin' would just head for the barn, no matter what kind of equipment happened to be harnessed to his flanks. One time he pulled a hay rake right through the fence, across Olive's kitchen garden, and wedged it into the barn door while he jammed his big ol' snout into a manger full of fresh soybeans.

G tugged at the trunk-like front leg and pounded on Lightnin's flank to no avail.

"Well, let's jest go on about gettin' outen this here hole. Then we kin git your hat. Sorry 'bout that Mr. John." G took the reins from Frank and gave a "Gaaaaduuup yhaaaarrrr. Lightnin'. Whoooooeeeee."

The big mule leaned into the harness and pulled the '36 Chevy back onto the center of the road without Mom ever getting the engine started.

"Well done! Well done!" Dad walked over and pulled his hat from a deep hoofprint of red clay. "Well done," he repeated, and slapped Lightnin' on the rear with the soggy hat, leaving a splotch of mud.

The mule lifted his tail and passed wind like the air brakes on a downhill coal truck.

G looked at Dad. Dad looked at Frank. Mary held her nose and stuck out her tongue. Mom stuck her head out the window and said, "Well done, Gingham," and everybody laughed.

"That last part weren't my doin'. Ol' Lightnin' runs on soybeans and hot air, I reckon."

Mom got out of the car with her sweater held over her head for shelter. "Frank, you'll have to clean up that dog. Take off your shoes and socks and take her over to that puddle and see if you can get some of that stuff off of her."

Frank got Chummy by the collar and urged her over to the puddle where he tried to clean off the smelly stuff by dipping his hands into the cold water and rubbing them on the happy terrier.

Meanwhile, Dad and Gingham had put the fence back in place and were hob-knobbing about relatives. "Jim and I and your daddy went over to Maybe on Saturday to see the traveling show. When we got there they were just setting up so we got a job helping put up the big old tent. There were a couple of girls about our age and—"

"John. It's time to go." Mom stood by the car holding the dirty towel.

"Oh yeah. Well thanks, G. It was a good thing you came along. No tellin' how long we might have stayed stuck. Here is something for your trouble." He held out a dollar bill, which was spendy for Dad.

"Oh no, Mr. Johnny. My daddy'ed skin me ifin I took anythin' for doin' for a ol' frien like you'ns. He tells about things you'all done when you'ns was young whippers. He'll be proud ta know I give you a help."

Gingham turned and slapped old Lightnin' on the rump and led him back to the mower to finish up the day.

Dad picked up his soggy hat, gave it a shake, and carefully hung it over the Chevy's hood ornament. "We'll take this along to remind us of Lightnin'."

"Just look at you all. Looks like you belong to that house back there with the ragged dirty kids." Mom was a stickler for clean kids. Her own in particular.

They went on up the road that climbed out of the slippery clay onto a rocky mountainside, switched back twice, and could see Uncle Jim's farm across a little valley where a glimmer of sunlight sparkled on the red roof of the barn.

"Look, I can see it, I see it!" Mary screamed. It was always a contest to see which one of them first caught sight of the barn and yelled the loudest.

In just a few seconds they came out of a patch of hemlocks, around a bend, and there was Uncle Jim and two Bluetick hounds standing at the opened gate.

"Helloooo there Johnny. Hellooo there folks. See you made it all right, what with all the wet. Didyah run into any of that road work down yonder?"

Uncle Jim slapped his leg with his old felt hat that sprayed water into the air, while the two hounds circled and sniffed.

"Well, I think we did see some of your neighbors down the rode a bit, huh kids?"

Dad grinned and reached out his hand to his kid brother, who took it and then gave Dad a hug.

"Come on then. Eula's got pot roast, pickled beans, and cornbread all a-waiten fer us up to the house. It'll be getting dark early today. Let's go."

The two hounds went running off into the blackberry briars while Uncle Jim climbed onto the running board. He held on with one hand, pointed with the other, and talked all the way down the lane to the red-framed farmhouse that showed a wisp of wood smoke from the kitchen stovepipe and a warm glow in the dining room window.

Frank Loudin in
the early 1940s

Teenage Frank Loudin
next to the family's '36
Chevy, site of his first kiss

Man's best friend

Fast break

Custodian Kid's custodial

Root beer floats all around

The Early Times

Aunt Lily's quilt

Stephen A. "Doug" Hartley (Granddad),
born 1856 in Cow Run, West Virginia

Loudins' Blue Rock, West Virginia

The classic Caddy

Groceries, goods, and gossip

Best of Show

Sugar plum

Gossip center

The Newton incident

It never rains

The three Magi

# *TEEZER'S TWISTS VII*

---

## *DRESS CODE*

*D*epending on the weather, dress at Teezer's can take some inventive turns, especially with the younger crowd. I don't know why we pick on the kids about their clothes. Look around. What am I wearing? A pair of jeans that are a bit too long. I have to admit that I am shrinking. The jeans fit just right when I bought them a few years ago but now they are too long so that the backs of the cuffs drag and as a result are dirty and frayed. The knees have lost most of their original indigo. They are held up to what used to be my waist by an ancient leather belt that was originally tooled by a Zuni craftsman from New Mexico, but now the traditional design is just a lumpy shadow of itself. I'm too cheap to buy a replacement even if I could find one. Save a cow!

I have my usual "Fly-In" sweatshirt, proclaiming that 1999 was a very good year. My newish shoes look pretty good because my old ones hurt my toes and leak on rainy days. My jacket testifies that I have been carrying in some pretty dirty chunks of firewood because my front is dusty with small bits of bark or maybe some icing from one of Carolyn's super cupcakes.

I sit there, comfortable with my crowd, observing the passing parade.

The most notable are the kids from high school. I think one of their requirements is a trip to Teezer's every day around 10:30. A teacher friend told me that when the kids get too rambunctious, a teacher will send them down to Teezer's for a latte.

Standard dress for a sophomore girl could be Uggs, probably the ugliest excuse for boot design ever, mid-calf high, over black tights. Then a ruffled top, maybe even a lace camisole hanging loosely from either a tight, too-small sweater or a too-big jacket. The sleeves of this jacket must be down to the tips of her longest finger and beyond.

Somewhere there must be a bit of underwear showing. This is a statement against any remnant of Victorian mores that might remain at Orcas High School.

An old gray hoodie is popular, pulled well forward so that just the nose and long stringy hair can be seen. This enhances that depressed, contemptuous look that teens like to display.

All boys are in denial of the human shape. The waist doesn't exist as such. However, the ever-present revealing of what is known as "plumber's slot" is popular in both sexes. Everything that once was considered a waistline can appear anywhere from crotch level to mid-thigh on some boys. One kid had his pants so low that he had to walk knock-kneed. I don't know how he keeps his pants on. Maybe that's the point.

Maybe their pants are held up by the tops of their huge, untied sports shoes that are splayed out wide with the flying laces approach. There's usually enough material in the pants to make two extra pairs.

On the other hand, the girls' jeans are so tight that the blood must be cut off to the lower parts. Their feet are blue from lack of circulation.

Hats are a statement also. Either a watch cap pulled well down over the ears or a baseball type with the bill twisted haphazardly right or left but definitely not centered. This adds to the bored, half-wit image. Actually, the mentally challenged man that I mentioned in previous chapters is better dressed than most of the kids.

Hairstyle can range from a bony shaved skull in either sex, to cornrows or dreadlocks, to a wild mop of rainbow-colored material that clusters around a face that may be pierced in various spots by small rings of stainless steel.

We more mature folks are wearing what we thought was cool some years ago and now may peg us as old duffers. It's difficult to get into the up-to-date dress when most of those elements of style are what we thought of as dorky. If you wanted to look like an imbecile, all you had to do was wear your cap backwards and folks would immediately take you for a numbskull.

We, the Teezer's Geezers, sit comfortably in our dated outfits and make clever observations on kids.

"Boy, I'm sure glad I don't have to worry about what girls think of me and what I'm wearing anymore," some guy will sigh.

"Did you ever?" his wife will reply.

"Yeah. My mother would inspect me at the front door on the way to school, then I would have to change everything around once I got out of her sight."

"You didn't dare have all of your buttons buttoned or your jacket zippered or even fastened. I had to work to get a lock of my hair to hang down over my forehead like Robert Mitchum. It took time."

Jannie gets into it. "Remember when we wore our dad's dress shirts with the tails out?"

"We wore our sweaters backwards and took the laces out of our saddle shoes," Dorothy adds.

Frank sips on his coffee. "If we did that today no one would notice."

Bob says, "It's my theory that as we get older, we become dimmer. Young people will walk right through us if we don't watch out."

"I think you're right. Just this morning I looked into the mirror and all I could see were my new six-hundred-dollar, state-of-the-art fillings and a loose crown," Frank laughs.

"And a worn and dingy collar," Jannie adds.

"My wife won't let me wear jeans that are getting pale in the knees. Then we go to Orcas Center for an event and most of the well-dressed young folks not only have worn knees but holes in the thigh with carefully rendered raveling."

"They pay extra for that feature at the Gap or someplace," Bill adds.

Two young women come in dressed to the nines. They have long skirts, long capes, and long boots with long heels. They have styled short hair and fine cosmetic decorations. One is carrying a laptop in a case and the other a sheaf of handouts for some unsuspecting citizen.

"I bet they're JWs," Dotty whispers.

"Maybe they're hookers from Bellevue," someone adds.

"Maybe they're JW hookers. You know the Muslims have their forty virgins, well, then the JWs must have an auxiliary of some kind, too," Frank suggests.

"You're really sick," Jannie nudges him with her elbow.

"Maybe they're talent scouts for the Hooters restaurant that is going in across the street," Bill adds.

"Hooters!" Dorothy snorts. "If they ever put in a Hooters on Orcas they will have to recruit in Texas. I don't see any girl that would qualify."

"Well, maybe you just haven't been looking," Frank takes a sip and nods toward two women sitting across the room.

"Is that all you men ever think about?" Elsie sighs.

"Well, sex is here to stay. That's what got us here in the first place. If your grandmother hadn't had sex, you wouldn't even be here."

"My grandmother?" All of the women shout in unison.

"Oh! Our grandmothers!"

"My grandmother never had sex," Bill announces.

"Yeah, I know. You came directly from Sears."

"In a plain brown wrapper marked 'This end up' and 'Do not stack more than four high,'" Frank adds.

They all laugh as the two missionary ladies leave with their laptop, handouts, and tall lattes.

"We gotta go," somebody says, and we all agree, milling

around getting our jackets, and cleaning up the tables.

Mark whips around with his bar rag, arranging the chairs and tables. He straightens one of the grandchildren's photos on the wall as the door slams again and the place is quiet. Silence reigns.

# *OZARK OCTOBER*

---

*E*very autumn after Jan and I closed our gallery and Harry and Barbara closed their restaurant on Catalina Island, we four packed our 25 pounds of personals and headed out to wherever the weather looked best. On this day, we were four carefree gypsy flyers cruising at 500 feet over the autumn landscape of Southern Missouri in our dependable Cessna 172, seeking experiences more than raw adventure.

My wife Jan and I had now enjoyed three autumn excursions with our friends. We had dropped into small town airstrips from Moses Lake, WA, to Corsicana, TX, to Fallbrook, CA, to Spearfish, SD, not to mention SFO and LAX.

Last night, we had been in St. Charles, MO, where, in a casual conversation in the Lewis and Clark Diner, a friendly stranger had extolled the virtues of a canoe trip on the Current River, down in the Ozarks.

Early this morning we had lifted off with the fog, followed the Father of the Waters down to the Arch in St Louis, and then headed southwest into the very heart of autumn.

The Ozarks are not really mountains, as in Colorado or Vermont, but, rather, gently rolling hills, mostly forested with crooked finger lakes here and there. A few farms take up the flatter places and the few small towns cater to sportsmen and lookie-loos.

Canoeing is a relatively new thing and several beautiful river courses around the country have been designated "natu-

---

153

ral" with the accompanying protection enforcement.

The brochure showed Van Buren as the jumping off spot for a trip down the Current River, half day, whole day or overnight, depending.

The weather was all blue sky and hot sun as we sailed over the rolling hills of colorful hardwoods and crazy quilt meadows. We spotted Van Buren and the Current River that split the town and trailed off to the southwest like a twisted silver ribbon.

An unpaved landing strip with one parked plane invited us to investigate further, so we did a 180 and touched down, taxied over to where the other plane was parked, and shut down. The only sign of civilization was a pole with the remains of a phone booth clinging to the side next to a gate that was off its hinges and lying in the weeds.

Once the hot engine of the Cessna stopped ticking, only the buzzing insects bothered the sultry noontide.

We had noted some kind of small warehouse, surrounded by parked cars, just down the hill from the strip and, with all the confidence in the world, we trekked on down through the beautiful woods.

"We make cap," said a stout lady with a beehive of indigo hair that looked heavily lacquered like a lampstand of blown glass. Her mascaraed blue eyes peered at us over rhinestone-studded glasses that perched well down on the tip of a long-freckled nose.

"Cap?" the four of us asked, almost in perfect unison.

"Yes sir, cap." She picked up a yellow baseball style cap on the counter that proclaimed Buffalo Lake, Arkansas, in bison brown lettering over a charging animal that faintly resembled a buffalo snorting crimson lightning bolts from its oversized nostrils.

"Oh, yeah, cap," Harry agreed, then inquired about the security of the airstrip.

"Nobody ever goes up yonder 'cept Nate Hickman. He is a forest ranger of some sort. Flies around sometimes, God knows where." The phone rang and she barked out, "Yeah? V.B. Cap and

Novelty."

Harry put the buffalo cap on sideways and looked at us cross-eyed.

"Lucille, can I borrow your phone?" Harry inquired.

"How did you know her name?" Barbara hissed.

Harry pointed at the nameplate on the desk that pronounced, "Lucille Poindexter, Office Manager."

"Lucille, we want to have a good lunch, take a canoe ride, maybe stay all night. Can we do that here?" Harry put the cap back on the counter and tried to look past Lucille into the back room where the sound of busy machines and muffled voices added to the stuffy office.

"Oh, sure. We don't have a taxi, but Flora drives folks around in her Impala when there is a call for it." She held the phone and gave Harry an inquisitive nod.

"Can we just walk to town or—"

"Better jest go on and get Flora. She knows about stuff," Lucille interrupted him.

She dialed, rattled into the phone, hung up, and with an air of superiority said, "It's taken care of. Flora is on her way. Where y'all from know-how?"

She leaned both elbows onto the counter, flashing her long, sooty lashes over the rhinestone frames.

"We're from Catalina Island out in California," Harry announced, with an air of pride.

"Uh huh, is that anywhere near Disneyland? My kids been there, but I never."

"Well, Catalina Island is—" Harry started.

"Here's Flora." A buzzer went off somewhere under the counter and Lucille yelled, "Yeah" and disappeared into the back room where we could hear Tammy Wynette whining about D-I-V-O-R-C-E, and a chorus of sewing machines making cap.

We stepped outside to meet not Flora but Shiloh, Flora's friend.

"Flora had to go to a cemetery meeting so she sent me. Whatchy'all be needin'?

Shiloh squinted at us like we were growing dim and flipped

a cigarette butt into a wet pothole clear out in the middle of the street. She looked pretty much like a boy except for the way she stood there with her hips swung to the left and her narrow shoulders pitched to the right. No boy could stand like that.

"First, we need to go back up to the airport, then down to town, Smiley's, and then we're gonna take a canoe ride." Harry took out a pack of Winstons and offered one to Shiloh. She put hers behind her ear and wiped her nose on her sleeve. "I'll take you to Smiley's then Flora will do the rest. I gotta get back to thu little'uns."

We got in the Impala, went back up to the airport and got our meager luggage, and headed on down to town. Shiloh didn't say anything, but squinted through the windshield, leaning forward like it was a foggy day, which it might have been for her.

There really was a plastic Jesus on her dashboard. I always wondered if it would be more effective if he was facing down the highway in order to fend off any looming dangers, rather than gazing blandly at the unfortunate person in the passenger's seat.

Flora's Impala was of recent vintage. The clear plastic seat covers and the extra rubber floor mats gave evidence of care. A large convenience carry-all clung to the drive shaft lump between the front seats. It was well stocked with Flora's daily necessities.

The town was one paved main street with a few gravel branches that meandered into chicken pens and wood lots. We could see a row of two-storied brick buildings on down the street but Shiloh suddenly whipped into Smiley's like she was evading a police blockade.

Smiley's was one of those L-shaped motels with the office at the street end of the L and parking along in front of each unit. There was a strip of flickering red neon tubing that skipped along the roofline and ended with a splutter that stuttered "Va ... cy."

A cluster of Adirondack chairs circled a low stone firepit in the front yard and a big old Bluetick hound languished on the welcome mat blocking the screen door.

Mr. Smiley himself was at the front desk but seemed pre-occupied. He was a big swarthy man somewhat gone to pot. A pot that was accented by a gigantic silver buckle that dipped low in the shade of his belly. He was pure western dude in costume except instead of the traditional boots, Smiley was wearing brown and white oxfords without strings.

"Y'all together?" Smiley growled.

"Well yes. We need two rooms with queens, back from the highway," Harry started.

"Non-smoking," Jan added.

"And a bathtub," Barbara added.

Smiley raised one eyebrow to give Harry a glare.

"I'm sure Mr. Smiley can take care of that," Harry announced to everyone in general.

Smiley scribbled over a form sheet, then, with a flourish, spun it about to face the front of the counter. Harry and I paid with credit cards while Jan and Barbara looked over a menu from The Riverside Resort Restaurant.

"Here you go. That'll be units 12 and 14. There ain't no 13 'cause we got enough bad luck around here the way is." Smiley almost smiled at his own humor.

We carried our meager luggage to our respective rooms and met Shiloh back out on the street.

"Shiloh, is there a good place for lunch?"

"Best place to eat lunch?" Shiloh bit at her lower lip. "I reckon that'ud be down at the Courthouse Café. They got the best chili con carne ever day 'cept weekends. All the folks from over at the courthouse go there, you know."

"Well, let's just go there. Can we walk?"

Harry peered down the street.

"That 'ud be jest on down there where you see them syc-amores. That'ud be the courthouse and the café is jest acrost."

Shiloh moved her hands in a direction that indicated a left turn.

"Y'all want's ride er jest walk?"

We looked at each other and hunched our shoulders.

"What the heck. Let's go get some chili con carne.

"I'll go get Flora. She'll catch up to you'ns down at the café."
Shiloh got into the Impala and left. Harry put his arm around
Barbara's shoulder and they started down the street. Jan and I
followed along the sidewalk, broken and cracked by time.

The courthouse was set in the center of a grassy town square
shaded by huge old sycamores. It was three stories-plus high,
not including a classic cupola of patinaed copper. The walls
were smooth, golden, river stones with long narrow windows
and a resident flock of pigeons that had decorated a Civil War
cannon that faced north and the ghost of U.S. Grant.

It was just about noon by the time we opened the Wonder
Bread screen door and entered the café along with a marmalade
tomcat and a collection of buzzy winged bugs.

Like stepping from a time machine into the '30s or maybe
beyond, there was a long, long counter with stools down one
side and a row of round oak tables down the other, clustered
with a collection of mismatched chairs. A pressed tin ceiling
must have been twenty feet above us with honest to goodness
fans that gently stirred the aroma of chili con carne and age.

"Hi, y'all. Here for chili con carne?"

There stood a thin woman with that kinda hair middle
aged women tend to have when the first flecks of silver appear.
Blue-black and dullish like the inside of a stovepipe. She was
wearing an official waitress uniform, black with a frilly white
apron. Embroidered over her left breast was "Golden."

"Golden, we came for your famous chili," Harry said, as he
fingered a menu that lay on a glass display counter full of candy
bars, knick-knacks, and chewing gum.

"The chili con carne isn't on the menu but that's what we
have on Tuesdays. That's today, except it ain't ready yet. He don't
get it done 'til 11:45. That's when folks from the courthouse get
off fer lunch. It's only 11:15 so we don't have no chili con carne
yet till more like noon."

"Golden. Is that your name? Golden? Can we get something now? You see, we want to take a river trip this afternoon
and so we don't have much time." Harry leaned over the candy

case using his best persuasive stance.

"I can see what Emory will do for you. Jest hold on there." Golden jabbed her pencil into a long ponytail that was entwined with strings of something that glittered.

"This ought to be interesting. I wonder what old Emory will feel like cooking up for outsiders." Barbara whispered.

"Do you suppose they have a salad of some kind?" Jannie asked.

"Maybe a cheeseburger," I thought out loud.

Golden came back and leaned over the table and whispered. "He'll make you toasted cheese." She looked over her shoulder like this was a drastic breech of some secret code of Ozark tradition.

"Well, okay. If that's what it is to be." Harry looked at us for approval.

"We'll take four toasted cheese sandwiches, ma'am."

Harry leaned back in his chair.

"Name's Golden. Don't like ma'am. Sounds like an old lady, huh?"

She carefully wrote four toasted cheese sandwiches in her receipt book.

"Golden?" Harry asked.

"Golden," Golden repeated.

"Not Goldie, like Goldie Hawn?"

"Golden, not Goldie. Actually it's Golden Delicious, like in the apple. Mama thought her golden baby was gonna grow up and be a blonde even if Daddy was part Cherokee. Mama thought Golden Delicious was the most beautiful name ever, so there you go. Golden Delicious Hickman."

"That's really nice Golden." Jan said.

We all nodded.

"What can we get with our cheese sandwiches?" I inquired, picturing something out of a school lunch.

"Well, I reckon we can give you a bowl of tomato soup, chips and a dill pickle."

"That would be great. Does your chef make good pies?" I asked.

"Chef? Oh, you mean Emory. Yeah. Folks rave over his Ritz Crunch Pie."

We leaned forward, all ears.

"Ritz Crunch?" Barbara repeated with a look of amazement.

"I want a piece of Ritz Crunch Pie." I stepped out boldly.

"You're gonna die, smarty," Jan hissed into my ear.

"I just hope he doesn't find out we're from California. He will probably spit in our tomato soup," I whispered.

"Remind me not to get the tomato soup," Jan snickered.

The swinging door to the kitchen slammed open and Golden came over to the back table where we had settled.

"Emory is gonna make y'all toasted cheese with tomato soup and saltines," she announced, as if this was really a special favor from the staff.

"Tomato soup?" Harry rolled his eyes over to the rest of us.

"What do you think, gang?" he chuckled.

"Sure. What do we care? We're probably going to perish this afternoon anyway trying to maneuver canoes on a raging river," I encouraged.

The tomato soup was really good but the cheese sandwiches were plain white bread and Velveeta with just enough mayonnaise to hold the things together. They had been toasted on a greasy fry-top that still carried this morning's sausage flavor. There was a slice of dill pickle that was strong enough to walk out of the place by itself.

Golden came over with the check and my piece of Ritz Crunch. It was not bad. A thick crust of crumbled Ritz crackers moistened with butter, a filling of kinda nutty flavored pudding, topped with a glaze of brown sugar and more crunched Ritz.

By the time we finished, folks from the courthouse came in, sat down, and were served chili con carne without any verbal order. Golden just served 'em up as fast as they sat down. Folks poured their own water or coffee, or got Coca-Cola from a cooler behind the counter. Golden just went to the kitchen and returned with bowls of chili and wrote up tickets and socialized with each table like a hostess at the Bel-Air Country Club.

"Hello there, folks. I'm Flora Willbanks. I guess Shiloh brought you."

A little woman with a face shaped like a triangle over a pointy chin stepped up to our table. She wore a flowery print housedress and a pale-blue knit sweater that was too big for her in various places. What hair she had was tied up under a loose lavender bandana. Her steel-rimmed glasses were big and round so that her eyes were magnified to the proportions of a wasp. A friendly wasp, but a wasp nonetheless.

"Hi there, Flora. Can we get you something to eat, a piece of pie, coffee?" Harry stood up and offered his chair to Flora.

"Oh my, no, but aren't you the one, though." She turned her head sideways and looked down at her sensible black shoes.

"Flora, we want to go for a canoe trip after lunch. How do we do that?" Harry looked at Flora in his most sincere manner.

"Oh surely. My cousin Willie Stark runs river trips all the time. We can jest go on down to his place and he'll fix y'all right up." She leaned back and looked out the window.

"That'd be his rig yonder, crost there by the Tap and Tip." Flora pointed her tiny chin in the direction of the front window. Sure enough, across the street, sat a pick-up with a rack on top that held four canoes.

"I'll jest step out and fetch him. Y'all rest easy. I'll be right back." Flora turned on her sensible heels and went out the door.

By the time Flora and Willie came back across the street, we had settled up with Golden and were waiting on the sidewalk.

Willie Stark was a stump of hickory khaki that displayed sweat stains like age rings in a tree. He was built like one of those modern stone sculptures with very little definition. He might have had squinty eyes but the reflective sunglasses hid all of his facial expressions. He would have made a great ventriloquist because he spoke or mumbled without moving his lips in any way. A deep voice came from somewhere inside of him like an echo from an abandoned coal mine.

"Y'all ever done canoe afore?" he grunted and spit a brindle stream of Bull Durham into a patch of weeds that clustered around a rusty fireplug there in front of the café."

"Yeah. Sure," Harry replied while Barbara, Jan, and I all shook our heads like a row of bobbleheads.

"Hain't nothin' to it, actual," Willie muttered and almost grinned.

"We just want to see the river and the autumn colors in the trees." Jan enthused.

"Uh huh," Willie replied in a noncommittal way.

"It isn't very dangerous, is it?" Barbara almost whispered.

"Nah. You jest watch out fer the snags."

"Snakes! Do they bite? Are they poisonous? Are they in the river?" Barbara asked with a frown.

"Poisonous snags?" Willie frowned over his dark glasses.

"Snags, he said. Snags, not snakes." Harry laughed.

"Oh, okay. I didn't want any of those slimy water things climbing into our canoe." Barbara relaxed.

"Oh, Willie hasn't lost a canoe this week," Flora said seriously, then tittered.

"All week," Willie confessed and chuckled.

"How much is it gonna be?" I asked.

Willie pulled a folded sheet of paper from is shirt pocket and handed it to me.

Stark River Adventures, it proclaimed, with accompanying prices and corresponding times and distances.

Harry pointed at the Stark and whispered in his loud way, "Poor choice of words, don't you think?"

We agreed on the two-hour trip for twenty-two dollars each and climbed into Willie's big pick-up that had a two-week collection of assorted garbage strewn on the seat, dashboard, and floor. Willie just cleared the seats onto the floor with a big hand full of sausage fingers.

"Where do y'all come from?" Willie asked, as he pulled the choke full on and tromped on the starter.

"We're from Catalina Island out in—" Harry started but was drowned out by the explosive cough of the big engine.

Willie pulled a U-turn right there in front of the café, almost hitting a police car in the process. The big cop's face just grinned and gave Willie a soft salute. He wore the same kind of reflective sunglasses that Willie sported.

"Cousins. They're all cousins," Harry turned from his place in the front seat and whispered.

In just a couple of blocks we came to the river where Willie took a dirt road that went down under the bridge to a gravel bar and a row of various colored canoes. Willie pulled two over to the edge of the turgid water, gave us orange life jackets and paddles, and helped us launch.

"I'll meet you'all down below. You'll see me there, no problem."

He stood there with hands on hips as the four of us fumbled about with the unfamiliar situation.

The gentle current carried us around the first bend as we tried to keep the canoes pointed downstream. There were a few mild ripples where the canoes tipped and bobbled, but mostly we just drifted through a dream-like setting of balmy blue skies and golden foliage reflecting off the twinkly surface.

A jon boat came roaring up the river. Driven by a big fan sticking up in the stern, the flat bottom boat is a favorite of guys in camouflage dungarees who strew the landscape with spent beer cans, shotgun shells, and Moon Pie wrappers. In the next two hours we saw only three of these offenders as they hurried by, churning up a wake to their glee and our consternation.

"Head into the wake," I yelled at Jannie, as we watched Harry and Barbara tip dangerously abeam. We actually nosed through the wake with expert aplomb, proud of ourselves.

"What a day!" I yelled at Jannie. "This is like a dream, or maybe the Riverboat Ride at Disneyland without the canned wildlife and background music.

Just ahead, Harry and Barbara were caught up in a little eddy that grabbed their canoe and tossed it around a fallen tree. While looking back to see if we could make it, they disappeared into a grove of willows hanging well out over the river.

Jan and I made it around the log with just a slight fright, tipping dangerously port and starboard. Our paddles didn't do much good as we waved them in the air frantically.

The glimmering stream reflected Ozark autumn awe as it

murmured along occasionally flashing platinum flakes in sudden stripes. All too soon we rounded a bend and spotted Willie's big white pick-up on a gravel bar that reached out of a grove of golden sycamores.

"I see y'all made it in fine fettle," he chuckled, as he waded into the shallows to pull us ashore.

"Oh yeah, it was just beautiful," Barbara answered.

"Did'ja happen to run into any of those poisonous snags up thar?" Willie grunted.

"Naw, it was a snap." Harry stepped into the water that was over the tops of his shoes.

"Damn," he grunted, hopping around like a frog.

I explained to Willie which button to push on my camera, and we posed with our canoes and paddles while Willie's big fingers fumbled with the camera. We helped Willie hoist the canoes up on the rack and climbed into his truck, three of us in the back seat and Harry riding shotgun.

The three of us became fascinated with a big boil on the back of Willie's neck that was the size of a half-dollar and looked like it was pulsating like the back-up lights on a trash truck. We weren't sure whether Willie was bald or just shaved his head, but it was smaller than his neck, smooth and shiny.

"Y'all make it around that big ol' snag back there at Bumble Bee?" Willie lifted his John Deere cap just enough to prove our speculations about his hairlessness. When he turned to look at Harry, we saw that he really didn't have any eyebrows either, just a ridge of pinched up wrinkles.

"Where can we get a good dinner tonight, Willie?" Harry offered Willie a Winston and lit up one himself. Willie had a cheek full of Bull Durham so he declined the Winston.

"I reckon Pete Hurley down there at the Resort has 'bout the best home doin's, I reckon. Y'all lookin' fer catfish, ol' Pete's as good as it gets. Yes sir." Willie ran a big hand over the back of his neck, including the boil.

Jannie, Barbara, and I winced but it didn't seem to faze old Willie.

As we crossed the bridge back into downtown Van Buren,

Willie nodded to the left, across the highway, to a rambling collection of add-ons that looked like they had run out of funds some time ago.

"That 'ud be the Resort, yonder. If'n y'all look in the glove compartment there, you can get a coupon for four free beverages, not booze though. Pete's too tight fer that," he chuckled.

"Well, thanks Willie." Harry fumbled through the pile of papers and came up with a wad of coupons, took one, and tried to get the mess back in place and slam the door. Willie glanced at the problem but didn't offer any help.

All was quiet at Smiley's Motel. We went to our rooms, changed out of our wet socks, and met at one of the picnic tables out front for a quick cocktail in the twilight. Flora pulled up in her Impala and Mrs. Smiley came out with a tall glass of ice and bourbon.

As the conversation proceeded, a light plane passed overhead, heading low toward the airport. We all paused and looked up.

"He's pretty low," Harry commented, squinting into the gathering darkness.

"That's a 172, like yours, Harry," I said.

"Yeah, and it has green trim." Jan added.

We all took a sip.

"Does it snow much around here?" I asked.

"Oh yeah. Sometimes it really—" Flora started but just then the plane came around again. Lower this time.

"That looks like your plane," Jannie said.

"Naw. My plane's not that fat," Harry scoffed.

We all took another sip and tilted our heads, listening to the sound of the airplane engine as it went away, then got louder again.

"Nobody else around here has an airplane, do they?" Flora asked Mrs. Smiley.

"Gee. I don't think so, though it might be—"

The plane came over again, lower yet, as darkness spread up from the ground, leaving only a fading purple sky. All grew quiet. Lightning bugs began to twinkle up from the lawn. We were all listening for the plane, but the sky was empty except for the first bats of the evening and a distant owl.

"I'm really hungry. Let's get on down to the resort." I broke the spell.

"I'm with you, buddy." Harry tossed his plastic cup at a trash barrel across the drive but missed miserably.

"Rebound!" I yelled and rushed over, scooped up the cup and slammed it into the barrel. "Slam dunk!" We all giggled like sophomores.

There were no cars parked in front of the resort, which is usually a bad omen for a highway café in a small town. We bravely marched through the weary front door to be met by the aroma of years of cigarette smoke and deep-fried everything. The interior reflected the same style of neglect that we had observed as we entered.

The entry had at one time been decorated with a montage of what could have been local river fish, featuring channel catfish that have got to be one of God's mistakes. Years of handprints and a border of AAA advertisements didn't make it any more inviting behind the bar.

It was too dark to make any judgments. It was a long room with a 30-degree bend in the middle to follow the natural curve of the riverbank. Windows all along the "view" side were semi-transparent due to long seasons of river mists, dust, and insect leavings.

A bar ran along the opposite side of the room where the lone bartender acknowledged our presence with a thinly disguised lack of interest.

"Dinner?" he growled, as he dumped a tin bucket of ice cubes into some noisy crusher.

"Right. We're told that you have the best catfish dinner in these parts." After only one brief afternoon, Harry had taken on an Ozark accent.

"That'll be four for dinner." The bartender turned and spoke to a woman at the far end of the bar who was so small that only her face showed through a swirl of cigarette smoke.

"Y'all jest take any table you ker to an' I'll get right with ya."

She spoke in a high childlike tone, but made no move to seat us.

Jannie and Barbara selected a table at one of the windows near the center where the room turned.

"This is gonna be interesting," I whispered to Jannie.

"Fried fish in this place is like deliberately squatting on the third rail," Jannie muttered.

"Y'all jest passing through, I reckon." The little woman came to our table with an arm full of menus.

She was well under five feet tall with tiny hands and feet. This made her head seem larger than normal, accented by a high and wide brow and a pair of enormously round eyes that seemed to be all iris. Her hair was a pile of sausage curls stuck on the back of her head like a dust mop. She looked like a bizarre attempt at a Shirley Temple doll that got out of control.

"Kin I fetch y'all sumpin to drank?" She almost curtsied.

"Maybe some decaf and a glass of water," Barbara spoke right up and we all nodded in agreement.

"Well I reckon we don't have no decaf right now but I kin jest add hot water to the regular if you want."

She smiled and showed perfect teeth and dimples.

"No, just the water will be fine," Harry ordered and picked up a menu.

"I'll be right back." She turned and flossed away across the room and disappeared through a set of swinging doors behind the bar.

"I'll bet she knows all the words to 'On the Good Ship Lollypop," I said, remembering the first movie I ever saw.

"Do you think it will be okay, eating here, I mean?" Barbara's eyes flicked around the room as she ran a finger along the windowsill.

"Whatever we get, they will probably fry the hell out of it. That should take care of any Ozark germs and all of the flavor," Harry chuckled.

"Are you really going to have catfish?" Barbara looked at us all for some sort of support.

Shirley Temple came back with a tray of glasses and a big pitcher of ice water. She managed it with professional skill.

"Y'all decide yet?" she asked in her lollypop voice.

"Yes ma'am. We're gonna have your famous catfish blue-plate dinner with all the fixin's," Harry ordered.

"They ain't no blue plates," Shirley giggled.

"Well, you know. All the fixin's," Harry added.

"That would be the catfish, deep fried onion rings, with green tomatoes, roasten' ears er limas er whatever he wants. Maybe it's okra tonight. There's potato cakes an' there's country butter and rolls and quince marmalade. Then fer after, we got buttermilk short cake with rhubarb and maple sugar topping." She put her hands behind her and strutted in place just like Shirley in *Curly Top*.

"Okay, we'll have all that."

Harry nodded enthusiastically as the little woman spun about and flounced away.

"Don't you wonder if that bartender is a cousin of Flora and Willie?" Barbara wiped the silverware on her napkin.

"Yeah, they are all cousins around here. Shirley Temple and some Cro-Magnon species, ex-Navy cook back there in the galley," I added.

When the waitress returned carrying a tray with four bowls of soup, we all passed around a look of surprise.

"J. R. thought y'all should have some of his leek an' potato dumplin' soup." Shirley nodded in agreement with herself.

"What's your name young lady?" Harry inquired like an English professor.

"Shirley. It's Shirley," she answered with a nod.

Harry spewed a mouth full of water and choked as the rest of us took in a collective deep breath.

"That's nice." Barbara tried her best to cover for all of us as we stared into our soups and tried not to snort.

"Mama always wanted a Shirley Temple doll but got pregnant instead and had me. She was only fourteen." Shirley spoke of the situation with a feeling of pride as if having a kid at fourteen was a major accomplishment.

"That's real nice." Jannie replied.

We all looked at each other in wonderment as she turned

and went into the kitchen.

Outside, a jon boat went roaring up the river trailing a wake of silver ripples and golden leaves. Four kids carefully inched out onto a fallen log that reached into the river from a bushy bank of brush. We watched in amusement as they tangled and re-tangled their four poles and lines. They looked like comic knights jousting for possession of a crude bridge in Sherwood Forest.

Shirley came back, followed by J. R. the chef, carrying four large U.S. Navy-type platters heaped with a breaded and deep-fried collection of lumps and gravy.

"You'all are lucky. I jest happened to have four ears a sweet corn. Goes real nice with catfish from rightcheer' on the river, jest down below thu fork." J. R. stood on his left foot and scratched his right armpit with a huge knobby fist.

"Looks just great," Harry enthused, as the rest of us gazed in awe at the pile of unrecognizable shapes on our plates.

"You'all be needen catsup?" Shirley inquired, being the perfect hostess.

I had the urge to gag with the thought of a gooey red decoration on my plate.

"No thanks. I think this will be just fine." Harry jabbed his fork into the stuff.

Shirley and J. R. went into the back as we approached our dinner with trepidation.

As Shirley had promised, everything was there and heavily breaded. It didn't matter what we bit into. It all tasted like greased cracker crumbs. The catfish was very dry, like it had been a long time out of the river. I couldn't help but imagining what those jon boat guys had left in the water upstream.

We each took at least one bite out of everything on our plates then sat back like after a fine Thanksgiving gorge.

There was no need to converse.

"I guess you'all weren't as hungry as you reckoned, huh?" Shirley took our plates and soon returned with four plates of buttermilk shortcake dripping with a gooey rhubarb and maple sugar topping. This was not bad, for rhubarb. The shortcake was still warm out of the oven, and light and moist.

We finished the dessert, settled up with Shirley, and walked back up to Smiley's Motel, satisfied that we had had enough of Ozark ambience for the day. Maybe forever.

The next morning we had bagels, apple juice, and very strong coffee at the motel, and phoned Flora to take us back to the airport.

She must have been waiting just around the corner because before we had brushed our teeth, she was standing there beside her trusty Impala with all of the doors open, just like a New York limo service.

There was still a fringe of frost in the shade as the Impala scattered golden leaves and gravel into the blue chicory along the edge of the road. Back past the "cap" factory and up the hill to the airport. We were in high spirits. Barbara claimed it was because none of us had died in the night from breaded gastronomy.

A light blue mist was just rising above the grass along the runway as we went toward our lonely plane that sat at the far end of the strip.

"Hey. Look at that," Harry said, a little too loud.

We piled out of the car to find that the plane had been moved, the pilot's door was ajar, the tie-downs were lying twisted on the ground, and scattered around were empty beer cans and a potato chip bag.

Harry looked in the front seat and found another beer can and a broken box of crackers.

"That *was* my plane that we saw last night." Harry looked at us with large eyes.

The thought gave us all chills. Someone had been flying our plane around, drinking beer, eating our crackers, and God knows what else.

"Look here!" Harry stood caressing the left horizontal tail. We gathered around to see that the tip of the horizontal tail was slightly bent up and showed a stain of red paint and scratches.

"Some son of a bitch stole my plane and then hit it with his car. Son of a bitch!"

Harry tried to smooth out the bent aluminum with his hand.

"That *was* our plane last night!" Jannie looked up as if she could picture it again.

We stood and watched as Harry went around the plane testing everything.

"I don't think we can fly it. We have to notify the FAA and the police too, I guess." Harry was glum for one of the rare times in his life.

"I know the constable. He is my cousin," Flora piped up. "He would be down to the fire hall. Vergil Carver would be him. Vergil, yes, Vergil." Flora's lips kept repeating Vergil, even after the sound had gone.

"Well, Flora. I guess you had just better take me down to the fire hall. Do you have time?" Harry asked.

"Oh yes indeed. We gotta get Vergil." Flora sounded excited. "We gotta find out jest who done it, I reckon." She wet her lips like a hungry dog and dabbed at her mouth with a tiny handkerchief she kept tucked up her sleeve.

"You guys stay here and I'll be back as soon as I call flight service and talk to the police."

We got our luggage out of the car and sat it next to the plane. Harry and Flora got back into the Impala and Flora spun it around, spewing gravel and dirt into our faces as they raced back to the gate and disappeared down the hill.

We were left sitting on our Samsonites in the warm Ozark sun with just the distant roar of a jon boat echoing along upriver.

"I guess we are lucky, whoever it was, that they didn't just fly away or crash. They certainly must have been drinking, if not drunk." Barbara sat on her little white Samsonite.

"Yeah. I wouldn't want them to hurt 44Golf," Jannie mused.

"Uh huh," I added. "I think I'll take a walk down to the other end of the runway. It is such a beautiful day." I got up and the girls followed. We strolled along in the balmy morning with a picket fence of multicolored hardwoods occasionally casting a leaf to the ground in silent salute. We made the far end of the runway and were about halfway back when we heard a car coming up the hill.

"They're coming back," I announced as we picked up the pace.

The first was a black and white pick-up with a whirling red light on top. Then came Flora's Impala followed closely by a white Dodge with a double orange diagonal and a roof full of fluttering red and yellow lights.

They nosed up to the plane in the traditional cloud of dust as a dark blue van with a gold star on the door came roaring up the hill and burst into the open, flashing its double red lights.

"Holy cow, it's the whole gol-dern posse," I said.

We walked over to the circle of lawmen that looked like the cast from *The Andy Griffith Show*. They were gathered around Harry, who just happened to be wearing a T-shirt that showed two bright yellow balls over green lettering. "Tennis players have fuzzy balls."

"I'll bet that shirt impresses those policemen," Jannie snickered.

"Yeah. They will probably arrest him for just the shirt," Barbara added.

Harry came out of the huddle. "I called flight service. They called the FAA and the FBI. It's a federal offense to steal a plane. There is an FAA inspector on his way over here with some gasoline. The plane is out of gas. They flew it dry, son of a bitch."

A plain black Plymouth joined the group, this one without the red lights. Two youngish men got out. They were dressed in dark blue business suits with conservative ties, well-polished Oxfords, and close-cropped hair.

"Could this be the FBI?" I whispered to Jannie.

"Hush. They are undercover," she replied, and we elbowed each other.

"I wonder what all of this has to do with catching the culprits?" I asked.

"They are probably down there at the cap factory stamping out little brown beavers right now," Jannie snickered.

A dusty Camaro came grinding up the hill and lurched

onto the field. It pulled to a stop behind the unmarked FBI sedan but continued to rock on its long-lost shocks.

"I jest had to see what's goin' on up'cheer." It was Lucille from down at the cap factory.

"Well, it looks like somebody took our plane for a joyride last night and in the process, dinged up the tail a bit," I informed.

"Did you notice anybody come up here yesterday late afternoon, just about dark?" Barbara inquired.

"You know, I did see a red Falcon go by the office yesterday, late. I stayed to get out some stuff in the mail, you know." Lucille frowned and looked back down the road as if to recreate the scene.

"Ma'am, did you notice if it came back down? Did you see who it was? About what time?" Jannie sounded like a real Jack Webb.

"Well I did wonder jest what anybody was a doin' goin' up there. Kids come up here jest fer no good an all, if you know jest what I mean. Jest look at all them deputies. Did ya ever?"

Lucille leaned around us and peered over her decorator sunglasses, curling up her nose like she smelled something bad.

"I just thought of it. You know those Hardens. They have a red car," Flora whispered.

"Yeah, and Til Gilmore's brother-in-law. What's his name?"

"Oh and that new fellow over at the feed store."

Flora and Lucille exchanged suspects like naming the lineup for a baseball game.

"You two know every red car in town?"

Flora and Lucille looked at us as if that was a given.

"Oh, not just the red ones. They ain't too many ya know."

Flora gave her little giggle with a shrug.

The FBI men got out a black pebble leather case and spread out a collection of crime scene equipment. They took off their coats, rolled up their sleeves, and started dusting for fingerprints over every possible service of the plane.

All of the posse had out their clipboards and were scribbling away with their ballpoint pens. There were yellow forms in triplicate, blue forms in triplicate, green forms in at least sextuplicate. They were milling around copying from each other like sophomore boys during an American Civics test.

A plane came low over the trees, touched down lightly at the far end of the strip, and taxied over to us. A young man that looked about eighteen hopped out and lifted two five-gallon cans out of the back seat, sat them on the ground, and lit up a cigarette.

Harry and the total law enforcement constabulary of Southern Missouri took a tobacco break. There were Luckies and Chesterfields and Bull Durham and Red Man enough to taint the whole county with a brown haze.

The law took a back seat to hunting season tales while the FBI fused and dusted. Harry and Earl from the FAA sat on the two gasoline cans innocently smoking and exchanging flight fantasies. Suddenly Harry jumped up and looked at the seat of his pants, which showed a dark wet spot.

The FAA expert had stuffed old rags into the top of his gas cans instead of real screw-on safety caps.

"Jesus Christ. I'm soaking up gasoline like a two-bit lamp wick." He tossed his cigarette butt into the dust and ran out to the middle of the runway and fanned his seat.

The gas had been soaking up through the rag stopper into the seat of their pants while they both were smoking nonchalantly away.

Earl stood by the gas cans looking at him, then suddenly it occurred to him that he might soon take on the characteristics of a Roman candle.

"Shit all mighty!" he yelled and jumped around like the flames were already licking at his pants.

The collection of lawmen broke into a demonstration of down-home snorts and guffaws as they stepped away from the gas cans and the two would-be wicks but they didn't toss away their smokes.

"Boy howdy. We could've all gone up in a cloud of smoke. Damn!"

The marshal took off his summer Stetson and wiped his forehead with his shirtsleeve. They all passed around a chuckle, did a little back slapping, got back in their respective cars, and trailed back down the hill and out of sight.

Harry came over to us. "I guess I have to go down to the courthouse and fill out a bunch of papers. It is a federal offense to steal an airplane. The FAA mechanic has to inspect the plane and decide if we can fly it."

He and Harry walked around the plane and fiddled with the controls a bit. Earl watched the left flap while Harry wiggled the yoke.

"Okay, looks good," he yelled.

"This is Earl. He is the FAA inspector mechanic. He gave me the go-ahead to fly if I take a little test hop first." Harry stood and looked hard at his plane. "Well anyway I have to go down to the courthouse. You guys can go back to the motel. Can you drive us around, Flora?"

"Sure, an' I can run y'all over, whenever."

Flora was a jewel.

"I gotta go back to the plant. Hope you catch them fellers, I reckon."

Lucille got back into her car and disappeared down the hill in the dust of the posse.

We piled our luggage back into Flora's Impala and jammed into the back seat with Harry in front.

We dropped Harry off at the courthouse and started back to Smiley's Motel.

"I got a kinda idea," Flora whispered, looking straight ahead, then making a quick turn down a dirt alley behind the Purina Feed and Grain.

"She is going to hold us for ransom in the feed store," I whispered to Jannie.

Jannie snorted and whispered to Barbara who spluttered out loud.

"Look there. That is a red Falcon. See over there by that trailer?" Flora hissed.

Sure enough. There sat a red Falcon, half hidden by a collection of topsy turvy appliances and waist-high weeds.

"That's those Hardens. A couple of no goodens if you asked

me."

"People like that could never fly an airplane. You have to take lessons and get licenses and everything." Barbara gave the red car a hard look.

Flora spun the steering wheel and started to pull up the rutted drive behind the Falcon.

"Wait a minute, Flora," we all shouted.

"We can't just go up there and asked if they stole a plane last night and they owe us for the gas," I said.

Flora pulled up behind the Falcon.

"I just bet it was them," Flora spoke through a grim mouth and squinted at the trailer like she could see inside with her superhuman X-ray vision.

"I'll keep the motor running an' one of you go see if there is white paint on one of their fenders."

"No siree. I'm not going over there. Those old boys might not like us snooping around you know." I wanted out of there.

"Flora, turn around and get out of here. We don't know if it was them or not. Anyway, it's for the sheriff to do."

Barbara's hand was on Flora's shoulder giving a little nudge.

"Well, I'll bet my old felt boot that it was them Harden boys. I lan."

By the time we got back to Smiley's, everybody in town knew all about what had happened. The place took on the air of an event. Everybody that had had contact with us spread their own version of the situation. Flora was in her glory. Shiloh reappeared as did Golden from down at the Resort. Old Willie Stark came by to suggest that it might have been an attempt to smuggle illegal whiskey, "er who knows what."

"I jest betcha I know who 'twas," Shiloh announced, then passed the information along to Golden in a whisper. Golden squealed and jumped up and down.

"I betcha. I jest betcha! Betcha betcha betcha." Golden was almost frothing at the mouth with the last betcha.

"Jest who'd you two be liken to anyhow?" Smiley asked in his deepest, most serious voice.

Golden and Shiloh stood and nudged each other for a minute. Then Golden blurted out.

"Everett and Stump Harden. That's who. They was inta the resort last night jest a hoopin' about sompin. They was already half-plastered and then took to throwin' down shooters. They was inta sompin' I lan."

Golden stood up proudly with her shoulders thrown back and her big blue eyes rolling around her freckled face like one of those bobblehead things of Dolly Parton.

"Didn't I jest tell ya?" Flora was convinced now. "We gotta get Vergil Carver up here to hear this."

"Who is Vergil Carter?" Barbara asked.

"Carver. That would be the Van Buren town constable. He's my cousin."

"Why am I not surprised?" I whispered to Jannie.

"Y'all get back in the car and we'll jest go get Vergil. He'll be over to Ruge's."

Flora opened the driver's door and looked at us like we were juveniles.

We had no choice but to get in the car. Flora made her trademark U-turn then an immediate right down the alley between Madge's Recreation Parlor and Joe Vail's Funeral Home. At the end of the alley was a one-time livery stable that now corralled wrecked trucks and John Deere tractors of ancient vintage. The yard looked like some auto assembly plant had blown up and rusted. I venture to guarantee that there was a used carburetor around there for every gasoline piston engine that had ever been built.

Ruge turned out to be a skinny little fellow in well-lubricated coveralls who at the time was banging on the battered bumper of a Studebaker stake-bed derelict that rested on its top in a helpless manor like a large dead swamp creature.

In assistance, holding the other end of the bumper, was himself, Constable Vergil Carver.

Flora pulled right up to Vergil and rolled down her window.

"Vergil, we got 'em, sure as you're born. They're right up there to home right now. We can jest go up there and get 'em."

Vergil spit over his shoulder into a fifty-five-gallon barrel of rusted drive shafts where a struggling morning glory climbed out of the dust and reached for freedom.

"Flora, what have I tole you about stickin' your nose inta police doings that don't concern yourself? Why don't you jest take these good folks on back up to Smiley's and go pick your peas 'er sumpin."

Flora gave the steering wheel a thump with her tiny fist.

"Vergil. Vergil, I know 'twas them Harden boys took that airplane last evening. Golden and Shiloh heard 'em snickerin' about it last night over to the resort. They got that old red Falcon and Lucille seen it go up to the airport jest as she was closin' the cap plant. What more do you need? I'm tellen' you. IT WAS THEM HARDENS."

Flora thumped out her last four words on the steering wheel, accidentally hitting the horn that blasted in Ruge's ear, making him drop the sledgehammer on his foot.

"Uck, Lora!"

Ruge couldn't say any "f" words because of the empty space in the front of his yellow grin, but he got his point across just as well.

"Well, dadgum, Flora. If you're so fired up, sure I'll go see the Hardens."

Vergil turned and climbed into his black and white International pick-up with the single red light on top and the faded star on the driver's door. He paused to roll and light up a twisted brown cigarette and ground the starter until an explosion shook the old truck and blew brown smoke out the back.

Flora stuck out her little chin and muttered, "Come on y'all, we a goin' with him. I know them Hardens better'n he'll ever. They used to live acrost thu road from me. They's dumb as dirt and pesky as pissants in yer pants."

We followed him out the alley and back up toward the cap plant to the Hardens. Vergil pulled into their driveway and Flora pulled right up behind. The two boys were setting out front on a car seat covered with a plastic tarp that said Missouri State Highways in big orange letters. The Hardens were peas from the same pod. They looked like their features were installed onto heads that were too large: small, almost lipless mouths, squinty eyes that were too close together to display much interest in anything, dishwater-colored hair that was already thinning on top but shaggy and greasy around the edges. Everett Harden was narrow and raw-boned while Stump (real name Quentin) looked like . . . well, a stump.

They didn't seem too put out when Vergil Carver stood in front of them with his thumbs tucked into his pistol-bearing belt full of huge cartridges. When Flora and Harry got out and stood support at Constable Carver's elbows, the boys began to look about for a quick escape route.

"You boys been up to the airport lately?" Vergil inquired.

Everett glanced sideways at Stump who muttered, "Jest maybe."

"Was you up there, say yesterday evening?" Vergil leaned forward.

Everett squirmed and Stump muttered, "Maybe, so?"

"Was you foolin' with that plane up there?" Vergil leaned forward even farther.

"Which plane would that be?" Stump dropped his empty beer can into the weeds behind the seat.

Vergil walked over to the red Falcon and ran his hand over the left front fender. "Looks like white paint. Did you boys run into somethin' white lately?"

"Don't recall. Reckon we run into lots a things with that old beater. Don't mean nothin'."

"Now listen real good. People seen you two go up to the airport last evening in this car. Then folks said you was carryin' on down at the resort about flying er sumpin'. This fellow finds out this morning that somebody done fiddled with his plane. Saw it flying around last evening while he was sittin' up at Smiley's. You fellows know it's a federal offense to steal a' airplane, not to mention state and county and even right here in Van Buren where we try to be tolerable to strangers, huh! Now, iff'en it was indeed you, best get it out right now." Vergil leaned back with hand on hips.

We all waited while, in the distance, a jon boat roared up the river and a dog barked and a screen door slammed. And waited.

Everett suddenly stood up. "'Twasn't us flew, 'twas him." He pointed over into a patch of sweet corn where we noticed for the first time an old fellow in bib overalls and maybe nothing else was slowly hoeing weeds.

Stump added. "Yeah, t'twas Uncle Gid. He always said he knew how to fly one of those planes but we never took no heed, him bein' blind in one eye and hard a hearing and loonie as a bucket a bats."

"You boys tryin' to tell me that your old Uncle Gideon flew that plane? Why he can't hardly find his own terwilliger."

Stump grunted and nodded. "Yup. Uncle Gid bet us a six-pack of Schlitz that he could fly, so we took him up there and kinda borrowed that there airplane fer a bit. Didn't intend no harm. I mean he jest got in there, hot-wired the switch, an took off. Went around once, came back and me an' Everett got in an' we went around again. Whooeee, it was a humdinger."

"Yeah an' . . . an' . . . we come in through those trees like a skeered buzzard and plunked right down, the motor cut on us and we rolled it back to where it was. Stump ticked it with the Falcon when we left. Didn't mean no ill to nobody." Everett nodded his whole body in agreement with himself.

We all stood and stared at Uncle Gid over in the patch of sweet corn. He paused, straightened up, blew his nose on his fingers, and wiped them on the seat of his overalls.

"You, Gideon Harden. I want to talk to you, get on over here." Vergil used his professional voice of command.

Uncle Gid threw his head back and looked straight up like he had heard the voice of God.

"Over here Uncle Gid." Stump walked to the old man and tapped his shoulder.

"Stumper. Where ya been? How's your ma? Time fer a beer?"

Harry came out of his stupor. "You mean to tell me that that old nut flew my plane, actually flew my plane?" He shook his head in wonder.

"Story herebouts is Gideon used to fly at county fairs and things. You know, upside down and twirlies with a woman standing on the wing and all that foolishness." Vergil rubbed his jaw.

"That old nut flew my plane around 'til it ran out of gas and landed it?" Harry looked at Uncle Gid like he was the eighth wonder of the world.

"You gonna cuff all of 'em Vergil?" Flora wanted action.

Vergil ignored her and frowned into a distant spot seeking wisdom.

"Well, I reckon we all better go on down to the courthouse and work things out. You boys get in the back of the pick-up. Gideon, go get on a shirt 'er sumpin.' We need to go down to the courthouse. Flora, bring these folks, sheriff's office, second floor in the back by the jail, you know."

"Jesus Christ, can you believe that old fart, flyin' my airplane?" Harry lit up a cigarette and got into the front seat.

"I jest knowed it'ud be them Hardens." Flora watched Stump and Everett climb into the back of the pick-up and set down on a tool chest.

We all sat for a while watching the door to the trailer, waiting for Uncle Gid.

Vergil gave an impatient toot on his horn and whistled through his fingers.

"Stump. Run and fetch him. We ain't got all day."

Just then Uncle Gid came into sight behind the rusty screen door. He was having trouble with the buttons on the front of his shirt.

"Come on Gideon, get a hustle on, will you." Vergil opened his door and started to get out.

Gid came out and walked toward us. He was still barefoot, wearing the filthy overalls, but now he had on the dress jacket of a naval aviator with one lieutenant bar hanging onto the left epaulette and some sort of name tag and a medal over the left breast. One button held the jacket pinched in over his belly, and his bony wrists showed at least two inches.

"Would you look at that!" we all said in unison.

"Uncle Gid was in the war with the Orientals. Story goes he did some deal of damage. I'm not sure whether it was to them er to us," Vergil said.

Harry turned and gave us a look of wonderment. We all laughed.

The courthouse was a classic river-stone edifice in the exact center of Courthouse Square surrounded by a river-stone wall and some grand sycamores. The root-broken walkway led past a statue of Brigadier Sterling Price, CSA, the hero of Wilson Creek, to broad steps up to the second-floor lobby.

Inside was old varnish, floor, and walls with a pressed tin ceiling that sprouted hanging lights on long stems of copper pipe. The pervading aroma of old—very old—paper and wood smoke hung in the air, like it had been cooped up since the cornerstone had been laid back in 1872. Every step gave out individual squeaks as we trooped up to the third-floor offices of the sheriff.

Sheriff Will Stover, Carter County, MO, was etched into a brass plate on the door that was propped open by a brass spittoon that looked like it had never been emptied.

We were greeted by the whole posse of local law perched around the large office on various pieces of bureaucratic furniture. Even this large room suddenly got crowded with large men with large hats standing around looking for some excuse to be there.

Vergil Carver pushed Uncle Gideon to the front of the bunch.

"Will, what we got here?" Sheriff Stover boomed in a voice well practiced at overpowering any competition.

Uncle Gid wiped his nose on his sleeve and shrugged his bony shoulders.

Sheriff Stover leaned forward over his desk clutter.

"You gonna tell me Uncle Gideon Harden here stole that airplane yesterday an' flew it around and brought it back down without doin' harm to nothin' and nobody?"

"'ccordin' to what I hear from these boys," Vergil nodded toward Stump and Everett Harden.

"An', this would be the owner of the vehicle?" Stover tilted his huge Stetson slightly toward Harry.

"'Twern't a vehicle. It was a' airplane," Vergil added.

"Well don't I know that Vergil? The term vehicle covers all motor-propelled things an' maybe even shit wagons and baby carriages. I don't know, don't give a damn."

"Yes sir. It was my plane. A Cessna 172. These people stole it yesterday evening and flew it around 'til it was out of gas, landed okay, then hit it with their car. They dinged up the horizontal stabilizer to where I will have to pay to get it fixed over at Springfield."

Harry stepped up to the Sheriff's desk.

"Jest where you from, mister?" Stover gave all of us a good look. "An' what are you doin' here, purpose-wise, nohow?" Stover was almost drooling with the exalted position in which the situation placed him.

"We stopped here to visit your town and take a canoe ride with Willy Stark."

Harry looked at us and nodded. We all nodded.

"Ol' Willy Stark, eh? He would be my cousin, you know." Sheriff moved some papers on his desk.

Flora crowded to the front.

"They'er with me, Will. I been showin' 'em around. I found the Hardens for 'em and helped Vergil fetch 'em all to here. At this time," she added to make it sound more like an official statement.

Will Stover and Flora were cousins.

Sheriff Will Stover suddenly got up. "Y'all come with me," he commanded, shoved through the crowd, and went out the door.

The whole troop, Flora and Vergil, Uncle Gideon, Stump and Everett, Jan and I, with Harry and Barbara, the four lawmen representing the county, state, district, nation, and maybe even the U.N. followed Stover out the door and down the hall, into a courtroom. Up on a judge's bench in the center sat a bald man with great bushy brows and horn-rimmed glasses. His tie was a black cravat and he had garters on each sleeve. His eyes opened wide, then squinted at the parade that had suddenly broken into his solitude.

C. Royal Kellebrew, Third U.S. District Court proclaimed a little black label holder that sat amid stacks of papers on the impressive judge's rostrum.

"What is this? Is it time for the Fourth of July Parade already? J. C., who are all these people?" C. Royal boomed to the back of the room and to the empty balcony seats above. A shocked pigeon fluttered around the room, then perched again on a stack of big blue court records in the corner.

"Your honor, these are the folks involved in a' airplane theft jest last night up to the airport, you know. Plaintiff, offender, offenders, witnesses, law enforcement, an' the like." Sheriff Stover nodded at each character as he called off the roster.

"And there is Flora. What brings you into my court room, Flora?" The judge peered at little Flora over his glasses.

"Why I knowed jest who 'twas stole this feller's plane right from the very beginning. Didn't I say so?" Flora looked around for agreement.

"Just how did all this transpire?" Judge Kellebrew's bushy brows canvassed the group.

There broke out a general hubbub while everyone but Uncle Gid recounted their individual take on just what had transpired the previous evening. Judge Kellebrew sat back into his horsehair chair, clasped his knuckles over his watch pocket, and seemed to take in every version simultaneously. The jabber slowly petered out like a rundown tractor engine and silence prevailed.

The pigeon made another sortie around the hanging light fixtures and landed on an open windowsill. A distant jon boat went upriver.

"What do you have to say for yourself, Gideon?" the judge asked.

Gideon reached out his hand over the rostrum and picked up the judge's personal gavel, gave it a complete inspection and tucked it into the front of his overalls.

"How's your ma, C. Royal?"

"Give me that gavel and tell me, how come you took this man's airplane?" Judge Kellebrew reached out a large, knuckled hand and Gideon gave it a good shake.

"Give him back his hammer." Stump nudged Uncle Gid and hissed into his ear.

"Jesus tempers the wind to the shorn lamb." Gideon carefully placed the gavel on the judge's stack of papers and pointed at the pigeon that had just pooped on the windowsill and was picking lice out of its wing pit.

Vergil Carver spent the next fifteen minutes recounting what had transpired in the last twelve hours, aided by comments and corrections from Flora and Harry.

Judge C. Royal Kellebrew leaned back, folded his hands across his vest, and in his most royal tones pronounced his findings.

"I can't incarcerate this poor nincompoop. Hell, he don't even know where he is. Just how he flew that plane will remain a mystery. But you boys," he nodded at Stump and Everett, "you boys need to perform some sort of restitution to Mr. Griffin here to indicate the integrity of Carter County and the fine folks herein. You got to restitute to Mr. Griffin here the cost of the repairs to his craft, the price of a tank of aviation gas, the amount usually charged to rent a like plane for three hours, a hundred dollars for inconvenience, and breakfast and lunch for four folks from California at their location of choice." With that pronouncement he slammed the gavel one good crack, sending the pigeon into an aerial display that would be the envy of the great Roscoe Tanner.

"Vergil, you take Mr. Griffin here and these young fellows on into the clerk's office and arrange some sort of reimbursement payment. Tell Fern I'll need a copy today. Now let's all get on over to Emory's for a bowl of his chili con carne."

Judge C. Royal Kellebrew took out his pocket watch, nodded, and with a flourish, whipped off his judicial robe and went out the door.

Harry went with the sheriff and the Hardens while Jan, Barbara, and I went out into the mellow Ozark October noon with

Uncle Gid, who took the time to snap his heels together and salute Brigadier Sterling Price before loping off across the lawn like a Bluetick hound.

"I'll be glad when we get out of this place. These people are driving me nuts," Barbara muttered as we headed toward The Court Café at the tail of the courthouse lunch crowd.

"I guess they are all related to each other. Did you ever see so many cousins?"

Jan took my hand as we crossed the street where Willie Stark had double parked his rig and was in conversation with four tourists.

Harry joined us at the café for chili con carne and Ritz Crunch pie.

"They gave me thirty-seven dollars and had to agree to send me fifty dollars a month until they have paid off the judge's fine. Comes to three hundred and seventy-seven dollars and twenty-seven cents. Don't ask me. Ask one of the cousins."

That afternoon, we sat in Flora's Impala while Harry took the plane up for a short test hop. He ran it back and forth on the runway until he was satisfied that the control surfaces were workable. He flew a couple of low passes over the town and landed.

"Everything seems to be in working order, so let's get out of here."

We started packing our stuff back into the plane when another car drove up. Lucille from Cap hopped out.

"I jest wanted to say goodbye to you folks.

Vergil Carver drove up.

"I jest wanted to see that you folks get out of here without no more fuss."

Willie Stark pulled up in his rig with Golden and Shiloh and Stump Harden. They were passing around a suspicious looking paper sack.

"We jest wanted to tell you folks that when you come next time jest let us know and we'll do somethin' special fer you."

Willie grunted and the girls giggled.

Harry gave Flora seventy-five dollars, we all hugged her and climbed into 44Gulf, and departed runway number three-seven.

The little group of cousins waved as we circled the town and headed west across the river that gleamed a silver ribbon through the Ozark October.

# TEEZER'S TWISTS VIII

---

## SECONDHAND PARTS

*T*f you had to describe today's weather, it would have to be in the "undeclared" column. Earlier, there was a bit of rain with some suspicious white flakes that made folks turn up the collars of their jackets. The wind is coming in gusts from every direction, favoring the north, then the sun pops in and out in a mocking sort of way like, "So, you thought spring was here?"

Well, spring is here. You just have to find it, like the hose nozzle you carefully disconnected last November before the first freeze. But just where did you put it?

Then some kids come in dressed in T-shirts and shorts. One young fellow is wearing flip-flops. His legs are a strange bluish, like feta cheese.

"Some people think spring is here," Dorothy remarks.

Bob pulls his jacket tighter around him. "They are so brain damaged by loud music that their whole thermostat systems are skewed."

"Yeah. They say the constant loud sound deadens all of your senses."

"That's why symphony orchestra leaders and jackhammer

operators can't stay married for long. It's a proven statistic."

"Maybe that's why Ethel Merman had such poor taste in clothes," Frank surmises.

"Ethel Merman? Jeez, you're a lot older than I thought."

"I'm a lot older than I think too, sometimes," Frank laughs. "I remember when American History class stopped at Herbert Hoover. The textbook ended with a full-page photo of FDR, 1932, and a question mark."

"Yeah. That was back when a telephone could only talk. Not make movies, start your car, open the garage door, and play your high school fight song."

Bill took a long sip of coffee. "Yeah, my hearing aid can pick up Hong Kong and Del Rio, Texas, baseball, but not across the room."

"Mine has a self-cleaning feature. Does that mean it will censor out all four-letter words? Or maybe I won't have to ever wash my ears again," Bob added.

"Mine can pick up long-ago messages from my wife about going to the grocery store for a pack of Benson and Hedges filter longs," Frank contributes.

Bill leans over the table. "Yeah, but can you hear me now?"

"What?" Bob shakes his head.

"Well, you can replace them anytime. Just wait 'til you have to get a knee replacement, or a hip, or a cornea, or a heart."

"Well, I just had a new tail light replacement. It cost me just as much as heart surgery. They don't just replace a little light-bulb anymore. You have to get a whole assembly from a factory in Tajikistan or someplace."

"Our car is so old we have to order parts from the Smithsonian Institute in Washington." Frank drops the last bit of his pumpkin scone on the floor.

"Yeah. They scavenge parts from a car that once belonged to Bonnie and Clyde."

"Do you have to take a driving test to renew your license after you're sixty-five?"

Dorothy is fumbling through her billfold.

"Mine is going to expire this July. I hate to do that test with the eyes and all."

There is a general scramble to check drivers' licenses.

"I can't read the date." Frank holds his license up to the window and squints.

"Here, use my glasses," Jannie offers.

"Oh good, I'm not due 'til next year," Frank sighs.

There is a general passing around of the glasses.

"Look! Here is my original Social Security card. I got that back in 1948."

"Don't you wish it had accrued interest all that time, like war bonds?"

"Yeah. If it had, I wouldn't need Social Security now."

Suddenly the lights flicker, go out, come back on, and then go out for good.

The three OPALCO employees get up without saying a word and hurry out.

"Do those guys work on the lines or are they just embarrassed about the electricity going off?" Bill asks.

"Wouldn't you feel funny if you had a big OPALCO on your shirt and the juice went off right here in public?"

"Yeah, it would be like going to a PTA meeting with your fly open."

"Did that ever happen to you?" Jannie asks.

"No, but I know a guy it happened to. Actually he got elected vice president at that meeting."

Bob leans back in his chair. "That's the way Bill Clinton got to be president."

Dorothy punches him on the shoulder.

Mark comes around the counter. "There's a short somewhere in this block."

"He's back again?"

"Yeah. I saw him going to the post office just a few minutes ago. He is about four feet tall all dressed in green with a tall, peaked hat."

Two strangers come in. Young men in suits with briefcases. The whole place gets quiet. The oldsters sip at their drinks, thinking how glad they are that they don't have to do that anymore.

Bill mutters, "I had to wear a suit every day for three years in New York."

"I had a suit once," Frank says. "I kinda grew out of it. I must have looked like Gomer Pyle."

"You were Gomer Pyle," Jannie snickers.

"Well, I was just an innocent country boy until I met you." Frank puts his arm around Jannie's shoulder.

"I don't think you were ever innocent. Maybe dumb."

The two handsome young strangers get their lattes, look around the room, then go outside to stand on the corner.

"Their head office sent them out here looking for any signs of life."

"Then they probably didn't notice us," Bob chuckles.

"If they are looking for life, they should go down to the dump. That's where the action is."

"Speaking of the dump, that's what I gotta do today. All of my cans are running over and the raccoons are beginning to come for dinner every night."

"We have to go to the bank and visit our money," Frank says, as he and Jan get up and leave. Others follow and Teezer's gets quiet. Mark makes a sweep with his bar rag, rearranges the chairs, carries a tray of dirty dishes into the back room, and the little place eases into quiet.

Outside, a shower of rain trails off to the east, pulling a swirl of winds and some flighty gulls.

# *OFF THE BENCH*

---

*T*t was all a matter of timing. The ball suddenly appeared there in front of my nose. There were long hairy arms and huge bony hands all around, but the ball was mine.

I had it in my grip. It was bigger than I remembered. Heavy and a bit slick with sweat. I felt its roundness. Beyond the ball I could see the basket high above me in the humid, noisy, popcorn-flavored atmosphere of the crammed gymnasium.

It would be my duty, my lifelong goal, to get that ball into that basket. I sprang with all I had, which was not much for a skinny fourteen-year-old. At the top of my leap, I released the ball with a flick of my wrists and just a bit of backspin. The ball continued on as I returned to the hardwood floor amid all the shoulders and elbows. I watched as the Spalding label bounced off the backboard, teetered on the rim for an eternity, and as if in slow motion, dropped through the orange circle and slid through the tattered gray net that was coming loose on the front side.

My heart soared with the eagles. I had scored. The measly two points that appeared on the scoreboard represented my achievement for the evening but really didn't have much to do with the outcome of the game as my team, the Carrizozo Coyotes, was well behind. So far behind that the coach had thrown in the towel in the human form of his number thirteen man, namely me.

Our little high school team had twelve maroon and silver

uniforms that represented the school colors. Actually, the silver always looked more like bleached cement and the maroon like a scab, but my uniform was red and blue, representing the fact that I was number thirteen on a twelve-man team.

When the coach motioned to me from the far—and I mean *far*—end of the bench, I jumped up, tripped over the medical kit that the team manager had left there on the floor, and started to report for duty.

I was that far down the bench. The assistant coach, the manager, and the student sports reporter were closer to the control center than blue and red number 32.

"Hey Franko. Coach wants you." Glenn Snow nudged me with his elbow.

My first thought was, "What now? I'm watching the game."

"Loudin, go in for Chapman," Coach grumbled.

That had never occurred to me. "You mean now?" I was so dumb.

"Don't wear that jersey. Here, change shirts with Morales."

Eduardo "Fatso" Morales ran at least six sizes larger than my willowy frame, so that when I put on his sweaty number 12, it looked more like a dress than a shirt. The armholes were so low that when I tried to tuck it into my undersized shorts, it looked like I was wearing some odd front and back tropical sarong.

But all that aside, I had indeed scored right there in the fury of the moment, and I was elated. I had justified the coach's faith in me. I realized later that he just didn't want any of his good guys to get hurt or to have their confidence destroyed while the other team ran roughshod over us in the fading minutes of the last quarter.

In my Jack Armstrong-enhanced imagination, I thought I could pull out a victory all by myself, but alas, that was the last time I saw the ball except for the time my face got in the way of a snap pass from somewhere that rang my bell and made my eyes water.

I had had my moment. I looked over to the stands where the pep squad clustered behind an arrangement of maroon and cement, I mean silver, pom-poms and megaphones.

Janet May was jumping up and down waving her arms in the air, screeching. She didn't think I looked like a geek with my floppy red hair and the remnants of sweat-streaked acne lotion that turned my face into a pocked trick-or-treat mask.

The major thing was that I had scored a basket right there between big Bill Luck and Maggi DeSilva. Either of them could have broken me in half. In fact, that's exactly what they tried to do less than two minutes later at the other end of the court when I got in their way.

I was very adolescent, six feet tall, one hundred and forty-five pounds of awkward limbs, not very fast, couldn't jump very high, not aggressive at all, and the pimples on my neck and chin caused more self-criticism than my big nose or the fact that I was a preacher's kid.

The status of being on that basketball team was indeed a dream come true. I was a sports fan. I kept track of all of my favorite teams, football, basketball, or baseball. I knew details about most of the top players. I fought to be the water boy at the high school games. That consisted of carrying an actual galvanized bucket of water and one tin cup out onto the field where my local heroes were usually struggling against overpowering odds to maintain some sort of pride for the Coyotes.

I was thrilled that the older boys accepted sustenance from me. Then the big day came when the coach called me by name.

"Frank. It is Frank, isn't it? Run and get me a cleaner towel. Somebody wiped his ass on this one." He tossed the soiled rag at my head and turned back to the game, which was going badly for our heroic lads.

Eventually I was privileged to follow him up and down the sidelines carrying his towel and anything else he might find necessary those days. He always kept a Lucky Strike between his thin lips but never lit it up, so that he was continuously spitting out bits of cigarette paper and tobacco.

Due to the fact that I was a good buddy to Fuzz Beamer and he had two brothers in high athletic esteem, I was selected to help Fuzz keep score for every home basketball game.

It seems unbelievable now, but at that time the scoreboard

was a cracked rectangle of ancient slate suspended high above the playing court where with one small piece of chalk and one old rag we would keep track of the game that went crashing up and down the court below.

To get up to our lofty perch we had to climb up a sewer pipe and crawl along an overhead beam to a rickety platform just big enough for two boys.

We had to lie flat on our stomachs in order for the throngs below to see the score, which was more than unfriendly to our locals.

We of the pre-high school age didn't have much of a chance to play basketball because, unlike football or baseball, you had to have a backboard and a hoop and a smooth piece of ground. We couldn't just go out in the meadow and play basketball. No one ever thought of hoops nailed to a piece of plywood over the garage door. We were so deprived.

My parents refused to let me play high school football because the son of a family friend had suffered a concussion while crashing headlong into a big kid from a nearby coal mining town and was never quite the same. They didn't seem to realize that same big kid also played basketball and his major contribution to the sport was eliminating opposing players by any means his anthracite brain could conceive.

I wanted to be a sports hero. Cheerleaders and letter sweaters and the camaraderie down at the barbershop when old men would recognize me for the star that I was.

I was very new to the game when I kinda made the team in my freshman year at the tiny high school in New Mexico. I probably owe part of this achievement to the fact that I was tall and not flunking in any subject, and the coach came to my dad's church.

I was honored to be any number if I could just be on the team. While the older guys scrimmaged and practiced plays, Mervin, Eugene, and I just shot baskets over and over again. Only ten guys could play, so the three of us never really got in the game.

We did get to go on most of the trips even if it was just to carry equipment and be gofers for the two coaches and a couple of seniors who took advantage of us. At the games we got to warm up with the real players and wear the uniforms, well except for my red and blue number 32. I didn't have a warm-up outfit either, so I had a red sweatshirt that didn't match any other maroon, scarlet, or red in the entire school.

Perhaps the greatest challenge of that first year on the bench was the acquisition of a supporter—an athletic supporter—a jock strap.

My dad didn't know about such things, I thought. My mother? Not on your life. The other boys? Not a chance. Then they would know what a dork was there among them pretending to be a regular guy.

I tried to fashion a jock strap out of a pair of jockey shorts that I had grown out of the year before. I tied knots in either side and hiked the whole arrangement up as tight as I could.

This didn't really work because right in the middle of a fast break or a rough scramble for a loose ball, I would feel my supporter coming untied so that instead of keeping my eye on the ball I was fumbling with my homemade harness.

One fateful day in the locker room, after a great practice session wherein I was allowed to play with the big boys for the first time, I whipped off my practice trunks right there in front of the whole junior varsity. Johnny Price immediately took note of my exotic loincloth.

"What the hell is that pansy-ass thing you got on Franko?"

All of the immediate guys turned to take note and add their personal expression.

"Did you steal that from the Girl Scout locker room?"

"Did your momma knit that for her darling dodo?"

"Hey guys. Franko's wearing diapers."

Thank God my memory has blanked out the rest of that episode.

Later that same day, I got up the nerve to casually ask Bill Dolan where was the best place to buy a jock strap. Mine were getting old and besides, I had outgrown them. With a funny look he told me that the best and cheapest was at T&G General

Mercantile.

Well, okay, I knew where to go now, but did they come in sizes? How much did they cost? Did they come in packages of a dozen? Were they just lying there on the counter? Did you have to ask someone? What was their real name?

Next day after school, I went into the men and boys' department down at T&G and scanned the counters and shelves. No jock straps. I was going to have to ask the lady that worked there, Tina something or other. We all just called her Tina. I couldn't ask an old lady for a jock strap. I went outside and rode my bike around for a while, composing my opening question.

"Well I guess I need another jock-strap." Naaaaah.

"Do you have all sizes of jock straps?" Nope.

"Do you have white jock straps for boys?" Uh-uh.

"I'm on the high school basketball team and the coach sent me down to ask about jock straps." Okay, that's best so far.

When I had decided on my opening statement, I went back into the store. There was Tina with a pencil stuck out of a salt and pepper bun at the back of her head. She peered at me over her tiny round glasses.

"Yes?" she said, as a little frown worked across her painted eyebrow.

"Yes," I repeated, examining the condition of my shoes.

"May I help you find something?"

"Yes. I need a special kinda shorts." I blurted.

"Special in what way?" The little frown between her brows rippled at me.

"You know. To play basketball in. That kind." I really wanted out of there. Cut and run.

"Doesn't the school provide those? The ones with the maroon and gray and the numbers and all that?" Both hands were on the counter as she tilted her head to one side.

"Well, I mean for under the uniform pants." My voice was wavering around the meteorite that was lodged in my throat.

"Oh. You want a supporter, a jock strap," she said loud enough to get the attention of two senior girls that had just come in.

Jock strap. Jock strap. There, it was out. Everybody in town knew I was buying a jock strap for the first time.

Tina came around the counter and looked at me head to toe.

"I'd say a small would do for you, you're so thin." Again, loud enough to entertain the two girls who whispered and giggled.

Before I could reply, she reached into a drawer under the counter and slapped down a small red, white, and blue box that called out "All-American" and then discreetly added, "small."

"Will one be enough?" She almost sneered, dropped the item into a paper bag, and shoved the glasses up on her nose while the little frown puckered down in pity.

My classmates whispered and giggled.

"Yes." I grabbed the sack and rolled it into the smallest possible shape.

"Well, that'll be one-eighty-eight with the tax and all." She rearranged a display of men's plastic pocket shields with her perfectly done-up red fingernails.

I unrolled the four dollar bills, peeled off two like I had seen Howard Duff do in *Sam Spade*, folded them lengthwise, and held them out to Tina.

She took them like they were contaminated with the black plague while the frown relaxed.

I had to go right past the two girls who now pretended not to be aware of my existence. I shifted my new athletic supporter to the hand away from the two girls and got out of there.

That was to be the most difficult play in my entire basketball career, except maybe the night three years later when we lost a game by forty-seven points. After the first few minutes, about all we could do was to not get injured while the bigger, faster, older boys whipped by us like our sneakers were nailed to the floor.

By the time I got into a real game and scored that first basket, the season was just about over. Hoyte Hobbs had quit the team and school to join the Navy. Alfonso Montaño had flunked out and was working for the telephone company. That moved me up to number eleven and a real uniform, number 57, to go with my collection of jock straps. I now had four. Tina down at the T&G considered me a regular customer, though I still wore size small.

The season ended that spring on a low note. We lost the first two games at the district tournament and were eliminated early. We didn't even get to stay for the final games but slunk home to mend out sprains and floor burns and to turn in our maroon and silvers.

All summer I worked as delivery and stock boy at the T&G. I was supposed to help clerk, but I avoided that as much as possible. Little old ladies like Mrs. Espy would come to the counter and fumble through their small black purses for a tiny shopping list written on the back of a remnant of last week's church program. She would hand me the list and I would scurry around the store filling her order while she stood there sharing gossip with Red Thornton the butcher. By the time I had stacked all of her necessities on the counter, she had changed her mind several times or was not pleased with the brand or the price or both, and would have me make an exchange.

I liked the back room where I organized the stacks of cartons, unloaded the trucks, and on occasion I got to drive the old stripped-down Model A delivery truck around town like a real person. I wasn't old enough to have a license but that didn't seem to offend anyone. After all I was the preacher's kid, made good grades, and was on the basketball team.

# STARS FELL ON CARRIZOZO

---

*D*eep blue skies seem to be much closer to the earth over the high desert country of New Mexico. Particularly at night. Stars are bigger and certainly more plentiful. The infinite stretch of heavenly bodies is clustered like the glitter sprayed overhead of a Las Vegas honeymoon suite. Resting right there over the surrounding mountains. Maybe even closer. And the most wondrous thing is that those very same stars are still there hovering over the front steps of that little house at the corner of Court and Sixth as they were on that certain glorious evening in the summer of 1944.

The movie that night of nights was one of those MGM musical extravaganzas starring Betty Grable and George Montgomery with the Tommy Dorsey orchestra and special appearances by Oscar Levant performing "Rhapsody in Blue," for no apparent reason. And for an additional treat there was a dancing performance by the fabulous Nicholas Brothers with their slip-sliding splits style. And plus . . . *Tom and Jerry, Captain Midnight*, RKO-Pathe News, and selected shorts. *Silver Screen*, that well circulated movie encyclopedia of Hollywood mythdom, which we starstruck teenagers swallowed as gospel, expounded upon the slightest tidbit of any possible lustful misgivings in Tinsel Town. Everyone understood and accepted that the lower extremities of Betty Grable were unquestionably the ultimate in feminine beauty. Pulchritude! We didn't know just what that encompassed but it was inviting, and the older, more sophisti-cated young studs of our clan elbowed each other vigorously at even the slightest hint of a female classmate's bare knee.

It was a "first run" movie, though, and that was good enough, even if Carrizozo was at the end of the line for anything of a cultural nature. Neither Betty nor George could dance or sing very well, but they could and did kiss a lot, and Betty didn't miss any opportunity to display her claim to fame.

The Lyric Theater was operated with an iron hand by Old Man Walker (old was anyone who didn't have to go to school anymore), who had no tolerance for kids of any size or per-suasion. The movie was the only release we kids had, now that the skating rink was shuttered again for unknown but highly rumored reasons.

It was the long summer of 1944 with the war raging furi-ously all over the world, supported patriotically by the folks clustered in this dusty little burg in the middle of New Mexico where the exhausted crews of the Southern Pacific main line west to California chowed down and changed shifts, while the big, orange-striped engines were serviced with coal and water.

I was a skinny 14-year-old with a spotted complexion and a newly discovered urge whenever Janet May Shaffer came near. In fact, I had the urge whether she was near or not. Just the thought of her gave me little tingle flashes that even a low-fly-ing pass by a P-51 Mustang, which happened frequently, could not match. Her daddy owned the local Ford garage and Janet May had the use of his new green pick-up. I kept a sharp eye out for any sign of that particular vehicle and was struck with goosebumps whenever it passed by our house.

Every day after school, she would sit on the crossbar of my new red Hawthorne bike as I proudly took her to her house there at the corner of Court and Sixth Street.

She would tolerate the discomfort of her position, occasion-ally leaning back to touch my chest with some part of her body or make sure a stray lock of her light auburn tresses brushed across my cheek. Then we would stand on the front steps nervously making small talk.

Usually we would agree to meet at the movie that night. That was the only thing we had to do. The onslaught of highly romantic movies of the time just encouraged this malady as a plague in every high school in the then-48. Janet May and I were "steadies." Well, as steady as sprouting youths can get. We secretly held hands in the secluded darkness of the rickety old movie house, encouraged by the screenland fantasies pelting us with romantic delusions. There was one troubling hitch. Even though I held her hand, held her close to the sultry rhythms of Glenn Miller's "String of Pearls" as we danced at the local women's club recreation hall, skated "couples" at the dusty skating rink, our perspiration mingling, walked her home from every event, and stood on her front steps talking for extended times, I could not get up the nerve to actually *kiss* her.

We never spoke of it but a mutual friend, Betty Jewel, informed me and assured me that Janet May wanted me to kiss her. In fact, I had better come through pretty soon if our romance was to continue.

It seems Danny Sharp was eager to step into my shoes with Janet May at the first opportunity. I didn't like Danny very much anyway, and the fact that he of all people was hanging around "my girl" made things worse.

Betty Jewel warned me almost daily that if I didn't come through after the movie that night, it was "Hello, Danny Sharp."

Night after movie night this went on. I was such a dweeb. I wanted to kiss her and she wanted me to, but I just didn't know how.

This situation grew and grew more desperate for me until one day a miracle happened in the back seat of my folk's '36 Chevy. My sister Mary was home from her freshman year at Highlands University and was just learning how to drive, so we had borrowed the family car for practice. This practice consisted of cruising the town's two paved streets looking for "action." The action proved to be picking up Art Doheny and Betty Jewel. Art had dropped out of school, or maybe he was expelled, to join the Navy but returned after a couple of months under mysterious circumstances to take up the highly desirable job of "skate master" down at the dilapidated old roller-drome. He retained the air of a sailor with a white T-shirt and a pack of Lucky Strikes folded up in the left sleeve, bell-bottom Navy work dungarees, and an attitude. He was the James Dean of Carrizozo. A stray lock of hair draped casually down over his forehead above squinty sullen eyes and a totally bored half-grin. The girls loved it.

I couldn't believe that Mary would take up with him but then I couldn't see what any boy saw in either of my sisters.

We picked up Betty Jewel on the way home from town lugging a huge sack of groceries because she was always lots of fun.

Betty climbed into the back seat with me and immediately started on my situation concerning Janet May and "The Kiss."

"I really want to but I just don't know how," I whined.

"Don't know how! You dumb-ass!"

And with that she grabbed me by the ears and planted her lips firmly on mine. And just held them there for what seemed like a long, *long* time.

"There Franko, did that seem so difficult?"

My whole head felt hot. I was out of breath. My hands belonged somewhere but I didn't know where. Now I was in love with Betty Jewel. IN LOVE WITH BETTY JEWEL!

"Now you do it to me." She punched me on the chest. "Do it. Do it, you dumb-nit."

So I awkwardly kissed the corner of her mouth, quickly.

"No, no, no. Like you mean it, Franko! Pretend I'm Janet May. Come on!"

So I did and thought, "Is the curse lifted? Will I be able to come through tonight?"

I could still feel the touch of Betty Jewel's lips that night as I headed toward the old Lyric Theater.

The movie that night, *Coney Island* with George Montgomery and Betty Grable, seemed to be extra short, but by the time Betty had stumbled through "Cuddle Up a Little Closer" and she and George had performed several kissing expositions, I was cranked up to the bursting point.

After the show, the walk down Court Street to Janet May's house went too quickly and there we were again, standing on those front steps where we had spent so many magic moments. My fate was sealed. If I didn't kiss her tonight . . . the grinning image of Danny Sharp hung over her shoulder.

I mumbled something stupid, took a deep breath, and kissed her full on the lips. A direct hit my first time. Wow! I had done it! I was now a cool guy, at last. It felt soft and moist. I pulled back a bit and our eyes met. I had never noticed that there were little golden specks in her deep brown eyes. Of course, I had never been this close to her before. There was an aroma of something sweet. It was warm like lilac, or my mother's linen closet.

I did it again. Better this time. Longer and with more emphasis. I felt like George Montgomery must have felt kissing Betty Grable.

I could feel the surge of my total heart, arteries, veins, and capillaries pounding out "Screw you, Danny Sharp." My brain, however, had deserted in my time of need. I hoarsely murmured, "See you at school tomorrow."

I turned and, without a backward glance, jumped down off the front steps and ran for home. I was young and healthy and in good shape and on the junior varsity basketball team and so cranked up that I ran full-tilt the eight blocks home. It wasn't until I was at our front steps that I stopped and noticed the stars of all colors and sizes. A grand spectacle. And they will be there again tonight. Will they remember? Do they even care? Here's to you, wherever you may be, Janet May.

# TEEZER'S TWISTS IX

---

## SMART ALEC

*T*t's one of those steely gray mornings when the sun is just a hint of a light spot over the mountain where a sunrise should be. The air is damp and cold enough to be raining, but it doesn't rain. It just feels that way.

A cup of hot Starbucks and a pumpkin scone sound like just the thing to brighten up the day.

Teezer's is jammed. We walk in like it is opening day of the House of Commons with all of our peers seated along the opposite walls east and west.

Our peers, in this case, are the usual crowd. Everyone is talking and no one is listening.

Lined up under the street windows are Valerie, a home care lady who from time to time threatens us with, "Your time will come." And then she just smirks.

Sitting next to her is Tex, who is there almost every day for hours. I have never heard what he says because he talks down into his flannel shirt and seems to mind his own business.

Dennis. A big ex-Marine who, from time to time, shows off a piece of his metal engraving. A pistol grip or a decorated plaque of some sort. He is really professional.

Eric, who is, I think, in insurance at some level, who can and will talk about any subject.

J.C. is here today bidding everyone farewell. He is off to Alaska for three months, working as a "bull cook" at a huge fish cannery on the north side of the Aleutian Islands. A bull cook does everything about the kitchen and adjoining camp, except cook. More bull than anything else. I can't imagine how he got the job, or why.

"I just packed my three pair of new long johns," J.C. announces.

"Will they last you?" Dorothy asks.

"Yeah. I put 'em on when I get off the plane and I take 'em off when I get back on."

"You don't change them or wash them?" Jannie asks.

"Heck, no. I wear all three of them all of the time. It's really cold up there."

J.C. struts out leaving the door open.

Dee Dee, a pretty, petite, silver-haired lady, gets a latte to go. She is about five feet tall and always well dressed.

"Where are you off to, Dee Dee?" someone asks.

"I work at Orcas Landing."

I pictured her standing out in the weather in an orange hard hat and DayGlo vest, directing semis and trash trucks with her lighted batons, saying "PLEASE" to every driver that goes astray.

"No, I work in the gift shop," Dee Dee giggles, blowing apart my image of her.

There is general shifting and sipping around the room while the next subject waits in the wings. Just name the subject and it will again go around the room like a game of Button, Button. Sometimes, there might even be a serious discussion, laced, of course, with spicy remarks.

The two telephone guys come in, get their lattes, and sit at a recently emptied table under the front window.

"Did you need a phone brought to your table?" Bill asks.

Frank points his scone at them. "You had a call from head office. We told them you were in a crawl space up on Buck Mountain and didn't wish to be disturbed."

Suddenly Mark comes from behind the counter carrying a muffin with a blazing Roman candle sticking out of its top, and sets it down in front of Fred, one of the telephone guys. Carolyn comes in to stand next to Mark.

They clap their hands, singing, "This is your birthday song. It isn't very long, HEY!" while the Roman candle spews sparks and flames eighteen inches into the air.

There is a general cheering and laughing as the fireworks continue with a plume of black smoke, and the candle sputters out and tips over.

Mark plucks out the dead candle and hurries back behind the counter where a line of smiling folks patiently wait.

There's a round of "Happy Birthdays" for Fred, who just sits and grins as the conversations regenerate from the large crowd.

"Are you still having birthdays, Bill?" Frank nudges Bill, who replies, "No, I ran out of numbers. Medicare wants me to prove that I'm still alive so they can extend their coverage to where no man has gone before."

"Yeah. They should send a field investigator in here some morning to see what the program is supporting."

"I'll bet the Republicans would close us down because we can't prove where and when we were born," Jannie adds.

"Yeah, or even why," Dorothy snickers.

Frank snaps his fingers. "We did that a couple of weeks ago, remember? None of us would be here if our grandmothers hadn't had sex."

A young woman comes in and goes to the counter.

Frank nudges Bill. "Watch that girl. Her body is moving all the time, even when she is standing still. Is that my imagination?"

"Well, it could be your essential tremors."

"You mean it's my eyeballs that are undulating and not really that girl?"

"If you can really do that, don't try to find a cure. It could be your last thrill."

Frank dabs his forehead with a handkerchief. "Whew! Thank God I can still have a thrill. I thought that had gone with my slam dunk."

"What are you guys talking about?" Jannie grabs Frank by the arm.

"We gotta go. I have a list that must be tended to."

Dotty pulls out her list. Elsie has one too. At the next table, Tony pulls out a scrap of paper from his jacket pocket.

"This is my wife's list. She writes so small I have to get a young person to read it for me."

Frank looks at the list. "My wife can write smaller than your wife. Jannie once copied the entire ferry schedule on a Band-Aid wrapper with a felt tip marker."

"Well, it's getting out of hand. I gotta go." Bill picks up his cup.

There is general movement as they all clear the tables and move over to the dirty dish trays.

"It's sure gonna be quiet in here, Mark," Frank says as he passes the counter.

"We love having you all here," Mark says, as he moves around with his bar rag, wiping tables and arranging the chairs.

The Geezers crowd out the door stops to pet a young Golden named Tyrone, then head off in different directions.

Teezer's belongs to the next setting who can't possibly be as clever as we are.

# *TIMETABLE*

---

*T*t was quiet in the waiting room of the remote little station, except for the night drones of insects. The pesky wind had died away as the sun went down, now sweltering heat along with a total lack of any air movement pressed down on the earth like one of Mama's mustard plasters.

As he stared at the hole in the battered screen door, a new swarm of bugs crowded through, circling about in search of the lone light bulb that hung precariously from a broken wall sconce.

His numb brain attempted to count the bugs as they paused on the broken screen before launching into the crowded flight pattern that filled the room like the approach to Chicago, O'Hare.

How long had he been here? Too long, too long. He was beginning to think there were no trains through here at all. Those shining rails were just iron lines on a kid's drawing that went out to the horizon and met, period. There was nothing beyond.

He had been sitting here since mid-afternoon, pondering his decision to try for the one and only local train.

This day had begun eons ago when he had hitched a ride with a guy in an eighteen-wheeler, carrying a load of anxious Herefords. The burly Texan never told him that he was only going so far. He got dropped when the driver suddenly announced that his delivery was off the highway thirty-seven miles north, so, adios buddy and good luck.

Here he had stood in Dingleshit, Nevada, with a dust storm so strong that you could actually lean into it like it was a 'dobe wall. A few trucks and one car passed him in the first hour, then nothing. Sitting on a pile of broken pavement, he began to take in the surrounding territory, as far as he could see, that is, what with the dust and stuff blowing in his face. At first, it appeared to be just desert or maybe prairie if you wanted to consider the hardy tufts of jimson weed that huddled in the lea of a scattering of bone-dry sagebrush.

From where he sat, the land sloped down to a railroad track that led into a scattering of buildings of a sort. Shacks really, but then he made out a familiar red Coca-Cola sign and licked his lips at the promise.

What the hell, he thought. I'll just amble on down there and get a Coke and maybe even catch a ride on a westbound freight. He had always wanted to try that, like in the good old days.

The odd collection of weather-worn buildings was scattered like tumbleweeds along a stretch of ruts that could be considered a street in that it had, at one time, been somewhat level.

The Coke sign was nailed to the side of a storefront that shied away from the prevailing wind, but other than some recent hand swipes on the dusty front door, there was no sign of life. He tried the rusty doorknob, then turned to survey the empty town.

The wind seemed to be settling down a bit as he rubbed sand out of his eyes. Across the street and down a ways sat what looked like a railroad station. He crossed the rough road and went around to the track side and was surprised to find a man sitting on a chair tilted back against the wall.

"Howdy there. Plannin' to catch the Golden State Limited, are ya, bucko?" the old fellow rasped in a high, dry voice. He wore a crushed old trainman's cap pulled down over a scarred face that looked like it had been blistered at some time and never quite healed.

"Don't know," he replied.

"She comes through here every day, more or less," the old fellow muttered, as he squinted down the empty track to the east and pointed with the stub of an empty sleeve.

"What time?" he inquired.

"Depends," the old guy grunted.

"Depends on what?" he asked.

"Depends if there's somebody wants a ride, I reckon." The old fellow got up and pulled a chain that raised a red semaphore on a pole above them.

"There now. They know you want a ride. All you gotta do is hunker down right here and abide." With that, the old fellow hunched his shoulders and shuffled around the corner.

He had been abiding all afternoon, evening and well into the night. The wind died down with the sun, and the stars came out in glorious profusion.

The clatter of a telegraph in the office roused him from his thoughts of the previous day. Maybe there was some hope. The clicking little instrument chattered to itself for a while, then quiet returned.

He looked again at the big Regulator clock on the far wall. Three forty-seven. It had been at three forty-seven since he walked in that afternoon. The big brass pendulum hung quietly, mocking the dragging seconds, refusing to neither tick nor tock.

There was a change in the air. He cocked his head and leaned forward toward the opened door. Held his breath in order to concentrate. A faint rumble came up out of the desert floor to the west. He stood and peered through the fly-specked and cracked window. The horizon showed a swinging light that got brighter even as he watched.

The rumble broke into hurrying chugs, and louder. Standing out on the undulating brick platform, he could see the swinging light become one sharp beam following the reflecting rails into the edge of town. Now he could feel the tremble of the earth. The stifling atmosphere rushed toward the approaching behemoth. He could feel it tugging on his jacket.

He looked up to make sure the semaphore was still up.

How in the hell could the engineer see that puny signal in time to stop? But it didn't look like the train was slowing down in the least. In fact, it seemed to be gathering speed and coming right at him. He stepped back and waved his arms as the ground began to shake and pulsate.

Then it was on him with a thunderous roar of blistering steam and acrid cinders. He fell to his knees to avoid being drawn into the grinding clamor of the huge drivers and the clatter of the rods. The thumping of the powerful pistons seemed to be in his chest. He rolled over and covered his head. He couldn't breathe. Tears came to his eyes. He tasted raw fear as he bit his tongue.

Then it was gone. The air cleared. The stars watched silently and a long low whistle came echoing back down the line.

"God damn. What the hell was that?" He got to his feet and looked down the track.

Nothing but the whisper of night and the drone of insects.

"Enough of this shit. I'll take my chances with my trusty old thumb." He made his way back up to the highway and reclaimed his seat on the pile of broken concrete, leaned against a fence post, and dozed off.

"Hey, bucko. You want a ride or not?"

He jerked up and ran his hand over his face.

"Well, whada ya say, buddy?" A red-faced guy with a mop of dirty hair that festooned a yellow Caterpillar cap leaned out of the window of a battered pick-up and slapped the door.'

"Coooooome on. Bus is leaving."

He jumped up and staggered around to the passenger's side. Climbed in, leaned back, and took a long, hard breath.

"What the hell you doin' way out here, dude?" The guy looked at him with squinty blue eyes.

"Well, I was hitching to California and my ride turned off back there, so I was tryin' to get a ride on the train."

The driver snorted. "You been smoking funny stuff, dude. There ain't no train through here for years." He pulled out a pack of cigarettes and offered one to his passenger.

"What do you mean no trains? I saw one but it didn't stop."

"Huh? You been out here too long, dude. There ain't no trains since that time when the wooden trestle collapsed and some old engineer dude crashed into the draw and burned up with his engine and a shitload of empties."

"Yeah, but . . ." He looked through the back window for the town or the tracks or something, but saw only a dust devil twisting out across the lonely prairie like the smoke from The Golden State Limited.

# *TORPEDOES FRESA*

---

"**T**oo cold to snow," some old codger would always remark to the usual gathering around the wood stove down at the T&G Mercantile and Feed. One of them will shake down the coals. Another will adjust the damper. They will all rearrange their old bones and ponder the big cold back in whenever.

Too cold to snow! I pictured some heavenly thermostatically controlled apparatus up north where all those delicate little flakes are stuck together, jammed up into a huge gray lump of ice.

As soon as the big chill lets up a bit, they will softly drift down to earth.

So my fantasies spun as I rubbed at the frozen moisture on my mom's kitchen window and squinted at the thermometer just outside.

The needle quivered there around zero, as if embarrassed to drop any further.

It was four-thirty a.m., my go-to-work time. Work was delivering dairy products to some seventy-five homes around town and then running a wholesale route to several small towns in the mountains of northern New Mexico. Towns like Sapello and Manuelita, La Cueva, Buena Vista, and Mora. Yes, still in the United States but just by geography. These towns were really just a combination of service station/store/post office, good old boy's hangout, etc.

---

217

I had flunked Spanish in college but I knew how to count and make change, some street talk, and dirty words. I didn't know what the dirty words meant but my sources were authentic. I could stumble through a very short conversation in Spanish but then went dumb when asked a question of any sort.

Yes, at the wise old age of twenty-five, I was back living with my mother after four years in college and two in the Marine Corps.

I knew what cold weather was like. I spent my college years in Boulder, Colorado. Then a winter living in a tent and a hole in the frozen landscape of Korea where the winds come down out of Manchuria with a bitter vengeance.

I would spend my afternoons down in Mom's basement working on a portfolio of self-conceived illustrations in order to submit to an art school in Los Angeles. I actually hoped to save enough money for the school by pedaling frozen ice cream goodies to residents of the frigid high country in January. What was I thinking?

Trying to ignore what the thermometer said, I buttoned every button and ventured out. Everything seemed to be frozen solid with a strange cracking sound coming from the trees and the earth itself. My car door was stuck tight so I had to pound on it until it finally opened with a loud creaking sound like I was ripping it off its hinges. Fortunately, it was a fairly new model so it started up after a few complaining growls.

While it warmed up I scraped at the windshield with a tool I had learned to keep handy.

By five o'clock I was down at the dairy loading the little delivery truck with the required number of regular and homogenized bottles plus a few cartons of cottage cheese just in case a housewife left me a request for same. We were a class operation!

The cases were stacked shoulder high and handy to the driver who drove the truck from a swivel seat. There was no need for refrigeration even in summer. I noticed that yesterday's driver had put on the chains and the useless heater was howling full blast but with the frigid air from outside it didn't have much effect. Thanks a lot!

My teenage assistant, Joe Maldonado, materialized out of the darkness, hopped into the other side, and punched me on the shoulder.

"Hace frío, eh Paco?" he muttered through his scarf-wrapped face as he leaned against the stacked milk crates.

"As an Eskimo's terwilliger," I replied, switching up the useless heater.

Joe rattled something else in Spanish.

"I know that was something dirty." I started up the motor and flicked the heater up to the red mark.

Joe picked up a quart of regular and a quart of homogenized in preparation of our first stop. He knew the routine better than I because he had been on the job for a year before I ever showed up.

He worked on Monday, Wednesday, and Friday. Another kid, Gene, worked Tuesday, Thursday, and Saturday. They were both good workers and wanted to do the job as fast as possible, particularly when the weather was bad. We ran at it most of the time. They would take the right side of the street and I would do the left. On the three long straight streets we would just let the truck drift down the middle by itself while we both were delivering to our respective sides, running all the time to see who would get finished first. Whoever got back to the truck first got to drive. Not legal I suppose, but it was five a.m. so who's to know, or care?

It usually took a couple of hours to do the whole town, then I would go home and have breakfast with Mom, oatmeal and biscuits, while the guys at the dairy loaded the truck with the wholesale stuff.

On Tuesdays I would go north up over the mesa and foothills into the mountains to a scattering of tiny Chicano villages—La Cueva, Sapello, and Mora—on a mission to peddle wholesale milk products that now featured a new gimmick called "Torpedoes."

They were cardboard cylinders about eight inches long, one and a half inches in diameter, filled with some frozen, flavored product that a delighted customer would eat by shoving up a plunger-like stick in the bottom, which forced the delicious, flavored ice milk out the top to be enjoyed by one and all. It was a colorful package all right.

By the time I had ground my way to the level of the first mesa, the sun was up. It was just a bright spot in the morning mist but a persistent west wind carried a promise of change that was discouraging. Thank God for the tire chains.

My first call was in Sapello, which on the road map is listed as a Phillips 66 station. That was exactly what the town consisted of. Mr. Morales bought a pint of cottage cheese, no Torpedoes.

Then off the highway and up a rough dirt road to Manuelita. A picturesque hovel of adobes. One with a highly weathered Coca-Cola sign that had a rough post office scribble over the trademark signature. It wasn't really a store building but just a house that sets close to the road. Inside was kinda like a store with a counter and shelves, etc. Four little Manuelitos were scrambling around on the floor building castles out of tomato soup cans and toilet paper. Señora Manuelita bought four, you guessed it, Torpedoes Fresa, for the little kids. But she just didn't have any room or call for more.

Back down to the main road and on to La Cueva in a biting wind that now included a scurrying of snowflakes. The La Cueva Mill was there when Hec was a pup but it is now a store/post office, of course. Close to the river in a handsome grove of huge cottonwoods there was a frontier-like ranch house from the 1800s.

The interior was dark and smelled of aged vegetation. The long, dark room was mostly empty except for one well-seasoned counter that ran the length of the bare adobe wall, and the tall ladder-backed rocker where the old lady proprietor sat shelling pinto beans into a huge pot. With mostly pantomime and a bit of stuttering Spanish, I convinced her to try one of my Torpedoes.

Her clattering false teeth couldn't quite manage the complexities of modern science. All she could offer was a jagged smile but no deal. She didn't seem to understand that I wanted to sell her a dozen of them. I bowed with a gracious adios and backed out through the heavy wood door.

Mora (blackberry) Valley was now getting picturesque with spitting snow and a herd of goats on the road into town. Mora was like stepping back into the old frontier. One of my customers was a trading post named St. Vrain's, whose ancestors had partnered with Kit Carson. They actually spoke with a mix of broken English and French. The building was partial log on the back with a 1930s "modern" front and an honest to goodness hitching rail out in front. There were all kind of skins hanging around with old rifles and snowshoes and beaded headbands and eagle feathers.

They only wanted Torpedoes Fresa, even though we offered them in six colorful flavors. It was bizarre to watch these rough old mountain men sucking on Strawberry Torpedoes. Their stubbly chins would turn pink from the drips and dribbles.

Back along the lone street was a drugstore of a sort run by a silver-haired fellow named Roy Eagle. He would buy two cartons of Strawberry Torpedoes every Tuesday, nothing else.

The people back at the dairy came up with all kinds of great flavors like nutmeg and cherry frost and eggnog and rocky road. But no. I just carried them up there and then carried them back.

My best customer was a Catholic school, Mt. St. Gertrude, that ordered three dozen pint bottles of milk, plain and chocolate, every Tuesday. I dealt with Mother Serene, who was anything but serene.

She was no more than five feet tall and had a deep voice and a hint of a mustache decorating her upper lip. She could have shaved every morning if she just got into the habit (sorry). The kids called her Sister Sam. She always had a complaint of some sort about the sanitary condition of my product. I told the guys back at the dairy about her comments and they just muttered something in Spanish that didn't sound good.

Across the highway, there was the T&G Market, the center of activities in downtown Mora. A big Texan named Red Thornton presided over the butcher counter like a royal. He was loud, red-haired, and freckly. Spoke Spanish better than

English but spoke a lot of each. The head clerk was a skinny little girl named Rosalina who flirted openly with me. Every Tuesday and Thursday she greeted me like a long-lost boyfriend with hugs and flirty talk.

"Cómo está usted, Rosalina poquita," I stumbled.

She rattled something in Spanish that I took for flirty. I didn't exactly mind.

She had a large, silken mop of the longest, black hair I have ever seen. It hovered around her doll face and shoulders down to her waist like a dark cloud as she flitted back and forth across the highway between the market and the Frenchman's trading post. She worked in both as interpreter, cashier, and greeter. They were my main reason for coming to Mora. Rosalina always bought lots of ice cream—vanilla, chocolate and strawberry. None of that exotic stuff, like rocky road or mint julep. Also milk, cottage cheese, and TORPEDOES FRESA. Lots of Torpedoes.

Up the road was the non-town of Holman. I don't know who Holman was, but I'll bet he had a Mexican wife. There was a Lutheran mission school that ordered two crates of pints for their flock, which made the trip worthwhile. I dealt with Helga, who was about my age, overly formal and gruff. I was never quite sure just which sex she favored. It varied from Tuesday to Tuesday, so I was never sure which one she would be on any given day. One Tuesday she might be in frills and heels. Next week she would be in plumber's coveralls or bib overalls and safety-toed boots.

On the way back down the valley to Mora, sometimes I would give Priscilla Montana a ride. She worked for Eagle as a general helper or something, and was cute enough to stir my imagination, until one time when we got back to Mora, she hopped down from my wagon and was greeted by a dangerous-looking young dude in a big black Stetson, a silver belt buckle that was as big as a manhole cover, and under-slung boots with silver tips on the pointed toes. He gave me a warning stare, muttering something in Spanish that I didn't want to know, but I got the general drift.

Back out of town, heading home, I pulled off on a side road that faced west and had my lunch break watching a small herd of white-face cattle drift down off the mesa into a cove of cottonwoods and a log corral as the flurries encouraged their progress then whipped off across the prairie.

Every Thursday I went up the road to Wagon Mound. Yes, Wagon Mound, New Mexico. It was named for a huge butte just east of town that was truly shaped like a Conestoga wagon with a yoke of oxen trudging down the Santa Fe Trail, which actually went through there back in the day. The ruts were still visible along the highway. The school there bought a regular amount of my pint milks. Across the street from the school was a tiny candy shop presided over by Padre Esteban who serviced the urges of a flock of teenagers with all the Strawberry Torpedoes they could afford.

Back down the road "Along the Santa Fe Trail" I occasionally stopped at an old stone store in Watrous where the trail crossed the Mora River, providing the first watering hole for a hundred miles.

The store didn't have a name but just hunkered under some huge cottonwoods. This old saloon has been there since 1849 to service the dusty cavalry men from nearby Fort Union. They patrolled the Trail for Kiowa and Comanche that scoured the area looking for ponies.

The place wasn't always open, but I just liked the idea of striding onto the front porch where Clay Allison, the notorious bandit, might have paused in the shade between lawless escapades to roll a relaxing cigarette. They only bought enough for the family, if anything.

It was just one long, dark room with a huge mahogany bar on one side and groceries on the other. A wonderful, curved glass candy display case stood empty except for a scattering of jaw breakers and a strip of red ribbon candy and a mostly empty Whitman's box of chocolate covered cherries.

Old Mr. Zebulon usually was seated in the barber's chair in the back with a week's old *Rocky Mountain News* in his lap and tobacco drippings on the front of his vintage denim shirt.

I would stride in feeling like Gary Cooper. "Howdy," I would grunt without moving my lips.

Mr. Zebulon would wake up enough to say. "Nothing today, I'm afraid, Darrell. She's got the freezer full of crabapple chutney and smoked perch." Darrell was the guy I had replaced, but I suppose Mr. Zebulon thought we all looked alike.

Then to complete my romantic tour of the Land of Enchantment, I got to venture out to Rainsville. There wasn't really a road out there across the prairie. Once you left the highway and went through the cattle guard, one had to select which set of ruts were the most passable on that particular day.

Rainsville was just a scattering of little adobes surrounded by a warren of corrals and feeding lots. There were huge drifts of tumbleweeds gathered along the southwest fences and walls, and dirty snow drifts on the north side.

I only went there on occasion. Their freezer (they did have REA electricity) was loaded with all kinds of containers full of chili; there wasn't room for any Torpedoes.

I would stop on the way home at a high spot where I could enjoy the view while I ate my mother's standard Velveeta and mayonnaise sandwich, a gingersnap cookie, apple, and a free quart of eggnog. The expansive scene included broad rolling prairie, the Santa Fe Trail ruts, the distant ruins of old Fort Union, a complete, unobstructed view of Truchas Peak, and the snowy Sangre de Cristo Range, occasional antelope, maybe a real cowboy, all covered by that unique New Mexico sky.

# TEEZER'S TWISTS X

---

## "IT'S SPRING! IT'S SPRING!"

*E*verybody is excited in the crowd around Teezer's door. Folks are coming and going like a commuter station in downtown Chicago.

The air is that balmy sweetness that mingles sunlight with the aroma of apple blossoms. The tree in Teezer's patio is tossing up its arms in a maypole dance as it scatters pink petals over the two black Labs that are circling below.

Polly and Jenny are catching the sunshine on the bench under the side street window. Polly is back from her winter home in Santa Barbara and they have a lot of catching up to do. Every day, from now until after Thanksgiving, they will get together for an intimate discussion. We don't know just what they talk about, but it goes on and on like schoolgirls discussing boys. Maybe it is boys. Wouldn't that be a kick?

I get in line for my regular pumpkin scone. "Hi, Annie," I say to my friend in front of me. "What a day, huh?"

"It is beautiful. I must get to my garden today. It's getting late you know."

She fumbles in her rather large shoulder purse. "Frank, can you lend me five dollars? I seem to have forgotten my billfold."

"Sure thing," I reply magnanimously.

"Mark, give this little girl anything she wants. I'm buying."

"Oh, thanks. I'll pay you back tomorrow."

"Good enough," I agree and pat her on the back.

So, what does she do? She steps up and buys the last pumpkin scone right out from under me, and I pay for it, then search around for my second-best choice.

Mark thinks this is hilarious as he hands me a coconut lemon scone, which is not my favorite, but the only kind he has left.

Annie takes her pumpkin scone out the door into the beautiful day with a smile over her shoulder for friendly Frank.

I turn to a collection of the regulars inside. We have one plumber, two communication specialists, a retired dentist, one computer/media technician, two real estate salespersons, one young lady from the bank, a covey of high school girls followed by a pack of high school boys, a healthcare lady, two art gallery persons, a gardener, an unemployed musician, an assistant librarian, and a gaggle of silver-haired retirees known as Teezer's Geezers.

I get a cup of Starbucks, hot and steamy, just the way I really like it, walk over to the table opposite Jannie, carefully place my cup on the table, pull out the chair, sit down, and tip the table up so that my hot cup of coffee skids over and dumps into my lap, then tumbles to the floor and shatters with a loud crash. I calmly get up while Sandie rushes over with a roll of paper towels and starts cleaning up.

"I don't know how that happened. I was just sitting there and all of a sudden the table lurches up and throws a cup of hot coffee into my crotch."

Bill chuckles. "That may be your best thrill of the week."

"Well, it has been some time since I have really felt anything there. Maybe since I came home from Hong Kong."

Jannie adds, "If you can remember that far back, there are still vital signs at least."

"Well, I suppose it will make the police report for this week, unless there is an incident at the Exchange," Bob chuckles and sips his latte.

All of these actors have been on stage before, but today we have a unique topic.

"I got a letter from the Neptune Society the other day. Did you know there is one in Anacortes?" Bill stirs his coffee with his finger and looks around for acknowledgment.

Jan pats his hand. "Don't worry, Bill. They won't come unless you call them."

"Do you have to get a letter from your doctor or a prescription or something to join the Neptunes?" Frank asks seriously.

"I think you have to have a completed license from the planning commission or a burn permit from the fire department," Dorothy adds.

Bob looks around the group. "Do you suppose they sell gift certificates for the person who has everything? I can think of several people I'd like to get one for."

"Wouldn't that be a real stocking stuffer for Christmas?"

I like to stretch my imagination a bit. "Do they have get-togethers to say mottos and pledges and give pins for the number of meetings attended in a row without missing?"

"Yeah. They have group ratings for fire insurance and different classes of membership. Like simmer, toast, broil, or barbeque and stuff like that."

"Do they give discounts for people who have been killed in a fire?"

Dorothy shakes her head. "Enough of this, you people. I don't want to think about it. We had my grandmother's ashes sitting on the mantel for three years before we could agree on what to do about her. I had to dust around her all that time because she was always such a good housekeeper. She was in a beautiful Chinese urn. People kept asking why I didn't plant one of my African violets in it."

"Maybe you should have. You might have grown some

exotic plant. You could have named it after your grandmother. She would have been proud."

"What did you finally do with her?" Jannie asks.

"She got lost when we moved into our present house. We don't know where she went."

I pat her hand. "Maybe one of the movers stole her, thinking it was a valuable vase and took it to the *Antiques Roadshow*. Now your grandmother is on TV."

"More likely she got sent to the Salvation Army and now lives in Darrington as a doorstop," Bill smiles and stares into his cup.

There is a period of grateful silence as you can hear the gears changing. It is a relief when the subject moves on with Jim announcing that he intends to sing at the open mike evening at Doe Bay. He builds stringed instruments and has composed a song that he'll premier Friday evening.

"Oh, yeah! We gotta be there!" I say, then wince as someone kicks me under the table.

"What time do you do this?" someone asks.

Jim shrugs. "I don't know. Probably around eight-thirty or nine."

"Oh, man, we can't stay up that late. Besides, we have to be home to let the dog out just before dark."

"Did you ever play any musical instrument?"

I laugh. "Yes. I was in a little musical group in kindergarten. It was like a juvenile Spike Jones. Everybody had a noise to make. Some of the girls had little bird whistles. Some of the nicer guys got to make ringing dings on a triangle. They gave me two sticks to hit together, like a caveman from the last glacial period. I just stood there until Mildred Bayless pointed at me. Mildred was our concert master. Not because she was particularly musical, but because she was the biggest kid in class. I think Mildred forgot I was there, so I just stood there with my two sticks and wet my pants."

"I played a flute in high school," Lois chirps in, not unlike a flute herself.

I laugh. "The rumor was that the flute girls were the best

kissers because of their strong, practiced lips."

Lois actually blushes, proving the theory.

Uzek, our town mechanic, comes in.

"Uzek, my car makes this groaning noise whenever I turn to the right."

"I had a girlfriend in high school that did that," Bob chuckles as Dotty punches him in the ribs.

I come back to the table with a refill. "My car has two noises. One under the hood and the other in the passenger seat. I fixed the one under the hood with WD-40, but there's nothing I can do about the other one."

"You better watch your mouth if you want any lunch today, big boy." Jannie hits me on the top of my head.

Hank comes in, walks in front of the Teezer's Geezers table. "I'm looking for a caucus."

"Hey, Carolyn. Fix this man a caucus latte with one-half whipped cream and some mocha stuff."

"Yeah, and a finger of Viagra," I say over the counter to Carolyn, who is at her station, working away on some exotic hot drink.

"I don't do caucuses, I'm a dictator. A benevolent dictator," Carolyn laughs from her post at the latte machine.

"You should dress like one, then. Like Muammar Gadaffi with all the fancy stuff," I laugh.

Someone starts talking about staying in the Fidalgo Inn in Anacortes.

Dave says, "Hey, Bob, remember the Pink Flamingo Motel in Coeur d'Alene?" Bob chuckles into his coffee. "I've been trying to forget that place for forty-five years."

All ears perk up to the subject.

"Yeah, Bob, what happened at the Pink Flamingo?"

He chuckles, "There was one of those Magic Fingers beds. We put in a quarter. It started its shaking and we started laughing, and then it wouldn't stop. We tried to unplug the thing. We tried to find an off switch on the coin box. Then we pounded on the box. We called the office, but they wouldn't answer. Finally, it slowly faded out with a groan and just lurched like a dying Model A Ford."

There was a round of Magic Fingers stories until . . .

"Well, there are things to do so we're out of here," Dotty announces.

The crowd stirs around clearing tables and giving goodbyes as Mark comes out with his bar rag and tidies up. He arranges the tables as we go out into the spring sunshine.

Teezer's will be there tomorrow with most of the same folks and a new card of subjects, but always entertaining and friendly. I hope every neighborhood has a Teezer's, where folks can come together, sit for a while, and exchange rumors and thoughts with a generous frosting of love and understanding.

# BEST AND WORST
# OF SHOW

---

"**W**hat is that tapping? It's driving me nuts."

Jannie was a light sleeper, and she liked to include me in her turmoil.

"I don't know. Is it morning yet? I don't have my eyes open and I may not open them today or ever again."

I was tired, really tired, and this was gonna be a big day. I was in charge of almost everything that was supposed to happen today. This was a situation that I really didn't savor.

Six months ago, in a weak moment, I had allowed myself to be nominated for vice president of our art association, foolishly thinking that the vice president didn't have much to do and besides, I wanted to be recognized not only as a good guy, but as an "artist."

We were relatively new in town and had participated in last year's Art Festival, without much of an effort. I had only eight paintings, sold six, and won several prizes.

This sudden appearance of a new guy in town made several of the old-time resident artists uncomfortable. One asked if I intended to be in town for very long.

Preparations for this event, which included the entire town, began early in the year. I just attended the meetings, sat in the back with little to say. What did I know? I was a new guy.

Avalon is a small tourist town on Catalina Island just off

the coast of Southern California. You know? "Twenty-six miles across the sea," as per the Four Preps back in the '50s. It is roughly one square mile nestled in a canyon around a crescent bay full of yachts and swordfish boats. A tourist mecca, the town is all bistros and boutiques serviced by a collection of small hotels and restaurants, from The Country Club down to Rosie's abalone burgers and fish sticks on the pier. It was all party time with a three-block-long promenade along the beach where just about everything could and did happen. At the end of each summer season there was an art festival arranged by the local art association and nicely sponsored and supported by the local merchants.

The city arranged display racks on the serpentine wall that ran along the promenade separating the pedestrian traffic from the beach that was always crowded with sun worshipers.

The Invitational Show was presented in the huge Casino Ballroom with The Judges Introduction Cocktail Party, dinner, and dancing to a live band. Prizes would be awarded. The next day featured the Street Show, the Children's Show, the Craft Show, and the Photography Show, with judging of everything and prizes for everything. All of these committee folks had done this before, so it was easy for me to follow along until . . .

Two weeks before the fateful date the Art Association president handed me a huge loose-leaf notebook and informed me that he was going on vacation, Yellowstone or Reno or somewhere, and would try to be back for the show. He gave me a grin, then went back to the little printing press where he turned out business cards and menus.

It was like getting on a train that is going full speed down a mountain to a burnt- out bridge over a bottomless chasm only to discover that the engineer is sitting drunk in the club car writing his own obituary.

The tapping continued. I got up to look out over the main street where the artists were to hang up their paintings to be viewed, judged, and hopefully, sold. It was up to the individual artist to handle his or her own work, first come first serve.

We were living in a classic old Victorian that stood on a

hill that looked out proudly over the little beach town. From our front porch we could see almost everything that happened along the promenade.

In the predawn mists I could see three shadowy forms gathered around the first set of racks. They were hanging paintings and it was still dark.

"I think it's Dennis Downs and his family," I whispered over my shoulder. Dennis was a short Englishman who painted sylvan brooks and glades and thatched cottages with dripping florals, though he hadn't been back to Yorkshire in twenty-five years. He did paint a few local scenes and was quite popular. He always won the Popular Prize because his collection of family and friends stuffed the ballot box. There was really no control over this situation, as most of us assumed that personal integrity would somehow keep it fair.

Dennis always complained about the location of his paintings. He had strong opinions about everything that happened during the show. He never volunteered to do anything because of his health, he claimed. He won his popular ribbon, sold his Constable-like paintings, and complained openly to every passerby.

"When are you going to have time to get your painting down there and get a place?" Jannie mumbled from under the covers.

"Well, first I have to go out to the Invitational Show and make sure the door is unlocked and check all of the paintings and see that my volunteer ladies are there to sell tickets and give out programs and all that stuff."

"You can't do that first. All of the booth spaces will be gone by then. Dennis Downs already has the best spot. There will be others right behind."

She threw back the covers and came to the window as I noticed more shadows gathering along the display area.

"See? Here they come. We gotta get down there."

I struggled into my clothes and hurried downstairs to my studio where there were sixteen new paintings all named, framed, and stacked against the wall. I had been working on these paintings all summer. I seem to get more done when there is some sort of deadline. I usually work from a collection of 35mm slides that I have taken through the years. Subjects that inspire me, from abandoned desert mine derelicts, Montana log barns, snowy back roads in Vermont, and now Catalina Island's rocky shoreline and boats, boats, boats.

They are all watercolors, from little eight by tens to twenty by thirties. All inscribed with poignant titles and signed. Working alone in my own little sphere I try to come up with subjects that will please some unknown person out there.

By the time we carried them down the front stairs, loaded them onto our blue hand dolly and wheeled them down the hill to the show area, it was daylight and there were artists all up and down the street nailing up their wares. There were breakfast lines waiting in front of Joe's and The Pancake Cottage. A few bleary-eyed boaters were having their first beers at Eric's. George the Mayor was selling the *L.A. Times* on the corner at the end of the pier. The town crew was hosing down the plaza, gulls and pigeons were flocking around last night's leftovers, and the early boat to the mainland pulled out from the pier with three loud toots, stirring up every gull in the harbor.

We wheeled along, stopping now and then to hear the first complaints about everything from the time of day to lack of nails and misspelled nametags. The only good display spot remaining was in front of the Busy Bee, an open-air restaurant that had put out last night's garbage in six smelly cans that were crowded around like chunky critics. A noisy flock of seagulls and ravens were picking their breakfast out of a lidless can, scattering stuff over the beautiful tile pavement.

"Think we should grab this spot?" I put my hands on one of the stands as Patty Stone came up from behind and plopped down a huge purse.

"Are you gonna take this spot?" Patty's two teenage boys stood there with big boxes of Patty Stone originals.

"Well, yeah, I guess so," I replied, as I took out my hammer and quickly pounded in the first nail.

"You islanders always get the best places. It just isn't fair.

What am I supposed to do?" Patty whined and looked desperately up and down the street, while her two hulking kids put their boxes down in my newly claimed space.

I quickly hung my largest painting on the one nail and drove in another nail right over one of the boxes of Patty's paintings.

"There is a good spot over there by Tom Cat's. Everybody goes in there." Jannie pointed across the street.

"But it's in the shade. I get chilly real easy. I have this low blood pressure condition and should try to keep warm." Her whine was now three pitches higher.

I put in another nail and hung up another painting. "I don't know, Patty. It's first come, first served, you know."

As we watched, Bob Walker pulled up in front of Tom Cat's and started unloading his paintings, hanging one huge seascape on an existing nail.

"Look, he took my place! Now, what am I supposed to do? You people should take care of the artists from out of town better. I might as well just pack up and go home." Her whine now included a little sob.

I hung up another painting.

"Look, Patty. There is a spot over there in front of Leo's Drug Store. It would be a perfect place for your delightful little paintings." Jannie was good at soothing feathers.

"Yeah. You had better get it now," I added with emphasis on the "now."

"It's in the shade and there are flowers all in the way and there is a postcard stand right next to it and . . ."

I picked up one of her boxes. The two teen boys had disappeared. I took it over to the spot in front of Leo's and sat it right in the geraniums.

"This is a great place, Patty. Everybody goes by here and the sun will be shining soon."

"Well, you should do better by your invited artists. We are guests and it cost a lot of money just to come over here and we have to get up so early to catch the first boat and . . ."

I was out of hearing range before she finished, but the

whine of her voice followed me across the street like the slip-stream of the X-15. By the time I got back to my spot, a man in a boater's outfit and narrow wraparound dark glasses had one of my paintings under his arm.

"How much is this one?"

I looked at Jannie. "Do you have the list of prices?"

"I thought you had it in your toolbox."

"I thought you had it in your cashbox."

"What's that in your shirt pocket?"

"Oh."

I pulled out the folded paper that Jannie and I had labored over, giving each painting a cogent title and reasonable price. I would rather they sell for a lower price than not sell at all. But then, what is a lower price?

"Your paintings don't sell because they are cheap. People buy them because they like them. They are good," Jannie has told me many times.

"That one is three-eighty-five, plus tax."

"Plus tax? He peeled four new hundred-dollar bills from a roll held by a huge gold coin clip and held them out between his index and middle finger. "If it is cash, I don't have to pay the tax, right?" He sat the painting down on a nearby bench.

"Well, yeah. We have to charge the state sales tax like everybody else."

"You don't even have to claim a cash deal. I never do. Just put it in my pocket for drinks later, you know?" He gave me a light nudge with his elbow. "Everybody does it." He looked at me with pity.

"We pay all of our taxes, including sales tax. The Safeway Store charges sales tax. Do you pay their sales tax?" Jannie stepped in.

The man put the four hundred dollars back into his pocket.

"Maybe I'll be back later. If you haven't sold that one by the end of the day, I'll give you three hundred dollars cash for it. You won't have to claim it. No tax."

He turned and joined some friends, muttering and then laughing as they walked away.

Jannie and I looked at each other, mouthing our own personal expletives.

I got busy hanging all of my paintings while Jannie greeted a crowd of locals that had gathered. They were beginning to discuss just which painting to buy and the competition was getting stronger and more vocal.

Roy Ross broke the logjam. "I want that one of the *SS Catalina* and that little one on the end. I'll be back later, after the judging."

Jannie quickly wrote "Sold" on the two nametags.

Katherine Long whined, "But I was going to buy that one." This was her style. She never bought anything, just whined that the one she wanted had already been sold.

A waitress from Joe's Place came up with a flat box full of fresh doughnuts and a big thermos of hot coffee and paper cups. "Joe sent this out to all you artists and he wants to buy that one on the end, of the fishing boat. He'll be out later, so save it for him."

Jannie wrote "Sold" on the nametag with her red felt tip.

"You sold four already?" Denise Brown, a friend who had set up her display next to ours, stood with hands on her considerable hips and a pouty scowl on her round face.

"No, just three. That other guy was just blowing smoke to impress his friends."

Denise had about a dozen paintings of women and kids on the beach in long white dresses of the style found in Portugal in 1880. On our beach just behind them was a real girl brushing out her long blonde tresses and wearing a white silk-looking bikini that I personally found much more artistic than any of Denise's.

Hovering around her like a vulture was Reverend Bob, a guy that claimed to be an ordained minister of some obscure religion, who prowled the beach daily, administering to young women. He would hover over the best-looking girls with his smooth talk, all the while boldly admiring their bodies.

"Don't you have one of the Pleasure Pier?" Three ladies gathered around with their arms full of packages and large tote bags. They had already been shopping and it was just nine-fifteen. The show didn't really open officially until ten, but most of the good spots were full of artists hammering, arranging, and complaining.

"Are you Frank Loudin?" She pronounced my name in the French manner, "Lou- done." "Could you paint one of the Pleasure Pier with my two grandchildren playing under it? Just a small one. I don't have much money to spend on art. We come over here every year and we love the pier. The kids spend all day on the beach. We always have fish burgers at Rosie's. We always stay at the Mac Rae Hotel, room 22. My husband stays on our boat, but it's too rocky for me to sleep on. We have had a mooring here for years. That's our boat out there, the white one with the blue Bimini top."

I looked to where she was pointing. There were at least thirty-four white boats with blue Bimini tops. Here was a lady whose husband owned a fifty-foot boat, staying in a beach front hotel, shopping armloads of tourist junk, and asking me to do a special painting, including her grandkids, but couldn't afford to spend much on art.

The three of them got into a conversation over grandkids so I finished nailing up my paintings, sipped my cold coffee, and ate the rest of Jannie's doughnut.

The show had started at a fast clip. The three sales would cover my total expenses plus. I was in the black and feeling good when Ivan Torgenson came up.

"How did you get this space? I thought we weren't supposed to put up our works until today. You must have put yours up last night. All of the good places are gone by the time most people get up and have breakfast. Have you seen my new print of the pier?"

I stood watching the girl on the beach arrange her towel, her hair, her sunglasses and . . .

"Don't you have a print of the pier?" Ivan was a bit taller than I with a pointed nose, icy blue eyes, close-cropped aluminum hair, and a landscape-size ego. He had the attitude that his paintings were so superior that he didn't really belong here on the street with us underlings.

"Yes, I do have a print of the pier, but this show is supposed to be just originals," I informed him, knowing that he was there just to sell his famous print.

"Yes, but my print is so popular that people want to see it."

"Huh?" I grunted.

Ivan moved a little closer. "Who is your printer?" Like a printer should be as important as the family psychiatrist.

"Oh, Standard Offset and Outdoor Display in South L.A."

Ivan's upper lip curled. "Mine was done in Rochester, N.Y. We used fourteen colors on one hundred percent rag stock from Brussels. You can see how the magnificent the blend of colors is faithfully reproduced. These are high quality archival pieces."

I watched the girl put suntan lotion on her thighs.

"How many colors did you use on your print?" Ivan was standing on his tiptoes so that he could see over me to where a man was inspecting his magnificent print with jeweler-like intensity.

"Oh, just red, yellow, blue, and black. Nothing special. I think they look real good. We have sold a bunch of them. It's going okay."

Ivan spun about and went over to the man with "This print was created in Rochester, New York, on expensive stock from Brussels ..."

"We picked a great spot between Ivan and Denise," Jannie whispered.

"Well, at least we will be entertained all day and my paintings will stand out."

We sold another painting to a couple of schoolteachers from Anaheim who collect windmill stuff.

"I'm glad I did that painting. You just never know what people will buy."

Over the years we must have sold ten paintings of windmills to a couple, then when the mister passed away several years later, she asked if I would buy them all back.

The street became crowded as folks finished their bacon and eggs at Joe's Place, or plates of maple syrup, butter, and strawberry pancakes at The Cottage. I always had a good crowd around my booth, causing Denise and Ivan to give me long hard looks of thinly disguised jealousy.

A man with a huge TV camera with KTTV stamped on the side came down the street, stopping occasionally to check out a prospective shot. He passed by Ivan and stopped at my place.

"Is it okay with you if I take some shots of your paintings with the bay in the background?" He pointed in the direction that he intended to shoot, and his assistant went over and moved one of my paintings so that his shot would include the pier and the girl.

"Do you want me to stand in here?" I smoothed back my hair and checked to make sure my fly wasn't hanging open.

He ignored me. "Cosmo, put that other painting aside so we can get more of the beach and boats."

Cosmo started rearranging my paintings.

"Why is he taking shots of your paintings?" Ivan growled in my ear.

"I don't know. It is a good angle for the pier and that girl, I guess."

"Are you from KTTV?" Ivan asked the guy with KTTV written all over his shirt, cap, carryall bag, and a little leather case he had slung around his neck.

Camera guy ignored Ivan. He moved back and forth, left and right, up and down. I noticed that he didn't really care too much for my paintings but rather the beach, the bay and, of course, the girl who obliged him by sitting up to adjust the skimpy top of her bikini.

"When will this be on TV?" I asked Cosmo, who was lighting up a Marlboro and sipping coffee at the same time.

"Tonight, local ten o'clock. Kelly Lange. She is right down there talking to some guy, the mayor, I think."

The camera guy moved on. Cosmo followed like Sancho Panza. I put my painting back in place. "We'll be TV stars tonight. You and me and Kelly Lange," Jannie snickered.

"Yeah, Lange and Loudin, or rather Loudin and Lange."

"Frank! You have got to do something!" Jane Jackson came

up to me with a specific purpose frowning up her face. Jane was always the first to find fault and was not shy about making sure everyone knew about it. She owned and operated a liquor store just around the corner and, as a result, had good opportunity to keep a grip on the pulse-beat of the town.

"About what?" I asked with trepidation.

"There is a nude over there," she whispered, as if just whispering the word was a mortal sin.

I looked to see if beach girl had taken off all of her bikini, but no, she had disappeared for now.

"What do you mean, a nude?" I backed away from Jane in order to escape her powerful presence.

She grabbed me by the arm. "It's over here," she hissed and pulled me down the street.

Halfway down the block, we came upon three little ladies clustered together, whispering, shaking their heads and making that clicking sound that somehow has gotten to mean "shame, shame."

"There!" Jane tilted her head toward a painting of the torso of a young and well-endowed woman, done rather nicely in a realistic manner. One could clearly see all of her female appurtenances. The group of ladies made sure that every passing person took notice of the offending art, expressing their unified disapproval with great shaking of their blue hairdos.

"See! See! We can't have that out here in public where children can see it. This is a family town where kids can safely walk up and down our streets and go to the beach alone." This from a woman who happily sold vodka to her neighbors who were raging alcoholics, and cigarettes to underage kids because she knew their folks wouldn't mind.

"What do you think I should do?" I was stalling because I saw Bob K. coming down the street and he was really in charge of this part of the show.

"Well, he has to cover it up or take it down, that's all." Jane now had the attention of her support group, who all nodded like a trio of bobbleheads.

Bob K. came up and stepped right into the group of agitators. He was the chairman of the Street Show and had a lot more guts than I, so I just turned and walked away. It wasn't my job. Later I noticed that the artist had put a piece of paper over the nude and written on it "Eighteen or older only." The three ladies spent the day making sure everybody was aware of the moral offense right there on our street.

"Is that on the island?" The man was pointing to a painting of a snowy schoolhouse in Kansas.

Jannie and I exchanged glances. "Jesus."

"No. That is a schoolhouse in Kansas. It is Christmastime. See the kids and the tree and the lights in the window?" I tried to be patient. It was still early.

"Were you there?" The man turned and stared at me, a little too close.

"Well, yes. I have been there, but I painted from a photo."

"So, you just copied from some magazine," he scoffed.

"No. It was my photo. I took the photo last fall. Then I decided to make a winter scene, so I snowed on it."

"So you just made the whole thing up. It doesn't really exist." He got even closer and I turned sideways to avoid his breath that smelled like yesterday's abalone burgers.

"Yeah. I guess that's what artists do. Just make things up."

"And you are trying to sell it for four hundred dollars?" I turned and made a quick conversation with Jannie. The man stood there for an eternity with another comment hidden behind his bad teeth but I continued to work around him. Finally he turned and went over to Ivan. Good, I thought. They deserve each other. I wonder if he will be impressed with Ivan's paper from Brussels.

The sun was full onto the beach, now crowded with devotees arranging and rearranging their colorful towels. The promenade was busy with lookers. On the stage in the plaza, a woman with a big mop of kinky black hair wearing some sort of gypsy (bohemian?) outfit with lots of beads and fringes was plunking out a mournful Spanish tune. The three judges and their helpers were slowly making their way down the street. The girl came by with more doughnuts. Ivan was sitting on a folding campstool in the shade.

Two women approached. They studied each of my paintings, then looked at the program where the artists were listed along with short bios.

"It says here that your work is like Andrew Wyeth?" It sounded like a question, so I tried to explain that Wyeth was one of my artistic heroes, that I had visited his farm and had seen his paintings in Maine and Pennsylvania. I was beginning to babble as the two ladies just stood and looked at me. I stopped babbling. They looked at me, my paintings, and the program, and scoffed. "We don't see that at all." They turned and left without another word.

Jannie and I started laughing so hard that passing people began to stare.

"How does that feel on your ego, Andrew?" Jannie snickered.

"I never said I was Andrew Wyeth. I just like his style. That's all." I went over and turned a couple of paintings away from the sunlight.

"Do you paint China?" A tall man in an iridescent green suit asked after scanning my collection.

"No, I have never been to China. I like to paint just the places I have seen firsthand. I have been to most of the states, all of the western ones, you know, Nebraska and Idaho, but not to the Deep South. I have even been to Andrew Wyeth's farm," I added for my own personal satisfaction. "I take a lot of slides, 35mm, you know because the colors are better, and I can blow them up to see the details."

I could see the glaze of boredom come over the man's face.

"I mean plates and teacups, not China, the country. With your attention to detail, I would think you might enjoy it. You could make a lot of money doing that. There is a place in Los Angeles that I have visited where they do custom designs on sets of china."

"Oh, that sounds exciting," I tried not to let too much disinterest show on my face, but the idea of sitting all day painting buttercups on gravy boats sounded like a bit of Hades.

"Do you have a card?" He handed me one of his. Ewald E. Everholt, Estate Executor.

I couldn't help but wonder what the middle E. stood for. He looked at both sides of my card as if expecting more information, or at least a title of some sort, or maybe a painted cluster of violets.

"Well, give me a call whenever you're in Pasadena."

The sunlight caught glimmers of unearthly shimmers from his green suit as he went over to Ivan.

"I hope he asks Ivan if he has ever painted China," Jannie murmured.

The judging party went right past Ivan and gathered around my booth. I stepped back across the street in order to not be involved.

"They should just give you all of the ribbons and be done with it." My friends Shirley and Char stopped by to chat.

"Who are those judges anyway? They have been sitting in the Galleon for an hour."

"Yeah, that one guy looks like he spent the night there."

The Galleon was a bar restaurant that featured an open piazza right off the sidewalk, where people liked to set and drink and watch the passing parade.

"I don't know any of them. I try to stay away from them so people won't think I have any influence in the judging. I get accused of it anyway."

The judges examined and conferred and selected three of my paintings, which their helpers carefully placed on a wagon to carry off to the library where the final selections would be made.

There were prizes for Best of Show with second, third, and three honorable mentions. There were special awards for best marine, best local by a local, best local by a non-local, best floral, portrait, figure, children, animal, not to mention several special prizes selected and presented by businesses or service clubs. Of course, there was the Popular Prize awarded to Dennis Downs for having the most admirers.

"Why did they take three of your paintings?" Ivan was back.

"I guess they are being considered for a prize of some sort."

"Why didn't they take my print?" Ivan grumbled.

"Because it is a print." I shrugged.

"They should have a prize for the best print," Ivan growled.

"Well, maybe, but then that would be a whole different kind of show."

Ivan followed the judges down the street.

"Maybe they should give an award for the most pretentious or the biggest ego or the best paper from Brussels," Jannie whispered in my ear.

A woman in a blue blazer with white slacks and high-heeled, red sandals approached. She had lots of blonde hair in a French twist and large sunglasses with heart-shaped frames. "I want that painting." She had out her checkbook.

Which one would that be?" I inquired politely, trying to remain nonchalant.

"That one of the Casino in the morning with the boats and all. That is our boat right there on mooring 47."

She pointed one shapely finger with a long red, white, and blue-striped nail.

Great, I thought. That is the one the fellow had wanted but didn't want to pay tax. When or if he comes back, I can tell him it had sold.

"That's three-eighty-five, plus tax," Jannie was quick to inform.

"I know. That was my husband who came over here a while ago and didn't want to pay tax. That's the way he is, the old poop. I don't know why he does that."

She took out her checkbook. "When he comes back, tell him you sold it to someone else. It's for his birthday next week."

"You sold another painting?" Ivan growled into my ear.

"Yeah. How are you doing with your print?" I tried to be friendly.

"A gallery owner from Beverly Hills wants to carry it. Mrs. Wayne has asked about it. Mrs. John Wayne." Ivan was a name-dropper.

"Oh yeah. I heard the the Duke was supposed to be here

today." He did show up in Avalon from time to time, and the prospects of hobnobbing with a celebrity got Ivan all in a dither. All day he kept asking if we had seen John Wayne.

"That was mean of you to tell Ivan that John Wayne might be here, but good." Jannie gave my arm a squeeze.

"Yeah, did you see how his eyes lit up? He is such a hamburger." We watched Ivan walking up and down the street looking for John Wayne.

Two young women were admiring a painting of a yellow crop duster that I had seen up in California's Central Valley. I approached them with "Hi there. Do you know about crop dusters? This is called an Ag Cat, built especially for the job of flying low over fields of celery or whatever, over fences and under telephone wires, around tall eucalyptus trees and really close to the ground. It is exciting to watch them. The plane was designed in . . ."

One of the women pulled out a wad of new hundred-dollar bills. "Five hundred, right?" She handed me five brand new bills.

"Plus tax," Jannie informed.

The woman peeled off another hundred-dollar bill and handed it to me without even looking at it.

"You like airplanes. Do you fly?" I asked.

"Fly, me? No way"

"You must like planes though?" I tried.

"Oh, not particularly." She rearranged her sunglasses and flipped her multi-colored ponytail that was sprinkled with glitter.

I was intrigued. "But you just bought this painting of a crop duster?"

"Oh, I just bought it because it's yellow. That's my favorite color. Where is the dinghy dock?" She looked out over the bay.

"It is right there by the pier. See the dinghies all tied up there?" I pointed.

"We'll pick up the painting later. We're supposed to meet at the dinghy dock. Come on, Candy."

"Here is your change." Jannie held out a handful of small bills.

"Oh. we'll be back." She waved off the money and they hurried off to the dinghy dock.

"Speaking of dinghy, she just likes yellow?" Jannie and I shook our heads in wonder.

So it goes at art shows. If you have the nerve to put your work out there for the public to view, you have to take whatever the public gives you in return. Somebody said, "It's like dropping your pants in public." If you are trying to make a living at it, you have to create something that others will appreciate enough that they want to have it for their own for any reason. I don't think any artist can anticipate this perfectly. Some just fall into it while others work and work and never quite get there, and there are all of us in between.

It is always rewarding when a painting is sold. It pays for your time and talent and inspires you to go back to your lonely little garret and paint some more.

We sold six paintings that first day with a couple of promises from folks who said they would be back tomorrow. We wheeled our leftover paintings back up to the house, had a drink or two, and crashed.

Dennis Downs must have spent the night on the street because when I looked out at the crack of dawn, he was already in place and we hadn't heard any of his tapping. Ivan was nowhere to be seen. Denise was in a better mood, having sold two paintings. The garbage cans were back in my booth with a swarm of gulls enjoying their breakfast. Patty Stone was also sitting there with her two large boxes.

"Do we have to take the same place we had yesterday?"

"Yes," I replied, making a quick interpretation of the rules for my own benefit.

One of the rumors that run through art shows is that some celebrity is going to be there. As if all it takes to make a successful show would be the appearance of Mary Tyler Moore. It is usually some movie star, like Bo Derek or Chevy Chase. On occasion, one will actually show up and pass right by without being recognized. In Catalina, there was a high likelihood that this would happen. Many movie and TV people either have boats or know someone who does, and the only destination for Los Angeles boaters is Catalina so we were used to the rumors as well as the actual sightings.

Today's rumor had to do with Howard Hughes. A likely candidate had been spotted last night at The Yachtsman, sitting at the bar, acting very strange.

This man came hurrying down the street. He was in all khaki, almost like a uniform except for the long red scarf and shower clogs. He had wild but shortly cropped silver hair and fierce eyes that seemed to be looking for some distant object, maybe Neptune or Krypton.

He suddenly stopped in front of my booth, made a sharp West Point right face and marched up to my painting of a Model T in the snow. He studied it closely like he was searching for some tiny flaw or, if it was really Howard Hughes, he was searching for germs. Then he backed off, stood up on his toes, leaned over backwards, and gave that painting his magic motion by wiggling both forefingers at it.

Having satisfied some obscure requirement, he whipped around and skipped, yes, skipped off down the street.

It's too bad Ivan wasn't there. It would have been an interesting confrontation.

"That's Howard Hughes!" Denise hissed. "He is nuttier than a fruitcake. He is on that big yacht out there. Last night in the Hurricane, he took off all of his clothes and marched up and down on the bar singing 'Give My Regards to Broadway.'"

"I hope he comes back this way" Jannie giggled. "He is the most exciting thing that has happened today."

"Yet," I added.

He never came back. We later heard that he had been picked up by the sheriff and it wasn't Howard Hughes at all, just some guy high on dope.

At eleven o'clock the prizes and ribbons were to be announced up on the small stage in the central plaza. I was getting my public appearance nervousness when the real president of the show showed up.

"Do you have a list of the winners? Do you know where the

judges are? Do you have the popular vote ballots counted? Do you, do you, do you?"

I tried not to punch him in his stupid nose. "No, I don't have any of that stuff. You'll have to ask Bob and Jeannie and Triva, etc., etc."

"I need you to come up on the stage and help me. I get nervous doing that kind of thing." He was already sweating a bit, just from the thought of it.

"Okay," I replied. "Let's go."

"Where have you been? We're all ready and one of the judges has to catch the eleven-forty-five boat." Triva, the judges' chairman, was efficient to a fault. The paintings were all stacked in order of presentation with the ribbons already stuck to them with scotch tape. She handed the president a combined list of awards and stepped back. The president adjusted his glasses and stepped over close to me and said, "What is your name? I can't remember."

I thought he was kidding but then I noticed that his hands were shaking and there was a sheen of nervous sweat on his brow.

"Frank. Frank Loudin," I whispered into his ear, trying not to show any emotion.

"Oh yeah. I'm kinda nervous." He fumbled through the list of ribbons.

We also fumbled through the awards presentation, mispronouncing names and forgetting a couple of people. Dennis Downs won the Popular Prize, surprise surprise. I received a blue ribbon for Local Marine and a red ribbon for Second Best of Show, also a yellow Honorable Mention ribbon.

The ceremony finally ended and I returned to my space where Jannie informed me that she had sold two more paintings including my red ribbon. The man wanted me to include the ribbon. Okay.

The crowds dwindled away with artists packing up and everyone trailing out to the Mole where the loaded boats were getting folks out of town in a hurry.

We never saw Ivan again. I guess he just couldn't stand the

awards ceremony and the lack of appreciation. The nude had been exposed again and a bunch of little boys were snickering and pointing.

The three young women who had bought the yellow airplane finally showed up at three-forty-five. The show closed at four o'clock, supposedly. They were all lugging huge bags of shopping stuff and some sort of cocktails.

"We have had soooo much fun. Yeah, we met these guys who have a yacht. What was it called? *Chicken of the Sea*? It's all white with a blue balloon top, 'er somthin'."

Jan tried to give the proper change back to Cheryl, the one with the money, but she didn't have a hand to spare.

"Can you carry the painting out to the boat place for me?" she asked, as she sipped on her gin and tonic, or whatever.

"Gee, I . . ."

Jan gave me a look that said, "No way."

"I have to stay here with my paintings."

"Can't she?" Cheryl pointed her glass at Jan.

"She has to stay here and help me with the paintings. We have to pack them up and all, you know."

We all just stood there looking at each other. "Look, there's Billy. Billy sweet, come over here," Cheryl chirped.

It was Billy Saldana, prince of our local studs.

Billy sauntered over in his skin-tight old jeans with his shirt unbuttoned down just far enough to show a tuft of curly hair on his chest. Cheryl's shirt was also unbuttoned down to about the same level of excitement. It made my imagination tumble.

With a bit of twitching and the laying on of hands, Cheryl convinced Billy to carry the painting and they all disappeared into the crowd of hurrying folk that were now streaming out to the dock where three boats were loading up for the last afternoon run.

"Is this a local boat?" A young couple dressed in baggy jeans with decorative holes and fringy cuffs pointed at my painting of a plank boat.

I was packing up and didn't really want to talk to anyone. "Yes," I mumbled.

"Is it all watercolor?" the girl asked.

"Yes," I mumbled again.

"How long did it take you to paint it?" he asked.

"Four days." I just picked a number without thinking.

"Is this the price?" He pointed at the little sticker on the upper right corner of the frame.

"Uh huh," I grunted. I really didn't want to talk about it or anything.

"Can we buy it?" He pulled out a clip of hundred-dollar bills that quickly got my attention.

"Why, yes you may." My enthusiasm sprang from nowhere when I realized that these folks were serious.

"We know the guy that owns that boat. Jerry something. He was at the Galleon last night. What a funny guy. It's the felucca or something Italian."

"Yeah. It's a plank boat. Jerry uses it for swordfish. It is setting right out there," I pointed.

"Cool," the girl said.

"Cool," the guy said, as he peeled off four hundred-dollar bills and handed them to me. I handed them to Jan, as she said, "Tax included."

"Well, you can never tell," I said, as we started gathering up our paintings.

"Yeah. Let's get out of here. My smile is totally worn out."

# TEEZER'S TWISTS XI

## CLOSING TIME

Today is crisp and clear. Crisp because the temperature is hovering around twenty and the wind is right off that huge glacier up in British Columbia.

The county road crew in their brown coveralls come in out of the weather for a large paper cup of strong hot coffee and sometimes a heart-shaped cookie with pink frosting.

If anyone appears to be overdressed, we know they are either speaking at today's Lions Club or on a mission for The Jehovah's Witnesses.

"Did anyone have a nice mother-in-law?" Jackie asks right out of the blue.

"Yes," I answer. "My mother-in-law loved me, even before I met Jannie. Then after she passed, my stepmother-in-law loved me. What do you suppose was my problem?"

"It must have been your aftershave," Bill suggests.

"Wouldn't that be a great name for an aftershave? Mother-in-law's kiss?" I laugh and shake my head.

Bill and the others raise their brows.

"No, not a kiss from a mother-in-law!"

"Yeah, if we were dropping it over enemy lines to demoralize the troops," Bob adds. "Do we try to demoralize enemy troops anymore or is the whole thing so bad that the troops are as demoralized as they can get? It would be a great waste of government money."

"Sounds like a great opportunity for political pork barreling or earmarking or one of those discouraging things we hear about."

The whole conversation was so weird that I decided to write down some of the snatches of conversation that I overheard that day.

"If they give you shots for glaucoma, do they do it right in your eyeball?"

"Yeah. First, they tell you not to blink."

"I'm afraid to have my knee partially replaced." One can imagine a knee with a collection of metallic mechanical parts sticking out of the side. "Well, they said it was a partial replacement!"

"They don't play hopscotch anymore." The middle-aged woman says it like maybe her whole life had been those fantastic hopscotch tournaments in Madison Square Garden back in the yesteryears.

"I had to sign out for the whole thing, including the tool to fix it with," one of the plumbing guys says. He had to sign out for something that needed tools before he even got the thing home. Was it a backhoe or a bidet?

"Did they make you sign for stuff when you were in the Navy, Bill?"

"Yeah, I think I signed out for an LST, and it wasn't a very good one either. It needed paint and a whole new galley crew. The bow ramp wouldn't totally close, so we went all the way to Okinawa at half speed, which to an LST is one knot slower than reverse."

Just then, the troubled guy that patrols the intersection there in front of Teezer's goes hurrying past the window, only to stop abruptly and hurry back in the other direction. He does this for hours.

"See that guy? He thinks the Feds are after him. That's the

reason he keeps on the move and a constant lookout fore and aft," Bob says over his coffee.

"Yeah. They say he signed out for an Atlas rocket, then lost it." I look around suspiciously.

"They'll never catch him. He doesn't even know who he is, so how could a GPS ever find him?"

"Did you notice the hair on that lady?"

"It was strange. You know, like those wigs that English lawyers wear."

"Do they still do that? Do they have to have them cleaned and shaped? Do they leave them at the beauty parlor? Do they have their names sewn into the underside?"

Gene, our legal consultant, informs us that in Canada they have a cage in the middle of the courtroom where the accused sits during the trial. Guilty until proven innocent. That's a good idea. We could use one of those in some of our meetings around town.

"I'm gonna get one for this place and set it right there." Mark, who usually doesn't say much, steps out from behind the counter. Mark and Carolyn are usually too busy to participate in our talk, but I think they listen a lot.

Dick has a new French coffee press that doesn't make a very good drink. So today he brought it in and Carolyn made up a thing full of Starbucks super blend. At a slow moment she brings it out and puts on a symposium on the use of same. We all give it a sample and agree that it's great. She expounds on technique as well as the selection of proper ingredients. After we empty it, she takes it back and cleans it.

"Yeah. We dropped another one. Had a beer and heated up a pizza."

It's two plumbers talking. Seems they were installing a new water heater for a lady up on Buck Mountain. They dropped it off the back of the truck and dented it severely. As it turned out, it was lunchtime so she invited them in for a beer and a heated-up pizza. They finally told her about the heater.

"Does it still work?" she asked.

"Oh yeah, I think so," plumber number one replied.

"Well, shit. Just turn the dent to the wall. It goes in a closet anyway. Finish up that pizza and have another beer." That lady was really cool.

Here is a list of subjects heard in just one sitting.

"You don't plant 'em 'til ya see an eagle building a nest."

"Yeah. It'll work out. Just keep your mouth shut when she starts."

"Oh really. Oh okay, then we won't need the instruction book."

"That sweeper just moves the dirt to the other side of the road and makes a lot of dust."

"Truffles are really easy to make. You just have to find the best chocolate and hold your mouth just right."

"Yeah. I put my boat in the Ditch." (That's a local small boat harbor.)

Subjects range from gardening, fishing, older sisters, health inspectors, how do they pasteurize eggs, long pants/short pants, dogs, waitresses, school bonds, new roofs and roofers, frozen pipes, veterinarians, ice on the road, births and deaths, and who is with who.

If you wait long enough, your topic of expertise will come along.

That's just one of the reasons that we all love Teezer's.

# *FRANKINCENSE*
# *AND GUMMY BEARS*

---

*A* blustery white Christmas Eve was bringing traffic to a standstill all along the eastern slope of the Rockies as the big Greyhound semi-cruiser mushed across the parking lot toward a display of colored lights. The bus growled to a halt with a wheezy hiss of air brakes as a highway patrolman in a yellow slicker motioned to the driver to open the door.

"The road is drifted over south of here. We just don't know when we can get it cleared, so I suggest you folks get on inside and try to keep warm."

A mutter of concern and dismay flickered up and down the narrow aisle as the collection of blue-collar folks peered out at the blinking red neon sign. "Half Hitch Café and Rec. Parlor."

As the hefty driver, Ponce Gutierrez, saw the last of his flock out into the weather, a loud snore came from the cowboy stretched out on the back seat. Ponce went to the back and nudged the fellow with his knee, getting a "humph" and a mumbled "Sh-e-e . . ." for his trouble. The cowboy waved an arm at some imagined assailant, revealing a pint-sized bulge in his jacket emitting a foul aroma like a well-seasoned bar rag.

Ponce returned to the front of the bus, shrugged into his jacket, and quietly closed the door as the big bus ticked and sighed in repose.

---

The passengers bundled into the already jammed restaurant, searching to find space amid the turmoil of impatient truck drivers and a few locals who just hung around for the excitement. The atmosphere was heavy with the aroma of frytop grease and wet wool overcoats, conflicting with a mixture of stale beer and overtaxed ash trays drifting in from the adjoining Rec. Parlor. One harried waitress, a bony blonde with a grin too full of teeth, responded to the truck drivers' flirting with a continuous repartee of over-the-shoulder wisecracks as she hustled about.

Eula was pouring buckets of coffee with both hands while Melchior, a barrel of gristle in a stained gray T-shirt and once-white U.S. Navy bell bottoms, yelled "ready" orders and sarcastic remarks through a chin-high opening between the counter and kitchen.

A young woman awkwardly lowered her ponderously pregnant self into the booth next to the back door under the STUDS and MARES signs. Her young son tossed his bulging backpack onto the marred and monogrammed table, then helped his little sister climb onto the cracked Naugahyde seat. The little blonde tintype of her mother held a well-used rag doll by the left leg and carried a red patent leather purse slung over her shoulder by a piece of silver gift-wrap ribbon.

Ponce, in a too-small gray uniform that was slick in the seat and knees came in last. Like a true captain of his ship, he dutifully went around the room counting faces and offering a few reassuring comments.

A lanky young man with thick glasses and a mop of black hair that fell down over his forehead was bussing tables, heaping dirty dishes on an ancient Navajo implanted at a rusty sink in the back of the kitchen.

It was Christmas Eve there in Wagon Rut, New Mexico, and some wiseacre kept punching up "I'll Be Home for Christmas" on the jukebox.

The bus people and the truckers had just settled into a tenuous comfort when the door burst open with a snowy blast and the cowboy from the back seat of the bus stumbled in muttering "Son of a . . ."

He stomped his boots and slapped his hat across the back of the cash register, splattering snow and toothpicks down the counter in front of Ponce, who raised one shaggy eyebrow and proclaimed, "I tried to get you up, but you was dead to the world. I figured that when you was beginning to freeze it'ould wake you up, and I see it did."

"She-e-e," muttered the cowboy, his soiled Stetson repositioned down over his eyebrows. He stepped in front of Eula, blocking her path to the kitchen. "Gimme some hot coffee and I mean HOT."

Eula do-si-doed around him with a "Kiss my grits, Buster Bean, can't you-all see I'm busy?"

He swatted at her rump as she passed and kicked at a suitcase on the floor.

Across the back of his denim jacket, studded lettering proclaimed, "Jingle Berry, Rodeo Clown, Ellensburg, WA." At the frayed cuffs hung two tiny bells that jingled with every move. The Stetson, now tilted back on his head, revealed an unruly shock of carrot-colored hair. His freckled face was hard and raw, decorated by a fresh scab on the considerable nose that divided two squinty blue eyes like a splitting wedge stuck in a juniper knot.

The tough Teamsters just ignored him, but the more easily intimidated passengers gave Jingle some space as he surveyed the room, daring anyone to meet his gaze. He crowded in at the counter, elbowing a route salesman and young Mexican seminary student.

"What a frickin' hole," Jingle muttered, as Eula slammed a mug down on the counter, splashing hot coffee over the back of his hand. He gave her a glare and pulled out a pack of Camels.

"If you intend to light that thing, you'll have to go into the smoking section," Eula said over her shoulder, as she reloaded the struggling coffee maker.

"Where the hell is the smoking section, Miss Kitty?"

Eula nodded toward the back door labeled EXIT. "Out there, Chester."

"She-e-e-," said Jingle, as he struck a match on the seat of his jeans.

"You think I'm just pokin' at you? There ain't no smoking in restaurants in this state no more and that's the law."

"She-e-e-." The match had burned down to his fingers and he flipped it out, dropping it on the floor.

Eula stood her ground. "That'll be fifty cents fir the coffee."

"How's 'bout two bits? That's 'most all I got left."

"Okay, but only 'cause it's Christmas Eve."

"She-e-e-," he smirked, thinking about the folded twenty tucked in his boot. He turned to look around the room, squinting over the steamy mug until his glance fell on the STUDS sign.

He stood, shook himself into a more impressive stance, and strode toward the back, pausing next to the last booth where the boy was playing with a short piece of twine tied into a loop.

"What's your handle there, Little Britches?"

"I'm Harland Elvis Petty, but my dad calls me Chigger, 'cause I can't sit still."

"Chigger? She-e-e, I knowed a mean ol' buckskin bronc by that name once."

"What's your name, mister?"

"Well, my professional name is Jingle, but back home they know me as Charles Goodnight Berry. My great-great uncle was ol' Charlie Goodnight hisself."

Jingle kinda strutted in place, trying to broaden his knobby shoulders.

"You got dirt all down your front," Chigger stated, as he eyed the cowboy from head to toe.

"Chigger!" his mother exclaimed. "That's none of your affair!"

"Well, that's the truth, ma'am. I kinda been pulled backwards through a knothole lately. I ain't at my best."

Jingle's denim jacket fell open revealing a huge silver buckle that covered a large portion of his scrawny midsection. It proclaimed SADDLE BRONC CHAMPION '19.

"My daddy has a buckle like that. He used to do match roping before he—"

"Chigger, leave the man alone. He don't want to hear nothin' 'bout that old stuff."

"Oh, that's okay, ma'am. Where you folks trying to get to nohow?"

"We're goin' to Albuquerque where my dad has a new job and a house and a Christmas tree and presents and stuff," Chigger replied. The little girl took interest in the mention of Daddy and presents. She popped in with, "We talked on the telephone and he promised that he had a place for Santa to come down a chimbly, too, and bring me a new Barbie doll and lots of candy and stuff."

Chigger continued, "Yeah, we got to get there tonight if Santa Claus is gonna find us."

Jingle snorted. "You don't still believe in that she-e-e-enanigan Santa crap, do you? A big feller like you? That's for yearlings that ain't broke yet."

Momma stepped into the conversation. "You jest tend to your own messed up fences. Looks like Santa forgot you 'way back down the road a piece."

Jingle gave them a hard look. "Well, Santa nor nobody is gonna find you in this gopher hole with this gol-dern weather."

The little girl climbed down out of the booth and stood by her brother, facing Jingle. "Santa is magic and he knows where all the children are all the time and if they have been good or not."

"Yeah," added Chigger. "Mom says if every kid would jest keep believing in Santa, the whole world could be happier."

Chigger and his sister Virginia, "Virgie," formed a solid front, with four big brown eyes staring at the ornery cowboy.

"Well, you little buggers jest keep foolin' yourselves if you want to, but I been from Mountain Oyster, Manitoba, to Frijole Fart, Texas, and I never seen no fat elf in no red union suit yet."

Jingle's turn came up and he strutted into the STUDS room like a bowlegged rooster.

"Listen up, folks!" A ruddy faced highway patrolman stood by the front door, brushing the ice and snow from his slicker.

The room came to attention and a booming voice in the passage to the pool room next door yelled, "Knock it off. We got the hot skinny from The Man."

The cop wiped his face with a bandanna and took a few steps into the room. "The storm seems to be letting up down south, but the plows are going to have a real tough job with some mighty big drifts up on Turkey Tail Ridge. We'll try to get you outta here by daybreak, so you just do the best you can right here for the night."

"Santa Claus will never know where we are if we have to stay here," Virgie whined. "And Daddy will be all by hisself."

Grumbles and mutters spiced with a few four-letter words came from the truckers. Some followed the cop out into the snow, but most just gathered in the bar and settled in for a night of beer and snooker. A slurry voice challenged "Rack 'em up, Fats."

In the café, the booths were full of people padding the hard benches with whatever they could find. A few went out into the dark with Ponce to collect some necessary articles from their luggage in the bus.

Jingle and Eula stood talking at the end of the counter.

"Can I get a bowl of soup or jest a cheese sandwich for, say, four bits?"

"We ain't got nothin' here for fifty cents, 'cept chewin' gum, an' besides, you said all you had was two bits."

"Well, two bits is all I got and I'm hungry as a lock-jawed magpie."

Eula shoved past him and said in a low voice, "A trail tramp like you ain't never worth four bits. Why should I give you any-thing?"

Jingle scuffed along behind her, using all of his acting tal-ent to seem even more pitiful. "But, ma'am, it's Christmas Eve an' the Holy Spirit wouldn't turn down a poor soul on a night like this. I swear, all I got is fifty cents and maybe in your heart you could find a way to—"

"I told you, we ain't got nothing for fifty cents."

By this time, they were standing next to the booth where

Chigger and his family were all eyes and ears. Jingle held out a hand full of change. "I'll give you all I got for some day-old biscuits." He looked down at his well-kicked boots.

Eula crossed her arms over an empty tray and leaned back pondering her next refusal.

A small hand reached out of a soiled coat sleeve and dropped a shiny fifty-cent piece into Jingle's leathery palm.

"Maybe they have something for two fifty-centses," Chigger said.

A shocked silence prevailed. Words failed everybody. Eyes met and looked away.

Eula broke the silence. "Yeah, sonny. I guess we can manage something."

"Gol-dern, Chigger, I can't—"

Chigger had it all figured out. "It's okay, Mr. Jingle. My daddy's got a new job and a house and presents and all, so I don't need the fifty cents as much as you."

Virgie butted in. "But we won't have any Christmas at all now 'cause Santa can't find us here." And her lips began to quiver.

"It's okay, Virgie. We'll be to our new home tomorrow," Mom soothed.

"But, but, Santa comes tonight and there ain't any chimbly or nothin' here." She started to cry and buried her face in her mother's lap.

Jingle looked at them for a minute, then turned and walked back to the counter where Eula presented him with a big bowl of Half-Hitch chili and a chunk of jalapeño cornbread.

Things got fairly quiet, except for the continuous snooker meet going on next door. Eula turned down the lights and was wiping the counter when Jingle engaged her in a whispered conversation. He seemed to be explaining something to her and, for the first time, she was listening.

"Eula, I hafta tell ya. I fudged a bit on being so broke and all. Ya see, I got this twenty here." He unfolded a wad of greenish paper that resembled a U.S. twenty-dollar bill.

"Why, you sneaky sidewinder. You claimed you was broke."

"I know. I know. But jest listen. I got a idear. Ya see, I'm really a performer, well, a clown, now, for the rodeos, ya know? I got this here get-up I wear as a clown and, with some assistance, I could do a bang-up Santa Claus fer those little fellers over there. Listen to my idear."

Eula frowned at him over folded arms. "Come on then, you four-flusher." She turned and went into the kitchen, motioning Jingle to follow. Melchior was scraping the grill and cleaning up for the next day. He had already mixed up tomorrow's buckwheat and blueberry pancake batter. Flat pans of cornbread sat steaming on the table. The three of them huddled in conversation as the swinging door swung shut and the café settled in for the night.

Outside, the snow was still drifting into ground swells of powdery dunes, but the wind was easing and a few stars glittered icily through an ebony hole in the scurrying clouds.

In the dim café, huddled bundles of blankets and jackets twisted and turned on the hard benches. Snores and wheezes were the only sounds from the Rec. Parlor. A thermostat clicked off and on encouraging the overtaxed furnace. Then from afar came the tinkle of bells and just the hint of music. Maybe a harmonica.

"Jingle Bells!" It was playing "Jingle Bells" and it was getting closer.

The swinging door to the kitchen swung open and a lumpy figure in red long johns and stocking cap scraped across the floor in run-down imitation armadillo boots. His face was hidden behind a raggedy piece of white fur and his shaggy eyebrows were coming loose, dropping bits of Q-tips on the floor. A gunny sack that smelled of Idaho Reds was slung over his shoulder as he jingled across the room toward the back booth.

Eula came waltzing along behind, whirling two sparklers over her head, singing "Jingle Bells" in a smoky rasp, while Melchior lumbered along behind, mouthing and spraying into his Marine Band harmonica. This tuneful trio marched over to the back booth where Chigger and Virgie jerked awake and stared, frozen in wonder. The Wagon Rut Christmas Pageant hovered over the awestruck children as other travelers stirred and observed.

"It's Santa Claus! Momma, look! It's Santa! He found us!"

In the flickering glow from the sparklers, Jingle began pulling out small brown paper sacks of Snickers, Baby Ruths, and Gummy Bears, and tossed them around the room for grabs.

Then for Virgie there was a special present. Wrapped in a piece of shiny red shelf paper, fastened with a strip of price stickers, was a glass paperweight encompassing a delicate silver snowflake. Her wide eyes reflected the pattern of prisms created by the snowflake and a blinking blue Budweiser sign from across the room.

Santa handed Chigger a shoebox with "Mayflower Van Lines" stickers all over it. Inside was a brand new Albuquerque Dukes baseball cap and a penny bank in the shape of a New Mexico Highway Patrol Car. The cap slipped down over his ears, but the grin was big enough to hold it up.

Virgie jumped down and hugged the well-worn knees of the red BVDs. Chigger held out his hand, trying to look up from under the baseball cap. The sparklers sputtered to blackened wires in time with Eula's last raspy screech. The cowboy Kris Kringle held his lopsided belly with both hands and hollered, "Merry Christmas!"

Melchior moved into his only other Christmas offering, inviting those witnessing the event to join in "Silent Night" as the First Wagon Rut Christmas Pageant wound down and disappeared back through the swinging doors into the kitchen.

Chigger and Virgie crawled back into the booth with their mother, who wrapped them in an old flour sack tablecloth and loving arms. A vision of sugar plums lingered in the glistening eyes of all those present as the room grew still. The tinny harmonica faded away in the kitchen and the thermostat clicked on.

Just at dawn, the first snowplow struggled in from the south. Soon the rumble of diesels filled the chilly air as the corral of semis circled and headed out, followed by Greyhound 2034 and a covey of cars.

Jingle Berry, the well-worn rodeo clown, was again stretched out on the back seat of the bus. A half-grin twitched at the corners of his tobacco-stained mouth as he pondered the twenty-dollar bill, his ace in the hole, that had preserved the spirit of Santa Claus, at least for a while.

Yes, Virgie, even in Wagon Rut, there is a Santa Claus.

# FRONT COVER PAINTING

*The Way We Were* by Frank Loudin

This painting encompasses many elements of my stories. That '36 chevy is the one that got stuck in the mud in "Ruts and Roots," and I got my first kiss from Betty Jewel in the back seat. The old house is where we lived in 1942, and the church is where I became a custodian for the first time. Mary and I rang the bell there on New Year's Eve in 1942. Just around the corner is North Street, where lived Catfish Erwin, Little Jim, Uncle Charlie, Tilly McGraw, and the location of "The Gutter Regatta."

Mary and I are on the front steps folding the evening *Sentinel* in "Paper Boy." Down the street behind the bus is The Candy Corner, and just out of sight on the right is Peck's Garage from *The Piston Ring* painting. The autumn color in the trees is from "Ozark October," and snow from "The Dreaded Grapevine" is almost in the air. This is truly the way we were.

~~~~~~~~~~~~~~~~

I don't pretend to be any kind of historian. These stories are just that. In my family back in West Virginia, any story that dickered with the truth was considered to be a yarn. It was intended to be just passed on down to a group of rapt youngsters. These stories do however reflect the life of a young whippersnapper living in a small town in the middle of 20th-century America, and could be a sort of chronicle of same. To witness my yarns all dressed up into a real book is a thrill and I hope you enjoy it.

—Frank Loudin, Orcas Island, WA, 2023